EDUCATIONAL
DAYS OUT

EDUCATIONAL DAYS OUT

A Handbook for Teachers Planning a School Trip

Christine Green

KOGAN PAGE

First published 1999

Apart from any fair dealing for the purposes of research or private study, or criticism or review, as permitted under the Copyright, Designs and Patents Act 1988, this publication may only be reproduced, stored or transmitted, in any form or by any means, with the prior permission in writing of the publishers, or in the case of reprographic reproduction in accordance with the terms and licences issued by the CLA. Enquiries concerning reproduction outside these terms should be sent to the publishers at the undermentioned address:

Kogan Page Limited
120 Pentonville Road
London N1 9JN

Many of the places to visit listed in this book have no set group size – teachers should enquire about this when making a booking. In instances where this occurs, the term 'N/A' has been used.

British Library Cataloguing in Publication Data

A CIP record for this book is available from the British Library.

ISBN 0 7494 2689 6

Typeset by Saxon Graphics Ltd, Derby
Printed and bound by Creative Print and Design (Wales)

Contents

Contents

PART 1
PRACTICALITIES

1 Planning a visit

All children, whatever their age, gender or culture, have an insatiable appetite for knowledge and the more experiences and thought-provoking situations they find themselves having to deal with, the more knowledgeable they will become. And one way in which teachers can nurture this appetite for learning is to provide pupils with as many thought-provoking and stimulating situations as possible. To this end, out of school visits have proved successful over the years, so much so that now they are regarded as being an integral part of a child's education, increasing pupils' social and personal development and offering them opportunities to demonstrate their inherent qualities of self-reliance, initiative and the ability to get along with their peers. But the actual organization of such a visit is quite an onerous task for any teacher to undertake, being in sole control of 10 or 20 pupils outside the confines of the school grounds. The success of the visit depends wholly on meticulous planning and preparation.

The actual physical exercise of organizing a school visit, choosing where to go, when to go and how to get together with some in-class preparation can take weeks, even months of arranging, so it is important that some basic guidelines are drawn up at the beginning, without which the overall success of the visit could be in jeopardy.

There are thousands of places to visit, museums, farms, countryside parks, art galleries, etc, many of which can be linked directly to the National Curriculum, while others may bear only a fleeting relevance but may nevertheless prove potentially useful and so could well be worth a visit. Take, for example, a visit to the local museum, which provides numerous opportunities for study where knowledge is more than a merging of facts but explores the past and present. There are endless opportunities for combining a variety of topics: a particular period in History, likewise English, Mathematics, Art, Geography and even for older students Architecture or Ecology. It is therefore necessary to consider this when deciding on a venue and to see how one visit can cover several topics. Obviously the more subjects it encompasses, the more valid it will be. Once the actual venue has been decided upon, a letter of enquiry should be sent and in turn you will receive all the relevant documentation about the place.

The primary questions to be considered when deciding on a visit include:

1. Why are you making the visit? Does it tie in with some project students are currently studying; or is it something which well could?
2. What subjects on the National Curriculum will it cover? It is better if there are several in which case the visit will prove even more beneficial to the students.
3. Is it meant as an introduction to the subject, the main core of the topic or perhaps a combination? In many cases a visit can actually instigate further investigation into a specific area.
4. What are the aims of the visit? What do you hope the pupils will derive from it – perhaps a better understanding of the topic, hands-on experience or a better understanding of the chosen subject?
5. What is the staffing ratio of adult supervision to pupils? Some Local Education Authorities have their own specific levels of supervision for off-site visits which schools must closely follow, and some 'sites' also have their own recommendations, but as a general guide under normal circumstances there should be at least the following: 1) 1 adult for every 6 pupils in school years 1 to 3; 2) 1 adult for every 10 to 15 pupils in school years 4 to 6; and 3) 1 adult for every 15 to 20 pupils in school year 7 onwards.

Once these questions have been fully and confidently answered it is then time to approach the Headteacher, who will in turn have to report to the Board of Governors or LEA to make sure all of the criteria and safety rules have been fully covered. Naturally the main concern of the Governors is that the visit will prove beneficial to the pupils and that there are no risk factors involved which could put both staff and pupils in danger. However, all managers of teaching establishments and LEAs provide guidance notes on the formal points of arranging school journeys, something with which teachers should be fully conversant. These points also generally outline the legal and safety requirements and therefore include details of insurance, transport, staffing ratios and responsibilities of the teachers.

Ensure that the following has been done:

☐ All the necessary information has been received prior to the visit.
☐ Any risk elements have been covered and it has been deemed safe to take the pupils.
☐ If there is any pre-training required, then this has been carried out.
☐ There is adequate supervision on site to fully accommodate the numbers of students attending.
☐ The governing body has approved the visit.
☐ Parents have signed any consent forms.
☐ Suitable travel arrangements have been made, and if there are any students requiring medication and special needs, these have been catered for.
☐ There is adequate and relevant insurance cover for the party.

□ The name and address of the visit's venue, together with a contact name, have been left at the school in case of an emergency.
□ And, finally, that parents and pupils know the travel times out and back to school and that all the names of the pupils and adults in the travelling group and the contact details of parents, staff, volunteers and next of kin have been left at the school.

Informing parents/guardians

Once the visit has been decided upon and been given permission by the Headteacher the next step is to contact the parents by letter explaining the reason for the visit. Most schools have a standard letter that they use in such circumstances but basically it should include:

□ Date and location of the proposed visit.
□ Details of meals out, if necessary. Most visits which cover lunchtime require children to take their own packed lunch, which is ideal for those who may follow a special diet. On some occasions when young children take school lunches arrangements can be made for the kitchen staff to prepare packed lunches for those children, but this depends on the individual school.
□ Expected time of departure and return home. The return home time is an important issue especially with parents out at work and who may well have a childminder picking their youngster up from school. Although secondary school children may well be allowed to return home directly (provided they have written consent from their parents), younger children should always be taken back to school and dismissed when their parent/guardian arrives for them.
□ Many children suffer from travel sickness and for them a 30-minute bus trip can turn into a nightmare, so it is a good idea to inform parents of the mode of transport being used so that they can supply a piece of ginger to chew on or a barley sugar sweet to suck.
□ If visiting an outdoor attraction, ie a farm or an archaeological site, it may be well worth mentioning that children should pack a waterproof nylon jacket or a pair of wellingtons to be prepared for any sudden downpour.
□ If money is allowed, then stipulate how much each child can take. This is far better than not stipulating a set sum of money as some children end up taking pounds while others cannot afford to buy anything.
□ And, finally, the all-important tear-off strip which should be returned by a specific date.

In the case of students who are of ethnic origin there may perhaps be some need for sensitivity in the pre-planning stages. For whatever reasons, ie religious beliefs, diet, or just the social aspect, some pupils may not be able to attend, while other pupils may have special educational needs, and in some instances language may be a barrier. Although most ethnic children speak English fluently, often their parents may not be so knowledgeable and in these circumstances it would be advisable for someone from their own culture, ie a health worker, to go along to the child's home and explain the purpose of the visit.

Pre-visits

Generally most places offer free familiarization visits beforehand, enabling teachers to go along and see what is exactly available and whether it caters for all their requirements, particularly if they have any pupils with special needs. Familiarization visits also provide an ideal opportunity to assess whether pupils would gain as much benefit as it was hoped from the visit. Because staff are all fully qualified and experienced in dealing with large groups of pupils, years of working alongside teachers have given them a much deeper insight into what students require and they can therefore supply whatever materials are needed. Some offer worksheets to coincide with the visit and handling sessions and workshops which can offer inspiration and add excitement to a visit. Tours and talks are also an integral part of many visits, and on many occasions role play can be included.

On the initial visit make a note of any potential areas and levels of risk; ensure that the venue can cater for the needs of teachers and pupils within your group, in particular if a group member has a special need, or requires the use of a wheel-chair; ask if there are any facilities for students whose hearing or sight is in some way impaired; are there indoor/outdoor eating areas?; are any activities under cover or outdoors?; is there a room where young children can leave their school bags etc? All of these points may appear irrelevant but they are as important as knowing that the venue can cater for your needs.

Some places may not actively advertise free pre-visits, but that is not to say they do not welcome teachers going along beforehand, and so if it is not clear then simply ask whoever is in charge whether they mind a staff member going along for a visit. More often it will simply have been a technical oversight in their adver-tisement and they will be only too happy to welcome a pre-visit. If this is the first time your school has ever been to the particular venue, and after your initial visit you still feel somewhat unsure, there would be no harm in seeking views from other schools who may well have visited the same venue in the past or even ask for further information from tourist boards.

Getting the most out of a site visit

So that students derive as much information as they can even from the briefest of visits it is important to do some preparation in class. Make sure that each pupil knows the object of the visit, what activities are organized, and what he or she is expected to do. If possible, get some information from the school library and set some homework to write out some questions they would like to put to members of staff. If the visit is to a historic venue spend time discussing how it may have looked, the lifestyle of the people at the time, their work, education, family life, etc. Provide pupils with enough information as to the reason for the visit and indicate the areas that they should try to develop themselves. The ideal visit should not only supply pupils with knowledge and experience but be an invaluable tool to learning. It should ultimately generate interest and stimulate their imagination to follow up studies, whether in class or separately as homework.

Furnishing each student with as much knowledge as possible will offer great rewards in that they will derive far more from the visit than merely the opportunity of spending time out of school, and so be able to utilize their knowledge further back in the class. Even with a half-day visit to a local museum every pupil ought to be made aware of the basic aim of the visit and the activities to be made available on site, otherwise it will be a total waste of time.

It is only by utilizing these off-site visits that lessons can be made more interesting and students' natural inherent learning capacity stretched and enhanced. But remember, prior to any student being taken on a visit they must be fully prepared and they must know the following:

☐ what is fully expected of them from the visit, ie how to record what they see. This could be with a map, photographic evidence, video recording, tape recording;
☐ if preparing a worksheet for use, then it should be designed in such a way that it can act as a useful support to their observations, ie are the questions challenging enough? From the evidence supplied, will they be able to make accurate deductions?
☐ they each should have the basic materials such as pencil, pen, paper, a packed lunch, camera, clipboard, measuring equipment and, depending on the visit, school uniform or casual clothes;
☐ finally, the things that can be touched and those that cannot; areas where they are allowed to go, etc.

Safety on site

Although most sites undergo regular safety checks to make sure that they maintain high standards, and doubtless the teacher will have already been on a pre-visit to look at the safety aspects, it is nevertheless an important issue and one which should be discussed with the children before the visit. Ensure they are made aware of the following:

☐ They should always remain together as a group and not stray away.

☐ If there are certain areas 'out of bounds' that is exactly what it means, and no one should be tempted to investigate.

☐ If going down a pit or exploring an archaeological site it is important that they listen closely to the instructions given.

☐ They should be warned not to touch things unless told it is all right to do so by a member of staff.

☐ When eating lunch they should always remember to take their litter home with them and be reminded that it is safer to take a plastic flask rather than a glass bottle which could fall and smash.

☐ Keep away if workers are busy at the site.

☐ Consideration of other people's property is of paramount importance and if visiting a church or museum they must be told beforehand not to touch anything unless permission is given. Similarly, when making a farm or countryside visit, make sure that they know the countryside code and abide by it. After all, they are the farmers and ramblers of tomorrow and if the land is not protected and taken care of there will be no land for them to harvest or walk.

☐ And, finally, manners. Hopefully there will be no need but remind students that they are visitors and should act like visitors, polite and courteous at all times.

First aid

Wherever you go there is a risk factor involved, even crossing the road, but when taking a group of students on a field visit it is doubly important that all risk factors are eliminated as much as possible, Acts of God notwithstanding. It is important to be prepared for any unforeseeable incident: a twisted ankle, a bleeding nose, even a headache can all put extra stress on a teacher and so it is sensible that at least one accompanying adult has some knowledge of first aid and that if going on a longer journey someone is designated responsible for taking along a first aid box. Most schools will have a fully equipped first aid box but it is important that you also have one for trips out. Further detailed information about first aid procedures and first aid courses is available from the British Red Cross and the St John Ambulance. However, the Health & Safety Executive have drawn up their own list of basic requisites that they feel teachers should have immediate access to:

☐ a leaflet providing general advice on first aid procedures;

☐ some wrapped sterile adhesive dressings;

☐ large sterile unmedicated wound dressing;

☐ two triangular bandages;

☐ two safety pins;

☐ individually wrapped moist cleaning wipes;
☐ pair of disposable gloves.

For further information on first aid in schools contact the Department for Education and Employment (DfEE) for their leaflet *Guidance on First Aid in Schools* (DfEE, 1998) obtainable from DfEE Publications Centre, PO Box 5050, Sudbury, Suffolk CO10 6ZQ (tel: 0845 602 2260; fax: 0845 603 3360).

Benefits of a visit

Teachers know the requirements of their students but staff know their displays and exhibitions and how they relate to certain subjects. Together a successful partnership between teacher and staff can be developed to ensure students get the full benefit from their visit. Although some aspects of the visit will be ironed out before the class attends, it is important prior to the visit that the teacher responsible has an idea of how they would like the visit to develop. An introductory talk by museum staff based on teaching from objects, guiding the students towards an investigative approach is helpful. This process will enable students to observe, discover and discuss the sharing of ideas.

Small group work or individual study is another option and towards the end of the visit there may be a question and answer session available, providing an invaluable opportunity to ask any further questions or address any issues.

Making sure your students get enough out of the visit

It is difficult to assess whether students have derived as much information as you had envisaged from the visit but it is a worthwhile exercise for future visits to sit down and evaluate the following:

1. Have you been able to reach your initial aims?
2. Was the visit too long or perhaps too short?
3. Did the visit match up to your expectations and did the pupils derive as much pleasure and educational value as you had hoped they would?
4. Did the on-site facilities meet your expectations?
5. If you were to go to the same place on a future date, are there any changes you would want to make?

Checklist for a site visit

Before going out on a visit check that you have covered all the following points:

☐ completed a planning form;
☐ made the purpose of the visit clear to all colleagues and helpers;
☐ checked the insurance cover;
☐ informed parents why the visit is taking place, date, time of departure and arrival back at school; made luncheon arrangements; stipulated how much money children might need (if any); and if there is any need for special clothing, ie wellingtons;
☐ obtained permission slips from all parents of pupils going on the visit;
☐ confirmed all bookings to the site in writing;
☐ booked the transport and checked all the relevant details;
☐ arranged that there is adequate adult supervision to oversee the pupils;
☐ compiled an accurate register of all pupils on the visit and left a duplicate copy at school with the secretary;
☐ left emergency contact numbers for the site back at school.

2 | Transport

When taking a class of students out on a field visit never underestimate the unknown dangers that may lurk. Excitement, distractions and the mere thought of being outside school can so easily culminate in thoughtlessness on behalf of the pupils, which in turn can frequently lead to accidents no matter how well planned the visit was. So be well prepared, do your initial preparation in the safety of the classroom and make sure that each student knows what is expected of him or her.

Going on foot

If you are simply going to a local countryside park, or taking a group of pupils along to the local museum and it is within walking distance, then obviously there will be no transport required but it still needs careful preparation. Think about the following:

1. Adult/child ratio – this is an important issue, especially with regard to the age of the pupils, as the younger they are, the more supervision they will require. Similarly, if some children have special needs.
2. Road safety – it just needs one child to start fooling around to cause an accident. Therefore it is essential all pupils know and adhere to the basic road safety rules laid down in the Highway Code and Green Cross Code. However, should their memories need a little brushing up it would prove a good exercise to get hold of some relevant literature on road safety from the Department of Transport and do work in class on road safety.
3. Walking in pairs – depending on the ages of the pupils it is sensible that younger ones are partnered off and that they keep with the same partner throughout the visit, particularly when going to and returning from the location. For safety's sake, and to keep an eye on any stragglers in the group, it is advisable that one supervising adult is at the head of the party and another one at the rear.

4. Supervision – constant adult supervision should be provided at all times and children should not be allowed simply to wander off alone. In some circumstances allotting five or six children to one adult throughout the visit is far safer and more convenient, thereby sharing the responsibility among several adults.
5. Crossing roads – when crossing busy roads full use should be made of the subways and crossings. If, however, none are available, then a suitable crossing area which provides clear vision in both directions should be selected. In order to facilitate safe crossing the teacher leading the party should take charge and ensure that the road is clear before taking the group across, paying due respect to motorists. Never make the children hurry across the road, hesitate or split up. They should be instructed to cross in pairs at the teacher's instructions and to wait in an orderly manner at the other side of the road until the entire party has crossed.
6. Getting lost – the worst scenario for any teacher on a school outing is to lose one of their charges. Some teachers taking a group of infant children out make individual name badges enabling any helpers who may be accompanying the party to readily identify the youngsters in their care, and if one should happen to go astray, then hopefully some responsible adult will be able to alert a member of the school. Although wearing name badges would not go down too well with older children, make sure that they have some basic understanding of the procedure to adopt if a child should happen to go missing. The teacher in charge should also take the register when setting off and also when returning to school.

Bus

For those visits that require some mode of transport it is the leader's responsibility to decide which is the best means, and if using a bus whether the numbers would befit a minibus, a single decker or a double decker. If the school has normally used the services of the same bus company in the past and has always been satisfied with the service provided, then there is little need to change. For those schools who have never used the services of a bus company, check around with other schools in the area to find out who they use and if they were fully satisfied with the service received, etc.

Although a bus driver is fully responsible for the vehicle and the safe arrival of the passengers, he or she is not responsible for supervising groups of schoolchildren and is it not fair to expect him or her to tell youngsters off if they become rowdy. The pupils are answerable to the teachers accompanying the party, who in turn should lay down some strict guidelines:

☐ pupils should be told to remain seated at all times and not move out of their seats until the bus has stopped;

□ windows on the bus should remain closed. If, however, they are open this is not an invitation for pupils to throw out litter, dangle their arms or worse still call out at passers-by;

□ pupils should in no way distract the driver, even if he or she is the next door neighbour or a relation;

□ if going on an overnight stay, luggage should be stowed away safely in the designated area and any cumbersome items stored in the boot;

□ ideally, teachers should be seated in various parts of the coach where they can easily supervise the party;

□ when disembarking, pupils should wait until the bus has come to a complete stop, and when told to get off, do so in an orderly fashion;

□ students should never attempt to cross the road from near a stationary vehicle.

An important point which many teachers overlook whenever involved in taking a group of students on a coach trip is to acquaint themselves with the emergency exits. If the bus doesn't have a first aid kit, take one along; and, finally, if the journey is a lengthy one, then arrangements should be made relating to toilet and refreshments stops *en route*.

Minibus

Many schools now own a minibus, thereby allowing pupils access to many out-of-school activities they otherwise might not have been able to attend, and on some occasions longer journeys too. Over the years there have been several accidents, some of which have involved school minibuses, and this has led the government to adopt stricter measures. It is vital that all schools should be familiar with these measures before a teacher takes on the responsibility of 'driver'. No teacher should be expected to drive the minibus. It must be done on a purely voluntary basis by a member of staff who has the time and commitment to take on the work and all the responsibilities it involves. But there are some excellent booklets which succinctly explain all the important requirements and information. One that makes good reading is *School Minibuses: A Safety Guide*, published by the National Union of Teachers (see Appendix for details).

The driver

Depending on the size of the school and the staff ratio it may be more practical and sensible to designate two teachers as 'minibus drivers', in which case their sole responsibility is for the general maintenance of the vehicle and to make sure that it is up to scratch at all times. As the law currently stands, the minibus driver must be fully qualified to drive the vehicle and hold a full, clean, driving licence. Providing the driver is over 21 years old and passed his or her driving test prior to

1 January 1997, then he or she is quite at liberty to be in full control of a minibus, but for drivers who passed their test after that date, they may only drive vehicles with up to a maximum of nine seats, including their own. Should they wish to drive the school bus they must take another driving test and also meet stricter medical standards.

Driving one's own vehicle is totally different from driving a minibus with eight or nine students in the back and that is why teachers are advised to receive training in minibus driving and the management of passengers. For further information about certain standards and the legal aspect write for a copy of *Safety on School Journeys,* published by the National Union of Teachers and supported by the Royal Society for the Prevention of Accidents. The leaflets are free from the NUT, Hamilton House, Mabledon Place, London WC1H 9BD (tel: 0171 388 6191). The Department of the Environment and the Regions (DETR) also can provide further information. Their address is Greater Minster House, 76 Marsham Street, London SW1P 4DR (tel: 0171 271 4800).

Checking the school minibus

Generally the driver of the minibus will also have to carry out weekly checks on the vehicle. There is also paperwork involved to make sure it is all in order, including: the service history; insurance, for example that the policy covers all the uses to which the minibus is used, eg transporting students to and from sports events, school outings, etc; the total number of passengers allowed; the full weight; and finally all the other people who are allowed to drive the vehicle. Comprehensive cover is necessary in order to ensure that the teachers are not held accountable for any damage that they may cause to the minibus as well as other vehicles.

Private vehicles

On some occasions it may be necessary to enlist the help of staff members to use their own cars. In such cases they should check their insurance policy cover and that they are fully covered, with a clause giving permission for them to use their car for business purposes. Generally teachers are allowed to use their private cars to transport passengers provided a) they do not carry more than eight passengers, and b) any money paid is purely towards the running costs. Similarly, if there are too many students, parents may be asked to help out with transport, but, again, they must ensure that they are made fully aware of their legal obligation for the safety of pupils in their car and parents' agreement should be sought for their children to be carried in other parents' cars. It is also advisable that the parents driving pupils are not put in a position where they are alone with a pupil but that there is another adult in attendance. Ensure that parents are fully conversant with the route being taken and likewise on the return journey back to school. Remuneration should be offered for petrol.

Train

Many children, even in this day and age, may never have been on a train and so the prospect could well be more exciting to them than the actual visit itself, and when children get over-excited they tend to get boisterous. A good idea is to reserve a compartment, thereby making supervision far easier and causing less upset to other travellers. But travelling on any mode of transport has its own inherent dangers and even waiting on the platform for the train to arrive can create problems. Harmless banter and pushing can so easily end up with items being mistakenly thrown on to the line, so before leaving the classroom children should be made aware of the need to act sensibly at all times. When aboard the train make sure that students remain in their seats and are not allowed to move around the train or make a nuisance of themselves running back and forth to the toilets. When it is time to disembark make sure that students allow other passengers to get off first, before they get off in an orderly fashion and then wait on the platform until everyone has been accounted for. Remember you don't want to lose any pupils or find out that one has stowed away on the train. It is better if one teacher remains on the train until all the pupils are off.

Travelling on the Underground

Although many cities have a network of underground travel, there are still some that don't and yet this is often the best way of getting from one part of a city to the next in the fastest time possible. For children who are unfamiliar with this type of travel it can be slightly overwhelming and dangerous, and so from the teaching side it is important that:

☐ groups stick together at all times, with a teacher at the front and also at the rear of the party;
☐ all children know the procedure if anyone becomes lost or strays from the group;
☐ they should know where they should meet;
☐ if some children are frightened of going on the moving escalators, then they should be led up carefully by an adult or, failing that, use a lift.

By sea

If a visit involves sea travel, then the amount of supervision required will depend on the age of the pupils. Obviously older students will want some time on their own in order to look around the boat, while younger children will need constant management. The main problem with older students is to make sure that they are fully aware of the implications of attempting to buy alcohol from the bar or duty free – it is simply not allowed, even if they do look old enough. And as regards customs, the allowances are only applicable to adults. If they should decide to disappear and investigate the facilities themselves even though they may be 15 or 16, warn them of the dangers of horseplay and impress on them that they must be back at the meeting place at a certain time.

By air

With better motorway systems, cheaper air travel and endless opportunities more schools are taking students abroad than at any other time. At one time a skiing trip to Norway was the one and only opportunity children had to go abroad with their school but now the field is wide open. There are cultural trips, exchange visits, sporting breaks and some schools organize their own language holidays, enabling students to spend a week or two in the country whose language they are learning, and one of the quickest, most convenient methods of travelling is flying. More information on this method of transport is given in the chapter on going abroad.

Children with special needs

Nowadays more children with special needs are being integrated into mainstream schools. Their requirements are just as important as the rest and so need to be addressed and given priority. For example, when travelling on a bus, are there facilities to allow a wheelchair easy access? Do they have a ramp or does the school have to provide a portable one? If travelling by train, are there facilities for helping people to get on board? Is there a special allocated area for wheelchair users? Are there disabled toilets on the train(s)? Will there be a porter to help?

Insurance

Another aspect of organizing a school visit is insurance. Although different educational councils have their own individual policies that schools under their jurisdiction are required to meet, it is a complex matter and one which must be looked into fully. Without being fully and adequately covered, no school visit should be allowed to take place, but it must be borne in mind that the type of insurance cover depends on the type of activity the pupils are taking part in. It is then the responsibility of the teacher to contact parents and inform them of the scope of the insurance in order that everyone is fully aware of this point.

Because insurance policies are legal documents they appoint fixed limitations and preclude certain people or activities. It can often seem slightly bewildering to wade through all the small print, so basically these are the types of insurance cover which may be suitable to school visits:

☐ Personal injury – although some educational authorities insure their own staff and volunteers against personal injury, they may not cover pupils. Therefore this should be looked into and parents should then be informed of what is and what is not provided, in which case they may decide to take out their own personal injury insurance for their children in the event of accidents.

☐ Public liability – this covers damages against the leader of the group, or other adult supervisors in the party.

☐ Medical and related expenses – often as a result of an accident extra expenses are incurred, such as having to get home quickly via some other means of transport, or if a member of the party has to stay in hospital after the others have returned home, etc. But when travelling abroad medical insurance is a necessity, particularly in the case of someone requiring hospital or doctor's fees, which may well not be reclaimable.

☐ Extra expenses – to oversee any costs that might occur as a result of a strike or transport cancellations.

☐ Personal baggage – the worst case scenario is to lose one's luggage or money and so taking out insurance cover is a good safety net.

☐ Hired equipment – in some instances it may be necessary to arrange for the insurance of hired equipment or items of clothing, especially if going on an activity break.

☐ High-risk activities – normal insurance policies do not include high-risk activities, eg rock climbing. If these types of activities are involved, insurance cover is a matter of necessity.

☐ Cancellation – in the case of a trip abroad or an expensive visit in this country it is advisable to include cancellation insurance in the package, thereby protecting against the possibility of incurring heavy financial loss to the school or families if the whole visit for some reason has to be postponed.

Other areas that it is worthwhile looking into include cover for: loss or damage to the hired equipment; programmed and non-programmed activities; legal assistance in the recovery of claims and failure or bankruptcy of the centre or travel company. Extra cover may be required for those people with medical conditions.

A lot of what is required legally to make the visit as safe as possible is basically down to common sense and so when it is a case of hiring coaches the teachers would, as a normal practice, check that the coach company they are intending to use is reputable and that they have appropriate insurance cover for school parties. If there are any concerns, then there are plenty of other highly reliable coach companies from which to choose.

Costing the trip

One of the important points when organizing an off-site visit is for the teacher to work out a budget whereby all elements of the trip are listed and duly costed, eg transport, insurance, any extra staff, entrance fees, miscellaneous expenditure and, in the case of a residential course, the board and lodgings together with the hiring of any items of equipment. To this there should be added a contingency sum which covers extras such as an entrance fee and charge for certain amenities, ie workshops, talks/tours. The costs should then be totalled and divided by the number of students who are going, thus arriving at a cost per student. Obviously there may be some families who cannot afford to send their child on a school visit, but this should be no reason why a child should not be allowed to derive the full benefits a school visit offers and so the school should look into ways of lending some assistance. Many schools have an emergency fund for such things or an arrangement can be made with the parents whereby they could perhaps contribute a nominal amount or alternatively pay off a certain amount each week.

Handling cash

In cases where the school is large and has a healthy administrative department the costings and handling of the fees could well be taken on by them, leaving the teacher more time to concentrate on the actual site visit. But in smaller schools it may well be up to the teacher him or herself to take on all the administrative duties, which include handling the money. Whenever this happens it is important that the teacher is fully aware that he or she is totally responsible for handing it over to the relevant bodies, ie the travel company, site to be visited, etc.

Costs should be totalled and divided by the number of students who are going in order to arrive a cost per student. This must all be written down on paper and kept so that if a governor or the Headteacher requests to see it, it is available and legible. If there is a surplus of monies when the visit is over, then the remainder should be divided equally and distributed to all those who actually paid to go on the trip. Up-to-date, clear concise accounts of all transactions should be maintained together with who the payment was to/from, the cheque number and the resulting balance. Whenever receiving any monies from students a receipt should be issued. Generally this basic account system should suffice with most off-site visits. However, in the case of a visit abroad where the cost runs into hundreds, it may be advisable to open a separate bank account to deal with it and the responsibility given to a member of the office staff.

Maintaining the accounts is only part of the successful financial planning of a visit. The first consideration is the necessity to travel and if there is a need, how far it is necessary to travel and by what means, where from and how much will it cost. Obviously the more complicated the visit, the earlier the start that has to be made on costings, which may well mean obtaining quotations from competing firms of travel companies. Accurate costings should include incidental expenses such as bus or underground fares between stations, baggage handling charges, airport taxes and an allowance for emergencies such as breakdown if travelling by road and delays at an airport.

It is only fair that parents are informed of the cost as early as possible, enabling them to save up if necessary and that whenever any money is received, a receipt is given in return. For a major visit it is normal to expect a substantial deposit on booking followed by regular instalments for the rest of the cost. Parents should be informed at what point it is no longer possible to withdraw from the booking without incurring a financial penalty. This will probably depend on the travel agent's own cancellation rulings.

Basic information issued at this stage

Make sure you have covered the basics:

☐ decide on the best mode of transport, ie on foot, by bus, by minibus, by private vehicles, by train, by Underground, by boat or by aeroplane;
☐ take out insurance cover – check the various types;
☐ cost out the trip;
☐ make secure arrangements for handling the cash.

3 Day trips requiring special consideration

It is well worth mentioning those day trips that require special consideration, ie visiting a farm, a theme park, an adventure activity centre, etc and noting that the safety aspect should be uppermost in the teacher's mind. Irrespective of the activity involved, there is always some element of risk. However, it is important that any such risk is minimal and that pupils are not placed in situations which expose them to unacceptable levels of psychological or physical risk. If the risk cannot be minimized or at best contained, then the visit should simply not be allowed to take place. Of over 1 million school trips arranged in England each year, the number of reported injuries and fatalities are few and the number of negligence actions against party leaders very small compared with the number of trips. However, it is unwise to become too complacent.

Adventure centres

Before the implementation of the Activity Centres (Young Persons' Safety) Act 1995 there was no guarantee to assure a teacher that all the relevant safety procedures had been enforced at adventure centres. However, since the Act was implemented there are over 900 providers who currently hold a licence demonstrating that they abide by the tightest safety measures. And so whenever planning to use adventure activity facilities provided by either a company or local authority the teacher should check whether the provider is licensable under law, and if so that the provider does hold a licence. For further information about providers contact: The Adventure Activities Licensing Authority, TQS Limited, 17 Lambourne Crescent, Llanishen, Cardiff CF4 5GG (tel: 01222 755715; fax: 01222 755757).

Holding a licence is proof that the provider has been inspected and the Licensing Authority is thus content that the relevant safety procedures have been carried out in order for them to provide such adventure activities. However, other facilities such as catering and accommodation do not come under their jurisdiction so should be checked separately.

Suffice it to say that those establishments that do not hold a licence are not necessarily dangerous; it may simply be that the particular activity being provided is not licensable, in which case it is advisable to check certain points:

☐ Are the staff fully qualified and experienced in the activity?
☐ Are the staff trained to instruct people in the activity?
☐ Do the staff possess the skills and qualities to lead pupils of the relevant age group?
☐ Have all steps been taken to ensure that staff have not been involved in any negligent or criminal civil actions in the past?
☐ Has the provider clearly defined roles and responsibilities for each member of staff?
☐ Is the equipment safe and has it been regularly inspected prior to use?
☐ Do operating procedures follow the guidelines of the National Governing Body?
☐ Is there provision for first aid?
☐ Are there emergency procedures on standby?
☐ Does the provider have adequate liability insurance?
☐ It is also a sensible precaution to find out the names of other schools that may have used the centre before and what they think about the centre, whether they had any problems, etc.

Farm visits

There are occasions when even people who have lived on a farm all their lives may be involved in an accident despite having taken all the precautions. Whenever taking a party of students on a farm visit there are certain guidelines that should be followed. Although pupils should be warned not to touch any items of farm equipment, or even animals without permission, there are occasions when curiosity gets the better of them. It is therefore advisable that a preliminary visit be arranged whereby checks can be made of the management of the farm: how well is it run? Are the tours and talks structured? Does it have a good reputation for safety? What are the standards of animal welfare? Are the public access areas clean and safe? Some farms have actually been built solely for school visits and so will be well aware of all the issues regarding school visits, but others that are termed 'working farms' may not provide all the amenities and facilities so readily. It is also advisable to check that the farm has facilities should any pupils have special needs, ie is there access for a wheelchair or for those visually impaired? Would it be safe for them to visit?

As regards safety rules and hygiene, the fundamental points to warn pupils about include:

□ Never attempt to feed any animals unless a staff member gives permission. Some animals may react in an unfriendly manner when being offered something to eat.

□ Never taste any animal foodstuffs or indeed touch them – a great deal of animal fodder contains additives that are not safe for human consumption.

□ Never place their faces up against the animals no matter how 'cute' they appear.

□ Never attempt to eat their own packed lunch until they have washed their hands.

□ Never drink water from the farm taps.

□ Never climb on any farm machinery.

Further information about farm visits can be obtained from the DfEE's letter of 9 June 1997, Pupil Visits To Farms: Health Precautions. Write to the Department for Education and Employment Publications Centre, PO Box 5050, Sudbury, Suffolk CO10 6ZQ (tel: 0845 602 2260; fax: 0845 603 3360).

Swimming pools

Swimming lessons are part and parcel of the school curriculum and as well as being educational can also be a pleasurable experience, but pools can also be dangerous if certain safety measures are not followed by pupils. It is therefore essential that the teacher check over the pool and its facilities:

□ Is the swimming instructor fully qualified and experienced in dealing with children?

□ Are there sufficient lifeguards around?

□ Is the water temperature appropriate?

□ Are there clear signs indicating the depth of the pool?

□ At the shallow end is the water shallow enough to stand up in comfortably?

□ Is there a poolside telephone?

□ Is there adequate first aid equipment?

□ Is there provision of swimming rings for people who may get into trouble in clear view?

□ Are there separate changing facilities for boys and girls?

□ Is there a safe place to leave one's clothes?

□ Will the pupils be instructed on how to behave in and around the pool?

□ Will the swimming instructor be able to see all pupils satisfactorily and so notice should anyone be in any distress?

□ If children have a hearing problem, are there facilities to accommodate them?

□ Are there extra staff available who may be able to go into the pool with the children?

Theme parks

One of the most exciting days out must be to a theme or leisure park, which can also be a very useful tool for education. There are a variety of such places throughout the United Kingdom to cater for all ages, some of which have specially designated classrooms and support amenities. Although they all regularly have safety checks carried out by the authorities to make sure that their attractions are safe, it is up to the teachers to keep a watchful eye on the pupils and make sure that they all remain together while on site. Because on many occasions they are also open to members of the general public at the same time as they are open to school parties, it is imperative that there are enough staff members to accompany the party of children and that they remain in a group throughout the visit to make sure that no one strays away. Remember whenever going on any school visit to make a head count both on arrival and before departure.

Obviously prior to deciding on taking pupils to a theme park it is advisable to make a preliminary visit and make sure that they accommodate school parties. Check whether they can accommodate a child with certain requirements, ie a wheelchair or in the case of a group with special needs whether there are adequate provisions to oversee a number of wheelchairs/prams etc.

For further information about the various theme and leisure parks in the United Kingdom write to: Information Management, British Tourist Authority, Thames Tower, Black's Road, London W6 9EL.

4 Residential visits

Years ago the idea of taking students on a residential visit wasn't even considered viable and yet now it forms an integral part of the National Curriculum, helping students develop both personally and academically. The benefits to be derived from residential courses include enhancing social skills and teaching students to interact with their peers outside the 'normal' school environment. Many teachers have acknowledged the difference they have noticed in students from disadvantaged backgrounds on their return from a residential course as they seem so much happier and confident about themselves. For the shy retiring student residential courses can be very character building, encouraging them to explore their inner selves and in doing so learn about and nurture their own abilities, often finding they are able to reach heights they never thought achievable. Surprisingly enough, the school 'pain in the neck' can sometimes be seen in a totally different light in the middle of the countryside endeavouring to be self-sufficient. The circumstances which have brought them together help young people to learn how to interact socially with their peers and can lead to a greater understanding of people's behaviour and why some people act as they do. By the end of the course the students begin to know themselves and others slightly better. Although relationships may be put under strain, this isn't always such a bad thing as it can often make people see others for what they truly are as opposed to what they thought they were.

Residential visits are also useful in developing and nurturing social skills not always available in school. This applies to the practicalities of being taught a new skill or improving an existing one. Generally the physical or academic structure of the visit may be more obvious than the social aspects. However, by living away from home and learning to work closely with fellow students, pupils do develop a high degree of social awareness; which may not initially be apparent. Many teachers have commented on the beneficial effects of a residential visit on those from the most difficult and disadvantaged backgrounds, enabling them to explore and learn more about themselves and their environment.

Many schools have their own residential centres for field studies and activities, but often if there are too many students they have to take advantage of the facilities provided by commercial centres for young people such as the YMCA or nearby commercial campsites, bed and breakfast hotels and other forms of accommodation.

Before deciding on the actual location of the residential visit, the reason for the visit must be decided upon: 1) the aim of the visit – is it purely to be a recreational or academic course and how does it tie in with the National Curriculum?; and 2) is it possible that the same activity/course could be undertaken just as effectively nearer school?

Most local authorities lay down detailed guidelines on the organization and conduct of school visits in general and it is the responsibility of the leader to obtain these guidelines and draw up plans in line with them in close negotiation with the governors and Headteachers. It may well be that the local authority demands specific staffing ratios and levels of qualifications and experience for teachers taking part in the proposed visit; the LEA may well insist on special insurance cover for certain activities and needs to be informed of and to approve the nature and extent of such visits prior to plans being finalized. As regards financial assistance, no child should be made to feel discriminated against if their parents are unable to pay or contribute monies towards any out-of-school visit. Most schools do retain a fund for such circumstances.

Preliminary visits

Before approval can be given by the Headteacher and Board of Governors or the LEA, they must all be fully confident that none of their employees, ie staff members or pupils will be exposed to any danger, however minimal, and that the venue can fully offer all that it purports to provide academically, socially and from a safety aspect. Therefore a preliminary visit is of prime importance to the organization of the visit. The teacher must check out the following:

- ☐ The type of accommodation available, and if relevant is it suitable for children with special needs?
- ☐ The exact location and nature of the surrounding area, ie middle of the countryside or close to a busy built-up area – both of which could determine the suitability from a safety aspect, depending on the age of the pupils.
- ☐ What role do the staff on site play in the running of the centre, ie are they on call 24 hours a day or simply available at certain times?
- ☐ Is there one designated manager?
- ☐ Does each staff member have a specific role etc?
- ☐ What types of activities and equipment are available? Are they fully up to date?
- ☐ Would there, in the case of it being an activity break, be sufficient equipment for each pupil to hire and, if so, is there a charge incurred separate from the overall costing of the visit?

□ What is the cost for pupils and accompanying adults?
□ What are the safety measures?
□ Is the venue fully equipped for any emergency, inside or outdoors?
□ Is there a member of staff who is a fully qualified first aider?

Only after the teacher is fully satisfied that the centre meets all these requirements should he or she take the students along.

Accommodation

Although technically 'a residential course', not all places are able to provide on-site residential accommodation. Some may sub-contract other local establishments, such as the local YMCA, bed and breakfast hotels or even campsites to provide the actual accommodation, while they offer the activities at the centre. This arrangement may well work for older students provided there is a member of staff supervising, but for younger children it may not be advisable and in such cases it is better to choose a site that has both the accommodation and activities. If the latter, it is necessary to check:

□ that staff sleeping quarters are in adjoining rooms to pupils;
□ that access to students' rooms is readily available to staff at all times;
□ that there are separate sleeping areas for female and male pupils;
□ that staff and pupils are fully conversant with the physical layout of the building and in case of any emergencies that students know of the procedures to be followed;
□ that there are adequate bathroom facilities in close proximity to the bedrooms/dormitories;
□ that there is adequate heating and lighting and that sleeping areas have sufficient ventilation;
□ that where the reception area is not staffed 24 hours a day there are some appropriate measures taken to prevent unauthorized visitors;
□ that should anyone take ill, there is a separate room and provision made;
□ that all electrical items are fully checked and deemed safe beforehand; and finally
□ if certain activities are to be arranged for the group by the centre staff, then the teacher should ascertain whether the resident instructors are fully experienced and also if they will provide any special clothing and/or equipment required by the participants.

These points may appear trivial but these are the main requirements that any teacher should check. Only after this information has been assimilated and any problems solved can the staff make a decision about the visit.

Parental involvement

It can be quite an anxious time for parents when their children announce they are going on a residential course with their school. The initial euphoria could well subside into sleepless nights and worry for both parties and so it is essential that parents and teachers show a united front and that they work together in contributing to the visit being a success. For some children it may be the first time they have ever been away from home and this can be quite frightening for the quiet child. Even the normally outgoing pupil can have moments of panic. Similarly, children who have special needs require extra consideration, and likewise those who are on medication or have a special diet.

Parents are sure to be aware of and concerned about the various stories reported in the press regarding school visits, where accidents have occurred despite all the necessary precautions having been taken. And yet despite all safety precautions being followed, it is no one's fault if a child accidentally trips and as a result fractures a leg, or falls ill with a tummy bug. Such things are inevitable and even the best laid plans can sometimes go awry. That is why parental involvement is necessary, so that any concerns or worries can be ironed out and any questions asked, ie will the pupils be supervised in the evenings?, will they be allowed to telephone home?, etc. The initial letter home will doubtless explain the important details, such as date of departure, the actual location, cost, etc, but at a later meeting other points should be raised and discussed, such as:

1. The aims of the visit and why it is useful for the child to take part.
2. The type of course and activities planned (also including those that may be slightly more adventurous).
3. The names and numbers of accompanying members of staff.
4. The methods of travel, which should also include the name of the travel company.
5. A breakdown of what the actual cost of the visit will and will not involve, such as extra-curricular activities or facilities available in the evening for students. While discussing money it is a good point to recommend how much students should take with them. Depending on the age of the students it is better to give a limit.
6. Parents should be told about insurance cover, what is and is not included. Some may want to take out personal insurance, especially if their child is embarking upon an activity course.
7. A list of clothing and personal requirements.

Staffing

Most LEAs issue guidelines on teacher/pupil ratios that must be closely followed. Where there are children with special needs, the ratio will be higher. On such occasions carers or qualified nursing staff may be called upon. It is difficult to know exactly how many staff members should accompany groups because it depends on the age, type of visit, location and the efficient use of resources. However, when group members are under the age of 18 staff to pupil ratios may well be: 1) 1 adult to 15 group members for a visit where the element of risk is similar to that generally encountered in daily life, eg visits to local places of historic interest; 2) 1 adult to 10 group members for all trips abroad; 3) schools may well want to consider that for children aged under 8 there is at least 1 adult to every 6 group members. The same could apply to groups which mainly or entirely comprise children with special needs, although schools may well prefer lower ratios. For higher risk activities it may be advisable to give higher ratios than indicated.

As regards choosing the right staff to accompany a group, the Headteacher may well have an overall say in the matter, but it is a very sensitive subject. The teachers who do accompany out-of-school visits should appreciate the enormous responsibility they are taking on. It isn't a 9–4 job then off home, it is virtually a 24-hour on-call job where they will not only have to act as teacher and instructor but also parent and if needed perhaps a nurse. Therefore the ideal persons must be fully committed and understand that their responsibilities will extend far beyond that of teaching. They should be able to contribute a lot to the course and through personal example encourage students to be reliable and responsible for their actions, teach them to make decisions and how to act independently.

Often it may be necessary to call upon voluntary helpers, ie parent governors or parents on the PTA. Again, selection is equally important and similar attributes should apply. It is equally important that volunteers realize they are not going on holiday but are in more of an administrative role and so it is sensible that they meet the pupils prior to the visit in order that everyone is well briefed in their duties and responsibilities. This also gives pupils an opportunity to get to know the volunteer helpers. Meetings involving teachers and helpers may help in actually formalizing the administration and organization of the visit, enabling each person to know what is expected from them, their legal liabilities, the social aims of the course, the insurance arrangements, the medical facilities and any other information deemed relevant.

Children with special needs

It is equally important, if not more so, that children with special needs are involved in school visits and actively encouraged to take part with their fellow students, especially as more children with special needs are being integrated into mainstream schools. Obviously more attention and planning are needed when children who have a wheelchair or difficulty in getting around are part of the group and so supervision and safety measures need to be addressed at the initial planning stages. Many places are fully equipped to facilitate wheelchair users and if not, then it may be advisable to take along some portable ramps. If there is no wheelchair access, then alternative arrangements should be sought, but a child should never be made to feel different or awkward.

In the case of a child who is epileptic, again additional safety measures and arrangements for taking medication may be necessary to support them. But it is vital that all members of staff are made fully aware of any students requiring medication or special diet, and the emergency procedures should anything occur.

Parents will be asked prior to the visit for the name and address of their child's doctor, who to contact in the case of an emergency, and also whether their child suffers from any medical condition and requires medication at a certain time every day. Other medical information such as dietary requirements, any phobias, allergies, even problems sleeping should be given.

First aid

As with any off-site visit there should always be at least one accompanying adult with knowledge and some experience of first aid. Other adults should be instructed to follow the advice of the first aid expert in the event of an accident or emergency until professional help is available. For further information on courses contact the British Red Cross or the St John Ambulance Association, both of which run regular courses on first aid and whose addresses can be found in local telephone directories.

AIDS

It is worthwhile mentioning a brief word about AIDS. Although people with the AIDS antibody do not present a health hazard to others in normal circumstances, if a party should include a carrier then all supervising adults need to be made aware of the fact. The Department of Education and Science and the NUT have documents explaining basic advice on hygiene precautions and what procedures to adopt when someone is a carrier.

Finally

The idea of spending a week away from school and home may seem an exciting thought for young people but what must be clearly borne in mind is the main object of this residential visit and that is why preparation in school before departure is important. Pupils must understand how this experience will help them in some aspect of the school curriculum and the social value of such a course: sharing with one's peers the difficulties which often occur when living in a group; taking responsibility for themselves and members of the group; and endeavouring to get along.

Practical aspects of the visit should also be discussed, ie what would happen if the luggage got mislaid? Draw up lists of clothes to take, jobs to be done on arrival, sleeping accommodation, etc. Preparing everyone before arrival will give everyone far more time to actually enjoy the visit and thereby reduce the time the teacher spends talking about things. Other issues that are well worth mentioning to pupils include the following:

- how much leisure time they will be allowed and how this should be spent;
- details about writing letters or telephoning home;
- some background information about other facilities around the area where they will be based, ie whether there are any shops;
- the programmed timetable they will be following;
- the number of staff and their respective roles at the centre;
- regulations on discipline and personal behaviour, hygiene and safety, and the importance of adhering to these rules at all times;
- the school's expectations on behaviour while away and reiterating the role the pupils have to play;
- emphasizing no smoking and no alcohol, explaining what could happen in such circumstances;
- any domestic duties they may be required to do, ie making their own bed; keeping the wash area clean.

Arrival

Provided initial instructions have been carried out relating to the allocation of accommodation at the centre, then everything should run smoothly. Doubtless the first evening it will take time for pupils to settle in but it is nevertheless worth-while to establish and enforce some basic bedtime rules which all students should stick to and after several days may be relaxed a little. Depending on the arrival time, after a good night's sleep the following day they should be taken on a tour of the centre, introduced to staff members and familiarized with the daily routine of the centre, ie meals and what is expected of all pupils who attend.

Homesickness should never be ignored. For some children the emotional upset they may be feeling can cause physical problems such as bed wetting and nightmares and thereby spoil a pupil's ability to enjoy the holiday. This is one reason why some people feel it is not a good idea to make a telephone call home. The sound of a parent's voice can so easily send a child into floods of tears and no end of calming advice can placate them. Although homesickness cannot be fully avoided, it can be minimized by organizing extra activities or giving the child who is particularly fretful some extra responsibility so he or she feels more important. In very rare cases some children are so upset by the break from home that they make themselves physically ill. On such occasions the parents should be advised and some arrangements made for the child to return home.

5 | Going abroad

The idea of organizing a visit overseas may initially seem a daunting prospect and it is true to say that it is certainly more time consuming and complex than organizing a visit in this country. Nevertheless, there is plenty of advice and support readily available from various sources whose job it is to assist such overseas visits, one being the Central Bureau for Educational Visits and Exchanges, who have vast experience in arranging school visits abroad (see Appendix for further contacts).

Much of the advice in earlier chapters can be applied to overseas trips but there are naturally additional factors, especially the legislation and regulations, which may well differ from those of the United Kingdom.

Why travel abroad?

Any school visit has to be justified to make it worthwhile and especially so in the case of taking a group of students abroad. It is after all a great responsibility taking a number of students to a foreign country where the food and language are different and where the climate and culture are unfamiliar. If you ask any student what they personally derived from an overseas visit, they are bound to say, 'an unforgettable experience'; 'the opportunity to find out more about foreign culture' or 'the opportunity of widening my knowledge of the language'. And from a social point of view, overseas visits can enhance relationships and help towards establishing a better understanding between different cultures. From a purely personal point of view, it enables students to take control of their own life, learn how to interact socially with their peers and taste a little independence.

Types of breaks

Recreational

There are several types of overseas visits, such as when schools take part in recreational and sporting activities, and these are always popular, the commonest being skiing in Norway or France. Although this activity-based visit may not be considered to have any relevance to the National Curriculum, some local authorities prefer skiing visits to take place during the school holidays as it could be argued that they are helpful to a student who has developed a talent for the sport and is contemplating becoming a skiing teacher. The visit can help to improve their knowledge of the language.

Exchange visits

Exchange visits have proved to be enormously popular and particularly helpful to students studying a foreign language. They enable students to exchange lifestyles for two or three weeks with a fellow student who lives in the country of the language being studied. Not only do they have a 'family' to live with but they also attend the school of their exchange partner, thereby allowing both students the opportunity to broaden their language, to learn more about living in the country and also to mix with their adoptive family. Sometimes these exchange visits are organized by the school that is the twin of the UK school.

Other schools may organize cultural visits that can be integrated with some aspect of the National Curriculum. Travelling abroad is the ideal way to broaden one's knowledge and provides people with an appetite for learning.

Preparing for a trip abroad

No one can really be totally prepared for a foreign visit but prior to going there are certain things that must be considered. The Foreign Office has do's and don'ts leaflets for the 25 most popular foreign destinations for British travellers. The leaflets outline specific points of advice about each country. Basically they include all the normal rules and regulations you would expect to follow when visiting a foreign country. However, it may well be useful to learn one or two of the more common phrases, as people always respect those who try to speak one or two words of their mother tongue, and even if it is totally wrong, it demonstrates that they have at least tried.

It is also equally important to respect your visiting country's culture, rules and regulations of behaviour, dress codes and local customs. Do not get involved with drugs and alcohol.

Hygiene standards in some areas are not very good and so in some countries it is advisable to drink only bottled water, never tap water, and take great care when eating raw vegetables, salads and unpeeled fruit. Raw shellfish should be avoided, similarly underdone meat or fish. Advise the pupils not to buy an ice-cream from an outside kiosk or vendor, it is much safer going into a café.

The planning stage

Obviously this part of the visit will require far more complex planning and preparation than any visit in the United Kingdom would and a pre-visit may not be feasible, although some tour companies may well make this arrangement. Because of the complexity of a school visit and the mammoth task of organizing one, many LEAs require so much information that the group leader must outline a plan of the proposed visit often 12 months before the visit itself so that formal permission from the governors and LEA can be obtained. The initial outline should include details covering the following:

☐ the purpose of the visit;
☐ the country to be visited;
☐ departure and return dates;
☐ the number of people attending;
☐ adult to pupil ratios;
☐ although it may be difficult to estimate, there should be an outline of the cost and whether there may be any claim for financial assistance towards any travel for students or adults in the party;
☐ insurance cover proposed;
☐ information regarding any hazardous activities such as canoeing or skiing, etc;
☐ how the trip is being organized, ie through an organization or via the teacher;
☐ arrangements in cases of an emergency.

And naturally it is important that the Headteacher and governors are kept fully up to date as the plans progress. Although there are many tour operators specializing in school journeys and who are responsible for organizing travel, hotels, visits and all the other necessary details, it can be a problem choosing the correct one for your needs. In this instance contact another school with foreign travel experience and enquire as to which tour operator they used. Tour operators have responsibilities under the Package Travel, Package Holidays and Package Tours Regulations Act 1992. Therefore it is up to the group leader to check the status of any firm being used and check whether it is a member of ABTA (Association of British Travel Agents) or Association of Independent Tour Operators (AITO) and have signed a code of conduct and can provide financial guarantees. One independent association with a members' code of good conduct and safety rules is the Schools and Group Travel Association (SAGTA), and all of its members are in ABTA. Consider investigating other groups, for example, the School Journey Association of London is a voluntary body established to promote school journeys (see Appendix).

In some instances teachers take on the role of organizing the planning themselves, in which case advice can be sought from the Foreign and Commonwealth Office's Travel Advice Unit or the Central Bureau for Educational Visits and Exchanges, which is government-funded. Teachers who organize their own visits should be aware of the EC Directive on Package Travel, Package Holidays and the Package Tours Regulations 1992, which imposes liabilities and obligations on the 'organizer' or 'other party to the contract' in the case of package travel. Schools arranging their own educational visits abroad should be able to justify why their visit is not within the scope of these regulations.

Preparatory tasks

A pre-visit to a location is a good arrangement and although this may not always be possible, the next best thing is that the teachers heading the party familiarize themselves as much as possible with the country to be visited. This advice may be obtained from: the Foreign and Commonwealth Office's Travel Advice Unit, Consular Division, 1 Palace Street, London SW1E 5HE (tel: 0171 238 4503/45040 (Monday–Friday, 9.30 am–4.00 pm); fax: 0171 238 4545); other schools who may have been to the area; a local educational authority or school in the area; national travel offices in the United Kingdom; embassies; travel agents; the Internet, books and magazines; and the Central Bureau for Visits and Exchanges, 10 Spring Gardens, London.

As when visiting sites in this country it is important that parents are given the opportunity of meeting the staff and discussing the visit overseas in order to iron out any worries. Similarly, there should also be regular meetings in order that parents, students and staff are kept up to date with arrangements.

Insurance

The insurance aspect of travelling abroad is not one to be taken lightly as it is essential that the group has fully comprehensive travel insurance and it is the responsibility of the teacher to inquire whether the LEA or the organization sponsoring the visit has sufficient policy cover to oversee any possible claims. If this is not the case, then a special policy should be arranged with an insurance company, with the premiums being charged to the cost of the journey. Further advice may also be obtained from the Central Bureau or from professional associations but the most important point for the teacher to remember is that the risk of loss, medical emergency or accident is far greater and may therefore be more difficult to deal with in a foreign country.

There are many countries which have no health care agreements with the United Kingdom, including Cyprus, Turkey, Switzerland, all of Asia including India, Thailand, the Middle East, etc and in order to secure even the most fundamental care in these countries it is vital to take out fully comprehensive insurance. If travelling to America, you should also make sure that you have an extremely high level of cover.

There are certain countries with which the United Kingdom has an agreement for the provision of emergency medical treatment, if not free then at reduced costs. These are the members of the European Economic Area (EEA) and include the 15 member states of the EC together with Norway and Liechtenstein. Should an accident befall anyone visiting these countries, then provided they have a valid Form E111, they will receive free or reduced cost emergency treatment. It is important pupils have this form filled in by the parent or guardian and take it along with them on the trip. It is also important to take out full medical cover whenever visiting a country outside the EC to avoid any financial complications should treatment be required. In these circumstances payment has to be made on the spot and can later be reclaimed.

In the case of any extra costs, ie a prolonged hospital stay or transporting the injured party and a member of staff back home, and in the case of a severe accident, any compensation or extra cover should also be taken out. Comprehensive insurance packages will also generally cover loss of money or baggage, and the cost of returning home via an alternative route.

Health and welfare

On the subject of travelling abroad and health, the teacher must find out whether any vaccinations are necessary and ensure that pupils have them in good time. The Department of Health provides advice on vaccinations in its publication *Health Advice to Travellers Anywhere in the World* (see Appendix). Some local authorities suggest that all pupils undergo a medical prior to going abroad, but it is important that it is ascertained in advance which pupils may have any special medical conditions which may require treatment on the journey or while abroad, in particular asthma, epilepsy, allergies, etc. Similarly, special care needs should also be taken into account. Girls should be advised to bring sufficient supplies of sanitary towels with them.

One teacher should be given the responsibility for all the medical requirements of pupils and should also be qualified in first aid and be in charge of a first aid kit. It is important that students are advised of the health risks when visiting a foreign destination.

Keeping safe and healthy

Every year thousands of holidaymakers abroad suffer an accident, many of which are preventable. Every year thousands end up spending their two weeks holiday in their bedroom as the result of food poisoning, which again is preventable. Every day thousands of holidaymakers go out in the midday sun and suffer from sunburn as a result. It is bad enough one person being poorly but when you are taking a whole class away and several of them fall victim to food poisoning or some other such condition, then somehow that holiday can turn into 'a holiday from hell'. The safest and best advice whenever going abroad is to spend some time doing general research into the country – its culture, customs, food, climate – so that you have covered every conceivable eventuality and are well prepared.

The commonest problem is travellers' diarrhoea, which is debilitating and can ruin a holiday. In order to avoid this, make sure that the students are well aware of how it is generally contracted and that they follow these guidelines:

- Always wash their hands after going to the lavatory and before handling and eating food.
- Always drink bottled water and avoid asking for ice in their drinks.
- Stick to drinking hot tea or coffee. Failing that, drink carbonated water and soft drinks such as bottled fruit juice.
- Eat only foods which are thoroughly cooked and so still hot. Don't eat any which have been kept warm on a hot plate, as you don't know how long it has been there.
- Unless you can shell or peel it, don't eat uncooked food, and the same applies to food which has been exposed to the weather.
- Buy ice-cream only from shops or cafés as it is far safer than buying it from corner kiosks.
- If drinking milk make sure that it has been boiled.
- If buying fresh fruit, make sure that the skin has been peeled.

Sunburn

Over-exposure to the sun can lead to sunburn and the closer you go to the equator the more powerful are the sun's ultraviolet rays. So never underestimate the intensity of the sun. Make sure that students remain out of direct sun between the hours of 12.00 noon and 2.00 pm and that they are well protected with sun cream, and wear sunglasses and also a sun hat.

Sunstroke or heatstroke often goes unrecognized until the person complains of a headache and a feeling of nausea, typical symptoms showing that they have had too much sun and that their body is dehydrated. It is essential to maintain fluid levels in warmer climates. Wear loose clothing, preferably made of cotton or other natural fibres.

Animal bites

Some people are more vulnerable to insect bites when abroad than others but there is little you can do about it other than use an appropriate insect repellent and when out walking make sure legs and arms are covered. Many tropical diseases are spread via tick bites, drinking contaminated water or eating contaminated food but these only occur in tropical countries for which vaccinations are readily available. For further information about these and other issues on travelling abroad there is a leaflet available called *Health Advice For Travellers* which can be picked up at any major post office or DSS office. And do remember to find out whether any party members in your group have an allergic reaction to insect bites, in which case they should see the nurse at their GP for some advice on preventative treatments to take.

Safety tips abroad

If taking part in a sporting activity which could possibly incur injury such as skiing, canoeing or mountain climbing, make sure that the school is fully covered and that all the relevant safety checks have been fully adhered to.

Most European countries drive on the opposite side of the road to Britain and so it can be pretty confusing when it comes to crossing busy city roads. Pupils should be told which way to look. Unfortunately traffic accidents are the major cause of death among travellers. Make sure that if pupils do go out unsupervised, they remember the direction flow of the traffic.

Travel documents: passport

It may well take several months to obtain passports for a group, especially if the party includes members who are not fully entitled to a full UK passport. Often in the spring and summer months it can take even longer to secure passports, so it is important to start the procedure in good time. The Central Bureau can provide detailed information on cost, procedures and special requirements such as visas for visits to specific countries, and in some circumstances a group passport may well suffice.

There are basically two types of passport available: 1) a full 10-year passport valid for 10 years (application form obtainable from a main post office); and 2) a group passport which can be issued to approved parties of UK nationals who are under 18 and travelling under the supervision of a responsible leader. Non-UK nationals and existing holders of a full UK passport cannot be included. The leader of the group using the collective passport must themselves hold a full UK passport. Applications must be accompanied by a supporting letter from the Headteacher or local authority governors. Some countries may well impose their own restrictions on the use of collective passports and on who may be included. Details and forms are available from the Central Bureau for Educational Visits and Exchanges.

It is worthwhile remembering that members of a group travelling on a collective passport are expected to travel and remain together throughout the trip. If, for some reason, a member of the group has to leave the group, then separate travel documents should be obtained from the British Consulate.

Essentials to pack

Although the cost of the trip will doubtless have been paid for and any other expenses incurred for travelling abroad should have been ironed out at the initial meetings, pupils will still require money to spend. It is advisable that a maximum amount of pocket money is specified and, depending on the age of the students, whether the teacher is held solely responsible for issuing money each day or the students themselves take full responsibility. Whatever is decided, most people tend to use travellers' cheques. Depending on the currency rate before departure it would be a good practice to take the pupils along to the nearest high street bank and cash some sterling into the foreign currency. Because exchange rates can differ so much and can be rather confusing, a rough calculation on what the exchange rates would be is a useful exercise to do in the classroom as part of the preparation work.

Luggage

Most people fall into the trap of taking too many clothes when going abroad, so the best advice for students is to take only what they can comfortably carry themselves, especially when they have to transfer their luggage several times from the coach to the plane, ferry or train and then off at the other end. Labels should be provided for both the inward and outward journey. All luggage should be clearly labelled.

Customs

The teacher in charge of the group should stress that duty-free allowances are not applicable to young people and so they shouldn't even bother trying to smuggle a bottle of whisky or cigarettes back home for Mum or Dad. They should also be made aware of the fact that they shouldn't take dangerous sharp items with them such as flick knives, and dangerous souvenirs will simply be confiscated.

Etiquette

Students visiting a foreign country are not only representing their school but are also ambassadors of their country and any rude behaviour is a bad reflection of their homeland. In recent years there has been a lot of media attention on youths who have gone on foreign football trips and behaved abominably and given the English a poor reputation. Courtesy and politeness can certainly improve relationships and if there is a member of the group able to speak the language so much the better. People respect and admire visitors who have taken the time to study their language and so will spend a little more time with them. But there are several other important factors to remember:

☐ Pay attention to the culture and local customs of the country you are visiting. Certain places have a strict dress code and will not allow people inside religious buildings without their arms or legs being covered.
☐ Never take drugs.
☐ When carrying money around it is safer to store it in a money belt or somewhere else concealed. Many people consider foreigners easy targets and will try to pick their pockets or beg money from them.
☐ Learn how to use phones abroad and know the dialling code for home. A BT phone card allows calls to be charged to the home number. Make sure that students are not allowed to roam freely outdoors in the evening or even in the hotel unsupervised, as there can be many unsavoury characters abroad.
☐ Make sure that all students are aware of and take notice of the No Smoking, No Drinking Alcohol ban.

There will be several meetings with staff and parents before departure, when it is ideal to bring up any last minute alterations to the itinerary and give everyone the chance to raise any questions. It will be at these meetings that the teacher can make these guidelines known: that students are fully aware of the local customs and laws of the country in relation to drinking and smoking, and the consequences of being found doing so. If students have free time in the evenings, it should always be supervised and they should not leave the main group and wander off without notifying a member of staff. Likewise they should not take part in any physical activity, ie skiing or swimming without permission and supervision.

Emergencies

There is nothing worse than being away from home when someone is taken ill abroad. The leader should know the location of the nearest British Embassy or Consulate together with the telephone number. Emergency procedures are a vital part of planning a school visit and if an accident should occur, the priorities are to attend to the victim immediately, make sure the remainder of the group are safe and inform the parents and school of the accident as quickly as possible.

Generally the leader of the group will take full charge and all those involved in the trip should be informed and know who is the back-up prior to leaving the school. But should an emergency occur when abroad, the leader must:

☐ establish the degree and nature of the emergency immediately;
☐ make sure that all the group members are safe;

- □ write down the names of the injured parties and seek immediate medical attention for the victims if necessary;
- □ make sure that a teacher accompanies any casualities to hospital and that the rest of the group is supervised;
- □ if necessary, notify the police and the British Consulate;
- □ notify the school of the names and details of the injuries of those involved, the nature, date and time of the incident, and the location;
- □ make sure that a complete written accident report is kept and written up as soon as possible.

It is important that no one discusses anything with the media and nor should legal liability be discussed or admitted. Drawing up an emergency plan is something which should be addressed at the pre-planning stages and all party members and parents should know what is involved.

Contact with home

It is not only children that become slightly fraught when they are going away for any length of time – parents too will worry, particularly if this is the first time their child has been away from home. The one way to allay any fears and put everyone's concerns at rest is to make sure that all students send a postcard home notifying their safe arrival. For those who want to make a telephone call, let them. Someone at school should have the official contact number for the duration of the visit and should have the names, addresses and telephone numbers of the parents/guardians of all students with full details of the itinerary, accommodation and telephone numbers and any other relevant information required. It is imperative for everyone that if there is any delay, if someone is taken ill or anything else, the contact person at home is informed. He or she can then relay any messages to the people concerned.

PART 2
DIRECTORY OF RESOURCES

6 The South West

THE AMERICAN MUSEUM IN BRITAIN

Address: Claverton Manor, Bath BA2 7BD
Tel: Education: (01225) 463538   Fax: (01225) 480726
Museum: (01225) 460503

Description:
Illustrating life in America from early colonial days to the late 19th century the main collection of items at the American Museum in Britain includes a series of furnished rooms covering the 17th century to the end of the Civil War. There are a selection of galleries depicting the work of American craftsmen and women; the North American Indians; maritime history, firemen's equipment and much more.

Ages: All ages
Subjects: History; Art; Design & Technology
Facilities: Guided tour; costume sessions; films; video; free teachers' pre-visit; library; car park, disabled access limited; refreshments; shop; toilets
Open: November–mid-March: Monday–Friday, 9.30 am–5.00 pm.
Mid-March–July, September, October: Monday, 9.30 am–5.00 pm; Tuesday– Friday, 9.30 am–1.30 pm. August: Monday–Friday, 9.30 am–1.30 pm. Closed January
Admission: Group rates upon application
Group size: Max 120
Length of visit: Half a day

BATH INDUSTRIAL HERITAGE CENTRE

Address: Camden Works, Julian Road, Bath BA1 2RH
Tel: (01225) 318348

Description:
Bath Heritage Centre has been recreated to reflect the life of Mr J B Bowler, who began his business in 1872 trading as an engineer, brass founder, gas-fitter, locksmith and bell hanger. His talents further extended to repairing and making soda

water machinery and running a fizzy drink-making factory. When his business ceased in 1969 the Heritage Centre recreated Mr Bowler's factory, enabling visitors to recall the atmosphere of a bygone age. There are also reconstructions of a Bath Stone quarry face and a local cabinet-making workshop, both of which played important roles in the city's history.

Ages: All ages

Subjects: History

Facilities: Refreshments; shop; hands-on activities; guided tours; slide shows; teachers' notes; resource materials available for loan; events

Open: Easter–end of October: Monday–Sunday, 10.00 am–5.00 pm. November–Easter: Saturdays and Sundays, 10.00 am–5.00 pm

Admission: Group rates upon application

Group size: Upon application

Length of visit: Full day

BLAZES – FIRE MUSEUM

Address: Sandhill Park, Bishops Lydeard, Taunton, Somerset TA4 3DF
Tel: (01823) 433964

Description:
With the help of exhibitions and the latest technology Blazes Fire Museum explores the history of fire and fire fighting, demonstrating the role fire can play in all our lives; making, using and preventing fire, traditions and mythology, as well as promoting fire safety and illustrating how fire affects our daily lives.

Ages: 5+

Subjects: Science

Facilities: Car park; disabled access; tearoom; outdoor eating area; presentation theatre; guided tour/talk; special events; shop; education room

Open: April–end October, 10.00 am–5.00 pm. Closed Mondays except Bank Holidays

Admission: Group rates upon application

Group size: Upon application

Length of visit: 2 hours

THE BOURNEMOUTH BEARS

Address: The ExpoCentre, Old Christchurch Lane, Bournemouth BH1 1NE
Tel: (01202) 293544   Fax: (01305) 268885

Description:
A new educational attraction celebrating the 90th birthday of the Teddy Bear from 1904 up to the present day and a valuable resource centre for teaching

visual perception in relation to the art and history of toys. A special display demonstrates the difference in the various textures of the early Teddy Bears compared with those made from synthetic materials. Old, new and limited editions and those of some TV personalities.

Ages: All ages

Subjects: Art; History

Facilities: Free teachers' pre-visit; teachers' notes; worksheets; introductory talk; outdoor eating area; shop; disabled access limited; toilets

Open: Seven days a week, 9.30 am–5.30 pm. Closed 24–26 December. Open Bank Holidays

Admission: Children £1.75; teachers/adults £2.50. One teacher free for every 10 pupils

Group size: Upon application

Length of visit: 90 minutes

BREWERS QUAY

Address: Brewers Quay, Hope Square, Weymouth, Dorset DT4 8TR
Tel: (01305) 777622   Fax: (01305) 761680

Description:

Travel back through 600 years of Weymouth's history; see, hear and smell the days of its exciting past at Brewers Quay. Begin your journey at the Town Museum, then pass through the special secret wall into the Timewalk Journey, before embarking upon the footsteps of Ms Paws, the brewery cat and her ancestors via 19 realistic scenes. It's exciting, spooky but entertaining.

Ages: All ages

Subjects: Science; Geography

Facilities: Free teachers' pre-visit; indoor eating areas; toilets; shop; disabled access limited; car park; talks; exhibitions; demonstrations; worksheets; teachers' resource pack; audiovisual facilities; regular special events; classroom

Open: Seven days a week, 10.00 am–5.30 pm. Complex closed 25–27 December, also last two weeks in January for maintenance

Admission: Entrance to Brewers Quay is free. Charges apply to some individual attractions

Group size: Min 20

Length of visit: 1 hour +

BRISTOL ZOO GARDENS

Address: Education Centre, Clifton, Bristol BS8 3HA
  Tel: Business: (0117) 970 6176   Fax: (0117) 973 6814

Description:
  Bristol Zoo offers a unique experience for everyone. Dedicated to educating, researching, conservation and entertaining it has earned a reputation for its role in international breeding programmes for endangered species as well as its exciting educational programmes. Learn of the plight faced by many creatures in the wild; see the reptile house and aquarium; tropical birds; sessions on animal care. A new education centre is opening in 1999.

Ages: All ages

Subjects: Science; Geography; Music; History; Art; English; Design & Technology

Facilities: Hands-on sessions; activity centre; teachers' pack; free teachers' pre-visit; education officers; worksheets; special events; tailor-made visits; talks; bug world; walk-through aviary; gorilla island; car park; indoor/outdoor eating areas; play area; zoo-Olympics activity trail; twilight world; disabled access; shop; toilets

Open: Summer: daily, 9.00 am–5.30 pm. Winter: daily, 9.00 am–4.30 pm. Advisable to pre-book

Admission: Group discounts apply to 15+. One teacher free with every seven pupils

Group size: Max 35

Length of visit: 1–1½ hours

THE BYGONES MUSEUM

Address: Fore Street, St Marychurch, Torquay
  Tel: (01803) 326108

Description:
  Open 364 days of the year 'Bygones' recreates the atmosphere of a busy Victorian Street, offering invaluable educational resources for all ages with

authentic smells and street sounds offering the opportunity to observe first hand and relate to the important aspects of the era. Topics to study include transport, communication, toys and games, homes and life in the trenches.

Ages: All ages

Subjects: History

Facilities: Guided tour; worksheets; hands-on experience; exhibitions; refreshments; indoor eating area; shop

Open: Throughout the year

Admission: Special rates for groups. One adult admitted free with six children aged under 8 years: one adult admitted free with 10 children aged 8 years and over

Group size: Upon application

Length of visit: Full day

CLOVELLY

Address: The Estate office, Clovelly, nr Bideford, North Devon EX39 5SY
Tel: (01237) 431200

Description:
Step back in history and find out what life was really like in the picturesque and historic North Devon village of Clovelly. Nestling on a 400 ft cliff with sledges and donkeys as the main means of transport and a cobbled street leading past cottages to a 14th-century harbour, Clovelly is one of the world's most unique villages, unspoilt and little changed by the 20th century.

Ages: All ages

Subjects: History; Geography

Facilities: Audiovisual facilities; disabled access; demonstrations; guided tours; exhibitions; educational pack; shop; playground; Land Rover service runs from the top of the village to the harbour from Easter to October; boat trips; car park; indoor/outdoor eating areas; visitor centre; toilets

Open: Every day, all day

Admission: Children £2.00; under 7s free

Group size: N/A

Length of visit: Full day

DAIRYLAND FARM WORLD

Address: Summercourt, Newquay, Cornwall TR8 5AA
Tel: (01872) 510246/510348   Fax: (01872) 510349

Description:
Learn about farm life; visit the Heritage Centre, which takes you back to rural life in the 1800s; a nature trail covering 75 acres helps you to explore and under-

stand pond life. There are also tailor-made visits available together with a brass rubbing centre, milking parlour, playground and park.

Ages: 5+

Subjects: Science; Mathematics; English; Design & Technology; History; Geography

Facilities: Free teachers' pre-visit; resource materials; quiz sheets; demonstrations; refreshments; outdoor eating areas; shop; guided tour/talks; toilets

Open: Daily, April–November

Admission: Group rates are available on application

Group size: Min 15

Length of visit: 4 hours

DINGLE STEAM VILLAGE

Address: Milford, Lifton, Devon PL16 0AT
Tel: (01566) 783425

Description:

Explore Britain's Industrial Heritage in a delightful rural setting featuring a collection of traction engines, steamrollers, vintage machinery and exhibits used by many of the original Dingle Family, one of the largest firms of road-makers in the area.

Ages: All ages

Subjects: Design & Technology

Facilities: Free teachers' packs; guided tour/talk; exhibitions; riverside walks; teachers' notes; education room; outdoor/indoor eating areas; car park; disabled access; play area; shop; toilets

Open: Daily from Easter Saturday until the end of October, 10.00 am–6.00 pm. Closed Fridays

Admission: Children (under 16) £3.00; adults/teachers £4.00; groups of 12+ 20 per cent discount

Group size: Min 15

Length of visit: 4 hours

THE DINOSAUR MUSEUM

Address: Icen Way, Dorchester, Dorset DT1 1EW
Tel: Museum (01305) 269741   Fax: (01305) 268885
       Bookings (01305) 269741

Description:

One of Britain's top attractions. The fascinating world of dinosaurs is brought to life in this 'new age' museum where visitors are encouraged to touch and use their senses. The museum relates the story of the dinosaur through displays and there are authentic fossils, skeletons, and life-sized reconstructions to amuse and educate.

Ages: All ages
Subjects: Science; Art
Facilities: Disabled access limited; shop; refreshments; outdoor eating area; free teachers' pre-visit; worksheets; guide; introductory talk and video
Open: Daily, 9.30 am–5.30 pm. Closed 24–26 December. Open Bank Holidays
Admission: Children £1.75; adults/teachers £2.50. One teacher free for every 10 pupils
Group size: Min 30; max 40
Length of visit: 90 minutes

ENGLISH HERITAGE

Before making a visit to any of the English Heritage listed buildings in the South West of England contact them for further information: English Heritage, Historic Properties South West, 29 Queen Square, Bristol BS1 4ND (tel: 0117 975 0716; fax: 0117 975 0701).

Avebury Museum
Berry Pomeroy Castle
Bradford-upon-Avon Tithe Barn
Chysauster Ancient Village
Cleeve Abbey
Dartmouth Castle
Farleigh Hungerford Castle
Fiddleford Manor
Glastonbury Tribunal
Hailes Abbey
Kirkham House
Launceston Castle
Lulworth Castle
Muchelney Abbey
Netheravon Dovecote
Okehampton Castle
Old Sarum
Old Wardour Castle
Pendennis Castle
Portland Castle
Ratfyn Barrows
Restormel Castle
Royal Citadel, Plymouth
Rycote Chapel

St Mawes Castle
Sherborne Old Castle
Tintagel Castle
Totnes Castle

For Stonehenge – English Heritage, First Floor, Abbey Buildings, Abbey Square, Amesbury, Wiltshire SP4 7ES (tel: 01980 625368; fax: 01980 623465).

FLEET AIR ARM MUSEUM

Address: PO Box No D6, RNAS Yeovilton, Ilchester, Somerset BA22 8HT
Tel: (01935) 840565   Fax: (01935) 840181

Description:
The opportunity of seeing examples of various types of aircraft covering World War I, World War II and Korea together with an aircraft carrier and two important British inventions of the 20th century, namely Concorde and the Harrier Jump Jet.
Ages: 5+
Subjects: History; English; Design & Technology; Art; R.E.; Mathematics
Facilities: Disabled access limited; indoor/outdoor eating areas; car park; toilets; shop; free teachers' pre-visit; education officer; activity sheets; introductory talk; adventure playground
Open: Daily. 1 November–31 March, 10.00 am–4.30 pm. 1 April–31 October, 10.00 am–5.00 pm. Closed 24–26 December
Admission: Children (5–16 years) £2.75; students (16+ years) £3.50. One teacher free for every 10 pupils. Extra adults £4.00
Group size: N/A
Length of visit: 2½ hours

HELICOPTER MUSEUM

Address: The Heliport, Western-Super-Mare, Somerset BS22 8PP
Tel: (01934) 635227   Fax: (01934) 822400

Description:
Students of all ages will enjoy the experience of seeing a collection of helicopters and autogyros to understand how helicopters operate. See the world's fastest helicopter, visit the Restoration Hangar and the Russian Hind Attack Helicopter. A rare and award-winning collection – unique in Great Britain and the world.
Ages: 5+
Subjects: Science; Technology: Mathematics: English
Facilities: Guided tour; educational pack; car park; cafe; shop; special events
Open: April–October: daily, 10.00 am–6.00 pm. November–March: Wednesday–Sunday, 10.00 am–4.00 pm

Admission: Special rates for groups of 15+. Children £1.70; adults/teachers £2.50. One adult free for every 10 pupils
Group size: Upon application
Length of visit: N/A

LONGLEAT

Address: The Estate Office, Warminster, Wiltshire, Wessex BA12 7NW
  Tel: (01985) 844400   Fax: (01985) 844885

Description:
  Longleat is steeped in over 400 years of history and provides a rare opportunity to see a selection of animals including zebra, elephants, llamas, camels, tigers, lions and wolves, many of which are endangered, living in as near to natural surroundings as possible at Longleat Safari Park. It is a truly remarkable experience and can prove an invaluable aid to the National Curriculum. Take a safari boat trip, go for a stroll in the Tropical Garden, explore the Science Fiction world, and browse around Longleat House which holds a rich treasure of priceless heirlooms and architecture. There is even a new exciting mirror maze to explore plus lots of other exciting attractions.
Ages: All ages
Subjects: Art; Design & Technology; English; Geography; History; Mathematics; Science; P.E.
Facilities: Exhibitions; museum; shop; tailor-made packages; car park; refreshments; tours; pleasure walk; The Total Animal Experience; Lancelot's Fun Time Ticket; Tiny Tiger Ticket; butterfly garden, pets corner; education packs; miniature railway; shop
Open: House: daily Easter–September, 10.00 am–6.00 pm; remainder of the year guided tours at set times between 10.00 am and 4.00 pm; closed 25 December. Safari Park: 14 March–1 November, daily 10.00 am–5.00 pm. Other attractions: 14 March–1 November, daily 11.00 am–5.30 pm
Admission: Grounds and garden – children and teachers free. There are group rates available for various amenities
Group size: Upon application
Length of visit: Full day

NATIONAL TRUST PROPERTIES

There are a number of National Trust properties in the South West of England. For further information about those in Cornwall contact: Assistant Public Affairs Manager, National Trust Regional Office, Lanhydrock, Bodmin PL30 4DE (tel: 01208 74281). It is advisable to book all school visits.

NATIONAL TRUST EDUCATION

The Ashridge Estate

Ringshall, Berkhamsted, Hertfordshire
Tel: (01442) 842488 Estate Office

The Ashridge Estate covers some six square miles in Hertfordshire and Buckinghamshire, running along the main ridge of the Chiltern Hills from Ivinghoe Beacon to Berkhamsted; it comprises over 1,619ha unspoilt open spaces, commons and woodlands; the main focal point is the granite monument erected 150 years ago to the third Duke of Bridgewater; wildlife is well-represented; a wide variety of birds is always in evidence; muntjac and some 400 fallow deer roam freely; badgers, foxes and grey squirrels also abound; and almost unique to the area is the Glis glis, or edible dormouse.

Teachers' resource book; study base (capacity 60); education warden to assist visits; National Curriculum links with Science, Geography and Environmental Education. Educational visits should be registered with the Education Warden, tel: (01442) 842488.

Claydon House

Middle Claydon, Buckingham MK18 2EY
Tel: (01296) 730349

Eighteenth-century house containing a series of magnificent and unique rococo state rooms with carvings; museum with Florence Nightingale and Verney family mementoes.

Written resource material available: National Curriculum links with Technology, Art, History and Science.

Hughenden Manor

High Wycombe, Buckinghamshire HP14 4LA
Tel: (01494) 532580

Bought in 1847 by Disraeli, Prime Minister during Queen Victoria's reign; contains his books, pictures, furniture and memorabilia. The estate is 226ha and includes woodland, park, formal Victorian gardens, walled garden and working farm.

Study base is available for groups (capacity 50); written resource material available; guidance notes for teachers; National Curriculum links with History (Victorians) and Environmental Education. Education Officer on site.

Osterley Park

Isleworth, Middlesex TW7 4RB Tel: 0181-560 3918
Educational visits should be registered with the Group Bookings Secretary on 0181-560 3918

Originally built in 1575, evidence of Osterley's Tudor origins is apparent in the splendid stable block and, with a little exploration, the interior of the house. In 1761 Robert Adam remodelled the house as a neo-classical villa. Today Osterley remains one of the country's most complete examples of his work. Osterley's 120ha of landscaped park and farmland area are a rare green lung in urban London. The lakes, trees and pasture are home to rich bird- and wildlife. The area is also a valuable resource for the local community and visitors.

Study centre (capacity 60); teachers' resource book; children's guide; house quiz, estate quiz, and Scavenger Hunt; National Curriculum links with History, Geography, Technology and Environmental Education. Education Officer on site.

Stowe Landscape Gardens

Buckingham MK18 5EH
Tel: (01280) 822850

Stowe, with its great house and gardens, is one of the supreme creations of the Georgian era and considered amongst the most important landscape gardens in the world; the garden, of some 202ha, 32 buildings and temples, lakes and over 3 miles of ha-ha, has links with 'Capability' Brown, Bridgeman, Kent and Vanbrugh.

Resource centre; National Curriculum links with History, Geography, Technology and Environmental Education.

Sutton House

2 & 4 Homerton High Street, Hackney, London E9 6JQ
Tel: 0181-986 2264

Early 16th-century Tudor house built on H-plan with later additions.

Study centre (maximum capacity 30); teachers' resource book; National Curriculum links with History, Geography, Mathematics, Technology and Science.

National Trust
EDUCATION
membership for groups

Cornish Engines
Cotehele
Lanhydrock
Poltesco
St Michael's Mount
Tintagel Old Post Office
Trelissick Garden
Trerice

For information on National Trust properties in Devon contact: Regional Education Officer, National Trust Regional Office, Killerton, Broadclyst, Exeter EX5 3LE (tel: 01392 881691).

Arlington Court
Buckland Abbey
Castle Drogo
Finch Foundry
Killerton
Lydford Gorge
Overbecks Museum
Plym Bridge Woods
Saltram Park

The Trust also owns over 80 miles of coastline and 12,140 ha of countryside in Devon, which is regularly used by schools for project work. The North Devon basecamp provides opportunities for schools to work alongside the Trust wardens on conservation projects and can also be used for field studies. For further information contact: The Warden, Exmoor Basecamp, 1 Town Farm Cottages, Countisbury, Lynton EX35 6NE (tel: 01598 741297).

The National Trust Wessex Region covers Bristol and South Gloucestershire, Dorset, Somerset and Wiltshire. For further information contact: Regional Education Officer, National Trust Regional Office, Eastleigh Court, Bishopstrow, Warminster, Wiltshire BA12 9HW (tel: 01985 843600).

Avebury
Brownsea Island
Clevedon Court
Corfe Castle
Dunster Castle
Dyrham Park
Golden Cap Estate
Holnicote Estate
Kingston Lacy
Kingston Lacy Estate

Lacock Abbey
Lacock: Fox Talbot Museum
Montacute House
Stourhead
Studland Peninsula

PAIGNTON ZOO

Address: Paignton Zoo Education Centre, Penwill Way, Paignton, Devon TQ4 5JS
Tel: (01803) 697510

Description:
One of the largest zoos in Britain, first opened in 1923. It accommodates hundreds
of animals, many of which are endangered. The main aims of the Zoo are to
promote wildlife and conservation, and offer visitors the opportunity to learn
more about animals and their natural habitats.

Ages: All ages

Subjects: History; Art; Mathematics; Geography; English; R.E.

Facilities: Worksheets; special events; car park; indoor/outdoor eating areas;
education centre; activity centre; trails; exhibitions; activities for under-5s;
shops; refreshments; special tours/talks and activities can be arranged; disabled
access (some limited); toilets

Open: Daily, 10.00 am–6.00 pm in summer and 10.00 am–dusk in winter. Closed
Christmas Day

Admission: Contact for rates

Group size: Min 20

Length of visit: 4–5 hours

PENNYWELL FARM

Address: Devon's Farm & Wildlife Centre, Buckfastleigh TQ11 0LT
Tel: (01364) 642023   Fax: (01364) 642122

Description:
With 65 acres to explore, a unique learning experience awaits pupils at
Pennywell Farm, where they can learn about nature and wildlife, conservation
and the environment in an exhilarating hands-on session.

Ages: All ages

Subjects: Mathematics; History; English; Geography; Science; Art

Facilities: Farm guides; wetland area; conservation area; farm animals; hands-on
activities including feeding and weighing animals; woodland wildlife area; toilets;
shop; indoor/outdoor eating areas; animal demonstrations; commando course;
pond dipping; introductory talk; car park; tailor-made sessions available; free
teachers' pre-visit

Open: Open daily, 10.00 am–5.00 pm. Contact for educational group bookings
Admission: Summer: children (under 15 years) £3.95; adults/teachers £3.95. Autumn: children £3.50; adults/teachers £3.50. One adult free for every five children
Group size: N/A
Length of visit: N/A

PLYMOUTH DOME

Address: The Hoe, Plymouth PL1 2NZ
   Tel: (01752) 603300   Fax: (01752) 256361

Description:
   Travel through time with a visit to Plymouth Dome and experience the voyages and adventures that shaped the world; stroll through the dirt and stench of an Elizabethan street and brave the high seas with Drake, Cook and *The Mayflower*, then see for yourself the amazing seascape of Plymouth Sound from the Dome's two observation galleries.
Ages: All ages
Subjects: History
Facilities: Free teachers' pre-visit; audiovisual facilities; disabled access; guided walks; car park; refreshments; shop; outdoor eating areas; resource packs available; toilets
Open: Throughout the year, daily from 9.00 am. Closed Christmas Day
Admission: Group rates upon application
Group size: Min 30
Length of visit: N/A

POOLE POTTERY LIMITED

Address: The Quay, Poole, Dorset BH15 1RF
   Tel: (01202) 669800/666200   Fax: (01202) 682894

Description:
   A visit to Dorset's number one attraction, the Pottery Factory, offers an unforgettable experience which promises to bring history and heritage vividly to life and where every part of the craft is explored. Visit the museum with its remarkable displays of work from master craftsmen; step inside the new cinema and take part in a 12-minute journey through 2,000 years of pottery with the help of Matthew Kelly; witness the fascinating processes involved in plate making; take part in creating some pottery.
Ages: 5+
Subjects: History; Art; Design & Technology

Facilities: Free teachers' pre-visit; classroom available; tour guide; museum; video show; craft village; hands-on activity areas; workshops; glassblowing demonstrations; shop; refreshments; worksheets; car park; disabled access; indoor/outdoor eating areas; factory tour

Open: Throughout the year, 10.00 am–4.00 pm. Advisable to check on times for school parties

Admission: Group rates upon application

Group size: Min 10

Length of visit: 45 minutes

RODE BIRD GARDENS

Address: Rode, nr Bath, Somerset BA3 6QW
   Tel: (01373) 830326   Fax: (01373) 831288

Description:
   A pioneer in the protection of endangered bird species from around the world, Rode Bird Gardens has over 200 different species from all climates. Studies can be adopted to accommodate various lessons on the National Curriculum.

Ages: All ages

Subjects: Art; History; Technology; R.E.; English; Geography; Science; Mathematics

Facilities: Car park; worksheets; pets corner; flower gardens; information centre; steam railway; play area; lakes; shop; disabled access; talks; refreshments; special events; toilets

Open: Daily. Summer, 10.00 am–6.00 pm. Winter, 10.00 am–dusk. Closed Christmas Day

Admission: Group rates for 12+. Children and adults/teachers £1.80 each. One adult free for every 10 children

Group size: Min 12

Length of visit: Up to ½ a day

ROMAN BATHS AND PUMP ROOM

Address: Stall Street, Bath BA1 1LZ
   Tel: (01225) 477757   Fax: (01225) 477271

Description:
   Discover the everyday life of a Roman city and see ancient treasures from the Goddess of Wisdom and Healing at one of the country's finest ancient monuments, the Roman Temple and bathing complex built almost 2,000 years ago.

Ages: 5+

Subjects: Art; History; Technology

Facilities: Disabled access; audio tours; guides; shop

Open: Daily. October–March, 9.30am–5.00pm (Sunday 10.30 am)
Admission: Group rates upon application
Group size: Upon application
Length of visit: 1–2 hours

ROYAL ALBERT MEMORIAL MUSEUM

Address: Queen Street, Exeter EX4 3RX
   Tel: (01392) 268585   Fax: (01392) 421252

Description:
   The natural history collection is the largest in the country with materials ranging from Antarctica to the Arctic, subject areas diverse as they are fascinating. There are collections of decorative art; a technology section which demonstrates the range of items manufactured in the 19th and 20th centuries; an archaeology collection; local history; ethnography; and an outstanding fine art collection.
Ages: All ages
Subjects: Art; History; Science
Facilities: Disabled access; indoor eating area; cloakroom; temporary exhibitions; resource packs available; special events; talks; weekend clubs for children
Open: Monday–Saturday, 10.00 am–6.00 pm; Wednesday open until 8.00 pm. Sunday, 12 noon–6.00 pm. Closed 24–26 December, 1 January and Good Friday
Admission: Group rates upon application
Group size: Upon application
Length of visit: 1–2 hours

SHIPWRECK AND HERITAGE CENTRE

Address: Quay Road, Charlestown, St Austell, Cornwall PL25 3NJ
   Tel: (01726) 69897   Fax: (01726) 68025

Description:
   An award-winning centre revealing the history of diving, salvage and shipwrecks from earliest times to the present day. Exhibitions of artefacts and relics recovered from sunken ships with many aspects of history to discover, from Roman and Tudor through to Victorian times.
Ages: All ages
Subjects: History
Facilities: Free teachers' pre-visit; worksheets; disabled access; indoor eating area; car park; radio-controlled boats; exhibitions; refreshments
Open: Daily, beginning March–end October, 10.00 am–5.00 pm
Admission: Children £1.95. Teachers and helpers free

Group size: Upon application
Length of visit: 90 minutes

SMEATON'S TOWER

Address: The Hoe, Plymouth, Devon PL1 2NZ
   Tel: (01752) 600608

Description:
   Built in 1759 on the dangerous Eddystone Rocks 14 miles out to sea, Smeaton's
   Lighthouse was moved stone by stone to its present site on the Hoe, since which
   time it has been Plymouth's most notorious landmark. Climb up the 93 steps to
   the top of Smeaton's Tower where you will be greeted by a panoramic view out
   over the Plymouth Sound to Devon and Cornwall. For further information tele-
   phone Plymouth Dome recorded information service on (01752) 600608.
Ages: 5+ (unsuitable for disabled)
Facilities: Gift shop; exhibition; refreshments
Subjects: History
Open: Daily
Admission: Free
Group size: Upon application
Length of visit: N/A

SS GREAT BRITAIN PROJECT

Address: Great Western Dock, Gas Ferry Road, Bristol BS1 6TY
   Tel: (0117) 926 0680   Fax: (0117) 925 5788

Description:
   Built and launched in Bristol in 1843 *SS Great Britain* was the largest ever ocean-
   going ship to be built of iron and be steam-driven by a screw propeller. The fore-
   runner of all luxury passenger liners and the only one to survive from the first half
   of the 19th century, the *SS Great Britain* is of great historical importance. Visitors
   can see the ongoing restoration work and experience a sample of life on board a
   passenger ship in Victorian days.
Ages: All ages
Subjects: History; Art; English; Geography; Science; Mathematics
Facilities: Teachers' pack; guided tour
Open: Contact for opening times
Admission: Party groups of 20 pupils. Children £1.90 each. One teacher free for
   every 10 pupils
Group size: Min 20
Length of visit: Up to ½ a day

THE TUTANKHAMUN EXHIBITION

Address: High West Street, Dorchester, Dorset DT1 1UW
   Tel: (01305) 269571   Fax: (01305) 268885

Description:
   A superb exhibition looking at Tutankhamun and ancient Egypt as depicted by accurate copies of the King's treasures. This is an indispensable resource which can readily be related to many aspects of the National Curriculum.
Ages: 5+
Subjects: History; Geography; English; R.E.; Mathematics; Art; Design & Technology
Facilities: Free teachers' pre-visit; worksheets; exhibition guide (charge); introductory talk; shop; refreshments; outdoor eating area; car park; disabled access; toilets
Open: All year, 9.30 am–5.30 pm (5.00 pm November–March). Closed 24–26 December. Open all other Bank Holidays
Admission: Group rates for 15+: Children £1.75; adults/teachers £2.50. One adult free for every 10 pupils
Group size: Max 30
Length of visit: 90 minutes

WELLS CATHEDRAL

Address: Cathedral Offices, West Cloister, Wells, Somerset BA5 2PA
   Tel: (01749) 674483   Fax: (01749) 677360

Description:
   Built in 1180, Wells Cathedral makes for a fascinating visit. See the second oldest working clock in the world which has three dials illustrating hours, minutes and date of the lunar month; the splendid West Front which holds 293 statues. The Quire is the oldest part of the Cathedral and the Chapter House was the place where many canons met to transact Cathedral business.
Ages: 5+
Subjects: R.E.; History; Geography; English; Design & Technology; Art
Facilities: Free teachers' pre-visit; guided tours; worksheets; educational packs; tours can be tailored to meet individual needs; restaurant; shop; outdoor/indoor eating areas; disabled access (most places); toilets
Open: Upon application
Admission: Free although donations gratefully received
Group size: Min 10
Length of visit: 45 minutes

WOODLANDS LEISURE PARK

Address: Woodlands Leisure Park, Blackawton, Totnes, Devon TQ9 7DQ
   Tel: (01803) 712598   Fax: (01803) 712680

Description:
   An educational and entertaining day can be spent at Woodlands Leisure Park
   with a collection of rare and domestic farm animals, undercover attractions, a
   circus playdrome with acrobatic funderland, circus ring and tumblers' tumbling
   zone, a falconry centre, bee talk, demonstrations, plus lots of play equipment
   designed by a sports teacher for children to have lots of fun with.

Ages: All ages

Subjects: Science; Art

Facilities: Education packs; indoor/outdoor eating areas; shops; car park; disabled
   access; commando course; indoor play area; rides; 14 playzones; various attractions

Open: 7 days a week, 9.30 am–6.00 pm

Admission: Group rates upon application

Group size: Min 10

Length of visit: Full day

WOOKEY HOLE CAVES

Address: Wookey Hole Caves Ltd, Wookey Hole, Wells, Somerset BA5 1BB
   Tel: (01749) 672243   Fax: (01749) 677749

Description:
   The notorious Wookey Hole Caves and Paper-mill create a magical experience
   for visitors who are led through an amazing underworld of caverns, pools and
   passageways, taking in the fascinating scenery which was carved out by the
   mysterious River Axe thereby combining legend, folklore and fact.

Ages: All ages

Subjects: Art; English; Geography; History; Science; Mathematics; Technology

Facilities: Free teachers' pre-visit; video for loan; schoolroom; indoor/outdoor
   eating areas; restaurant; car park; activity sheets; disabled access (except for
   caves); shop; resources available for the disabled and access (except for caves);
   hand-made paper shop; magical mirror maze; arcade; working water-wheel;
   toilets

Open: Summer, 10.00 am–5.00 pm. Winter, 10.30 am–4.30 pm

Admission: Group rate for 15+: Children (4–19 years) £2.90; adults/teachers £5.00.
   One adult free with every 10 pupils

Group size: Upon application

Length of visit: 2 hours

7 London and the South East

1066 STORY IN HASTINGS CASTLE

Address: Castle Hill Road, West Hill, Hastings, East Sussex
Tel: (01424) 781113

Description:
Explore the ruins of King William's castle at Hastings to commemorate his victory in 1066, the remains of which stand proudly on top of a cliff jutting out to sea. The castle includes whispering dungeons and the amazing eastern gateway, and once inside visitors are transported back with the aid of an audio guide reliving the battle.

Ages: 5 +

Subjects: English; Science; Geography; Technology; History; Art; R.E.

Facilities: Guided tours; worksheets; toilets; indoor/outdoor eating areas; audio-visual facilities; exhibition; children's themed activity area; dairy; icehouse; shop

Open: Daily. Easter–end September, 10.00 am–5.00 pm. October–Easter, 11.00 am–4.00 pm. Closed for 2 weeks in January

Admission: Group rates upon application

Group size: Min 10

Length of visit: N/A

APSLEY HOUSE

Address: The Wellington Museum, 149 Piccadilly, Hyde Park Corner, London W1V 9FA
Tel: (0171) 499 5676   Fax: (0171) 493 6576

Description:
One of the capital's finest residences, Apsley House, built between 1771 and 1778, is also home of the first Duke of Wellington and the first house met past the tollgate into London. Its magnificent interior accommodates the Duke's collection of paintings, silver, porcelain, furniture, medals and memorabilia.

Ages: 5+

Subjects: History; Art

Facilities: Toilets; cloakrooms; tailored visits organized; guided tour; disabled access limited

Open: Tuesday–Sunday, 11.00 am–5.00 pm. Closed Mondays (except Bank Holidays), Good Friday, May Day Bank Holiday, 24–26 December and New Year's Day

Admission: Children (12–17 years) £2.50; adults/teachers £4.00. Children aged under 12 years free

Group size: Max 30

Length of visit: 45–60 mins

ARCTURUS DAY CRUISES

Address: Cassio Wharf, Watford, Hertfordshire WD1 8SL
Tel: (01438) 714528

Description:
A popular barge cruise which passes under four ancient bridges of great historical interest and two locks, travelling along some of the most picturesque countryside in Britain and giving an insight into the working of locks and also the opportunity to take in the flowers and fauna *en route.*

Ages: 5–16

Subjects: Mathematics; English; Science; Geography; Technology; History; Art

Facilities: Free teachers' pre-visit; worksheets; quiz sheets; project books; drop-off point at entrance; outdoor eating area; shop on board; disabled access; live commentary

Open: Term time: Easter–October

Admission: Upon application

Group size: Min 25; max 54

Length of visit: 2 hours

ARUNDEL CASTLE

Address: Arundel Castle Trustees Limited, Arundel Castle, West Sussex BN18 9AB
Tel: (01903) 883136/882173   Fax: (01903) 884581

Description:
Situated in splendid grounds overlooking the River Arun, Arundel Castle was built at the end of the 11th century by the Earl of Arundel, Roger de Montgomery. Badly damaged in 1643 during the Civil War it was eventually restored to its former glory and has amongst its treasures a collection of tapestries, paintings, clocks, furniture, possessions of Mary, Queen of Scots and many other historical artefacts.

Ages: 5–15

Subjects: History; Art

Facilities: Car park; shop; restaurant; Arundel festival at the end of August; disabled access

Open: 1 April–last Friday in October: Sunday–Fridays, 12 noon–5.00 pm. Closed Saturdays and Good Fridays

Admission: Groups of 20+ children (5–15 years) £3.70; adults/teachers £5.20

Group size: Min 20

Length of visit: N/A

AUDLEY END HOUSE PARK AND GARDEN

Address: Saffron Walden, Essex CB11 4JF

Tel: (01604) 730320   Fax: (01604) 730321

Description:

Built by the first Earl of Suffolk in the 17th century, this is one of the finest examples of Jacobean country houses in England, which was used by Charles II until 1701. In 1760 Capability Brown landscaped the park.

Ages: 5+

Subjects: Mathematics; English; Science; Geography; Technology; History; Art; R.E.

Facilities: Free teachers' pre-visit; welcome talk/demonstration; car park; outdoor eating area; toilets; disabled access

Open: Grounds from 10.00 am. House from 12 noon

Admission: Free

Group size: N/A

Length of visit: 2 hours

BANK OF ENGLAND MUSEUM

Address: Bartholomew Lane, London EC2R 8AA

Tel: (0171) 601 5545   Fax: (0171) 601 5508

Description:

Located within the Bank of England in the City of London the museum traces the history of the Bank from its very beginnings by Royal Charter in 1694 to the present time. The tour gives a fascinating look behind the scenes, with exhibits of gold bars dating from ancient times and documents relating to famous customers such as Horatio Nelson and George Washington.

Ages: All ages

Subjects: History; Mathematics

Facilities: Audio guides (available for hire); disabled access limited; slide shows; interactive sessions

Open: Monday–Friday, 10.00 am–5.00 pm. Closed weekends, public and Bank Holidays

Admission: Free
Group size: Contact Visitors Liaison Group (0171) 601 3965
Length of visit: N/A

BASINGSTOKE CANAL

Address: Basingstoke Canal Authority, Canal Centre, Mytchett Place Road, Mytchett, Surrey GU16 6DD
Tel: (01252) 370073   Fax: (01252) 371758

Description:
Learn more about the environment, wildlife and the history of the Basingstoke Canal. Find out how a lock is constructed, the workings and engineering of it, together with a look at traditional canalware painting.
Ages: All ages
Subjects: Art; Design & Technology; Science; Geography; History
Facilities: Free teachers' pre-visit; study room; exhibition area; indoor/outdoor eating areas; shop; boat trips; pond dipping site; pets' corner; worksheets available; canal ranger available (by arrangement); scavenger hunt and discovery trail; disabled access
Open: Two sessions are available: morning, 10.00 am–12 noon; afternoon, 12.30 pm– 2.30 pm
Admission: Children £2.50; adults/teachers free
Group size: Max 30 per session
Length of visit: ½ a day

BATEMAN'S

Address: Etchingham, Burwash, East Sussex TN19 7DS
Tel: (01435) 882302

Description:
Visit the home of Rudyard Kipling, from where he penned many of his famous works. See his Rolls-Royce and his delightful gardens, where you will find one of the oldest working water-driven turbines in the world.
Ages: 8+
Subjects: English; History
Facilities: Car park; toilets; education pack; shop; tearooms; refreshments available; disabled access; guidebook available
Open: House, garden and mill: 4 April–1 November, Saturday–Wednesday, 11.00 am–5.30 pm (also open Good Friday)
Admission: Group rates available upon application
Group size: N/A
Length of visit: 1–2 hours

BATTLE ABBEY

Address: High Street, Battle, East Sussex TN23 0AD
  Tel: (01424) 773792

Description:
  Explore the battlefield where William the Conqueror defeated King Harold on 14 October 1066. Relive the terrifying experience with the aid of an audio-guide of the battle and find out what really happened on that tragic day in the words of a Saxon soldier, a Norman knight, or King Harold's mistress.

Ages: 8+

Subjects: Science; Technology; History; R.E.

Facilities: Shop; outdoor eating area; exhibition; themed activity area; dairy; icehouse; disabled access; teachers' handbook

Open: 1 April–31 October: daily, 10.00 am–6.00 pm. 1 November–31 March: daily, 10.00 am–4.00 pm. Closed 24–26 December

Admission: Group rates available upon application

Group size: N/A

Length of visit: N/A

BEACHY HEAD COUNTRYSIDE CENTRE

Address: Centre Manager, Beachy Head Countryside Centre, Eastbourne, East Sussex BN20 7YA
  Tel: (01323) 737273

Description:
  Beachy Head Countryside Centre is an innovative exhibition, the ideal location to explore all areas of the environment; listen to the talking shepherd reflecting on life on the Downland, visit the Bronze Age man in his hut and see wildlife displays.

Ages: 5+

Subjects: History; Science; Art; Mathematics

Facilities: Car park; guided walks; study room; restaurant; disabled access; special events; exhibitions; worksheets; free teachers' pre-visit; shop; play equipment

Open: Daily (check on times)

Admission: Group rates upon application

Group size: Upon application

Length of visit: Full day

BECKONSCOT MODEL VILLAGE

Address: Warwick Road, Beconsfield, Buckinghamshire HP9 2PL
   Tel: (01494) 672919   Fax: (01494) 675284

Description:
   Take a look back in time to find out what village life was really like in the 1930s.
   Beckonscot is reportedly the oldest model village in the world, where life has
   virtually stood still and where visitors can browse through the six villages and see
   people going about their daily chores. It is a fascinating look back at English
   history as never seen before.

Ages: All ages

Subjects: History; English; Art

Facilities: Car park; indoor/outdoor eating areas; shop; education pack available;
   toilets; disabled access; play area; refreshments; Enid Blyton's house

Open: 14 February–1 November: daily, 10.00 am–5.00 pm

Admission: Children £1.40; adults/teachers £2.80. One adult free for every 25
   paying persons

Group size: N/A

Length of visit: N/A

BENTLEY WILDFOWL AND MOTOR MUSEUM

Address: Halland, nr Lewes, East Sussex BN8 5AF
   Tel: (01825) 840573   Fax: (01825) 841322

Description:
   Conservation and the breeding of endangered species are the main aims of
   Bentley Wildfowl, a 23-acre nature reserve where you will find over 1,000
   geese, swans and ducks from all over the world; a 12-acre mixed wood with
   an activity trail and a motor museum housing a superb collection of vintage
   cars and motor cycles. There is also a Palladian-style mansion, once a 17th-
   century farmhouse, which is renowned for its fine collection of paintings and
   furniture.

Ages: All ages

Subjects: Science; Geography; Art; Design & Technology; English

Facilities: Free teachers' pre-visit; classroom; slide presentation and talk; indoor/
   outdoor eating areas; tearoom; shop; audiovisual; woodland activity trail; worksheets; adventure playground; gardens; exhibition; special events

Open: Subject to arrangement, Bentley is open to school parties any time

Admission: Group rates available upon application

Group size: N/A

Length of visit: Up to one day

THE BETHNAL GREEN MUSEUM OF CHILDHOOD

Address: Bethnal Green Museum of Childhood, Cambridge Heath Road, London E2 9PA
Tel: (0181) 980 3204

Description:
Be entertained and educated with a visit to this museum, which has the largest toy collection on public display in the world. There are doll's houses ranging from Victorian mansions to small home-made cottages; 65 showcases of dolls from the 17th century to the present; puppets from all over the world; a range of toys and games and in one of the galleries changes are being made to transform it into the Social History of Childhood.

Ages: All ages
Subjects: History; Art; Design & Technology
Facilities: Shop; changing exhibitions; workshops; teachers' pack; disabled access (limited but help provided if informed beforehand)
Open: Throughout the year, Monday–Thursday and Saturdays, 10.00 am–6.00 pm (including Bank Holidays). Sunday, 2.30 pm–6.00 pm. Closed every Friday, May Day Bank Holiday, 24–26 December and New Year's Day
Admission: Free
Group size: N/A
Length of visit: N/A

BEWL WATER

Address: Southern Water, The Estate Office, Lamberhurst, Tunbridge Wells, Kent TN3 8JH
Tel: (01892) 890661   Fax: (01892) 890232

Description:
Owned by Southern Water Services, Bewl Water is a 770-acre reservoir set amidst the beautiful Kent countryside and is the ideal location to study conservation and the journey water takes until it reaches the consumer's house.

Ages: 7+
Subjects: Science; Technology
Facilities: Introductory talk; classroom; guided walk/talk; car park; indoor/outdoor eating areas; adventure playground; visitor centre; nature walks; visitor centre; ferry boat rides; disabled access (advisable to check)
Open: April–October, Monday–Thursday
Admission: Children £1.30; adults/teachers free
Group size: Min 30
Length of visit: 1½–2 hours

BEXHILL MUSEUM

Address: Egerton Gardens, Upper Sea Road, Bexhill-on-Sea, East Sussex TN40 1RL
Tel: (01424) 787950

Description:
A small museum with permanent exhibitions depicting the natural history, archaeology and geology of the area. Changing exhibitions.
Ages: 8+
Subjects: Technology; Art; R.E.; Science; Geography; History
Facilities: Classroom; toilets; indoor/outdoor eating areas; educational material; disabled access; shop; free quiz sheets available
Open: All year. Tuesday–Friday, 10.00 am–5.00 pm. Saturday and Sunday, 2.00 pm–5.00 pm. Closed Mondays and 24 December–3 February
Admission: Group rates upon application
Group size: N/A
Length of visit: N/A

BEXHILL MUSEUM OF COSTUME AND SOCIAL HISTORY

Address: Manor Gardens, Upper Sea Road, Bexhill-on-Sea, East Sussex TN40 2HA
Tel: (01424) 210045

Description:
Located in the old manor library the museum exhibits a collection of costumes, dolls, toys and other items dating from the early 18th century to 1960 cleverly displayed in tableaux and scenes. An excellent way to bring history alive.
Ages: 8+
Subjects: Technology; History; Art
Facilities: Disabled access; toilets; educational material; guided tour available
Open: April–October: Monday, Tuesday, Thursday and Friday, 10.30 am–5.00 pm and also Wednesdays in June–September; Saturday and Sunday, 2.00 pm–5.00 pm. April, May, September and October closes 4.30 pm
Admission: Group rates upon application
Group size: N/A
Length of visit: N/A

BLENHEIM PALACE

Address: Administrator's Office, Blenheim Palace, Woodstock, Oxford OX20 1PX
Tel: (01993) 811091   Fax: (01993) 813527

Description:
Set in 2,500 acres of parkland landscaped by Capability Brown, Blenheim Palace is an outstanding example of English architecture and birthplace of Sir Winston

70

Churchill. Its present owner is His Grace 11th Duke of Marlborough. The Palace, gardens, park and estate are available to study a wide range of topics and subjects on the National Curriculum or for leisure and are suitable for all ages.

Ages: 5–17

Subjects: English; Mathematics; Science; Technology; History; Geography; Art

Facilities: Free teachers' pre-visit; shop; indoor/outdoor eating areas; classroom; car park; educational packs; maze; worksheets; adventure playground; park; butterfly house; rowing boats; giant draughts and chess adventure; gardens; motor launch and train; introductory talks; exhibitions; tours

Open: Mid-March–31 October: daily, 9.45 am–5.00 pm. In winter by arrangement

Admission: Group rates upon application

Group size: N/A

Length of visit: N/A

BODIAM CASTLE

Address: Bodiam, Robertsbridge, East Sussex TN32 5UA

Tel: (01580) 830436

Description:

Built in 1385 to defend the country from the King's enemies, Bodiam Castle is one of the most popular castles in the country, especially for children, and has established a reputation as being a fairytale castle. This is probably because it looks very much like a fairytale castle, with its long bridge over the moat which leads you into its mysterious inside.

Ages: 5–16

Subjects: Science; Geography; Art; History

Facilities: Shop; tearoom; car park; toilets; regular events; restaurant; disabled access; children's activities; guided tours; education pack; classroom; video on medieval life

Open: 8 February–2 November: daily, 10.00 am–6.00 pm. 4 November–4 January: Tuesday–Sunday, 10.00 am–dusk. Closed Christmas holidays. Open New Year's Day

Admission: Group rates upon application

Group size: Min 15

Length of visit: N/A

THE BODY SHOP TOUR

Address: The Body Shop International plc, Watersmead, Littlehampton, West Sussex BN17 6LS

Tel: (01903) 844044   Fax: (01903) 844055

Description:

An educational tour around the Body Shop is an unusual but popular attraction where visitors can find out all there is to know about the company and are given an insight into how raw ingredients are made into finished products, and the launch process of a new product from the initial concept to its final place on the shop shelves. It can prove to be an invaluable resource to all students, even those studying higher diplomas.

Ages: 5+

Subjects: Science; Geography

Facilities: Car park; refreshments; shop; tailored tours available; disabled access limited; resource pack; guided tours; audiovisual facilities

Open: Tours all year around. Advisable to arrive 20 minutes before tour begins. Monday, Tuesday and Thursday, 9.20 am–3.40 pm; Wednesday, Friday and Saturday, 10.20 am–3.40 pm

Admission: Groups of 20+ children (5–16 years) £2.95; adults £3.95

Group size: Max 26

Length of visit: Up to 2 hours

BOOTH MUSEUM OF NATURAL HISTORY

Address: 194 Dyke Road, Brighton BN1 5AA

Tel: (01273) 292777   Fax: (01273) 292778

Description:

Over 525,000 insects and other animals; 50,000 fossils, minerals and rocks; 5,000 microscope slides; 30,000 plants and 11,000 books and maps – all under one roof at the Booth Museum. This was the brainchild of the Victorian ornithologist Edward Booth. Initially built in 1874 to accommodate his collection of stuffed British birds, and despite them still holding the limelight, the Booth Museum displays over half a million other specimens covering three centuries, many of which have only ever been seen in books.

Ages: 5+

Subjects: Science; History; Art; Design & Technology

Facilities: Car park; children's holiday activities; shop; temporary exhibitions; workshops; handling sessions; talks; library; loan service; disabled access limited

Open: Monday, Tuesday, Wednesday, Friday and Saturday, 10.00 am–5.00 pm. Sunday, 2.00 pm–5.00 pm. Closed Thursdays
Admission: Free
Group size: N/A
Length of visit: N/A

BOWMAN'S OPEN FARM

Address: Coursers Road, London Colne, St Albans, Hertfordshire AL2 1BB
Tel: (01727) 822106   Fax: (01727) 826406

Description:
A working farm with cows, piglets, lambs, chickens, William the Bull, Ben the shire-horse, a super falconry display and an opportunity for a tractor ride.
Ages: 5+
Subjects: Science; Geography; Technology
Facilities: Free teachers' pre-visit; teacher/pupil resource packs; worksheets; quiz sheets; project books; classroom welcome talk/demonstration; guided tours; indoor/outdoor eating area; toilets; shop; disabled access
Open: Daily, 10.30 am–2.30 pm
Admission: Pupils £2.25. One adult free with every 10 pupils
Group size: Max 100
Length of visit: 4 hours

BRIGHTON MUSEUM AND ART GALLERY

Address: Church Street, Brighton BN1 1UE
Tel: (01273) 290900   Fax: (01273) 292841

Description:
Opened in 1873 the museum houses collections of national and local importance. There are many artefacts including Stone Age tools, Egyptian household goods, Indian and African artefacts and an assortment of fine watercolours and exhibitions.
Ages: 5+
Subjects: Art
Facilities: Worksheets; talks; shop; outdoor eating area; toilets; teachers' packs; disabled access limited; refreshments
Open: All year. Monday, Tuesday, Thursday–Saturday, 10.00 am–5.00 pm. Sunday, 2.00 pm–5.00 pm. Closed Wednesday, Good Friday, 25–26 December and 1 January
Admission: Free
Group size: N/A
Length of visit: N/A

THE BRITISH MUSEUM

Address: Great Russell Street, London WC1B 3DG
Tel: (0171) 323 8511/8854   Fax: (0171) 323 8855

Description:
What can you say about the British Museum other than it is one of the greatest museums in the world, exhibit illustrating objects from prehistoric times to today, with information and resources to accommodate all ages.
Ages: All ages
Subjects: History; Art; Design & Technology; Geography
Facilities: Free teachers' pre-visit; lunchroom; cloakroom; toilets; shop; disabled access limited; teachers' packs; worksheets; videos available for short-term loan; CD ROMs
Open: Throughout the year, daily. Monday–Saturday, 10.00 am–5.00 pm. Sunday, 2.30 pm–6.00 pm. Closed 10 April, 4 May, 24–26 December and 1 January
Admission: Free
Group size: No limit provided there are sufficient adults to accompany. Primary children: one adult for every eight pupils. Secondary and older students: one adult for every 15 students.
Length of visit: N/A

BROOKLANDS MUSEUM

Address: Brooklands Museum Trust Limited, Brooklands Road, Weybridge, Surrey KT13 0QN
Tel: (01932) 857381   Fax: (01932) 855465

Description:
Opened in 1991 Brooklands is the birthplace of British motor sport and aviation and is also an excellent example of life in the 1920s and 1930s. An ideal venue for studying many National Curriculum subjects at all levels. Accommodating over 30 aircraft depicting 80 years of aviation, there is so much to see: a collection of Vickers and Hawkers aircraft, a genuine motoring village complete with its 1920s Shell and BP Petrol pagodas and the world's first Flight Ticket office from 1911.
Ages: All ages
Subjects: History; Science; Art; Geography; Technology; Mathematics; English
Facilities: Free teachers' pre-visit; teachers' resource pack; toilets; shop; refreshments; guided tours; introductory video; car park; regular events; disabled access; exhibitions; picnic lunch (room available in bad weather); worksheets
Open: All year. School visits (which are arranged during term time) are on Tuesdays, Wednesdays, Thursdays and Fridays

Admission: Children £2.50; adults and helpers free
Group size: Min 10
Length of visit: At school's discretion

BROUGHTON CASTLE

Address: Banbury, Oxfordshire OX15 5EB
  Tel: (01295) 262624

Description:
  Although Broughton Castle is now a family house lived in by Lord and Lady Saye
  and their family, the original manor house of which much still remains was built in
  the 14th century by Sir John de Broughton, on a location surrounded by a 3-acre
  moat. Between 1550 and 1660 renovations were undertaken in which the house
  was enlarged and adorned with splendid plaster ceilings, panelling and fine fire-
  places. Today visitors can see many historic artefacts on display from the Civil War
  and other periods.
Ages: 5+
Subjects: History
Facilities: Car park; shop; toilets; outdoor eating area; guide book; guided tour;
  opportunity to try on period armour; disabled access; tearoom
Open: 20 May–13 September: Wednesday and Sunday. July and August: Thursday
  and Bank Holiday Sunday and Bank Holiday Monday (including Easter), 2.00
  pm–5.00 pm. Groups welcome any time of the year
Admission: Group rates 20+: children (5–15) £1.75; students £3.40; adults/
  teachers £3.40
Group size: Min 10
Length of visit: 1 hour

BUCKLEYS YESTERDAY'S WORLD

Address: 89–90 High Street, Battle, nr Hastings, East Sussex TN33 0AQ
  Tel: (01424) 774269   Fax: (01424) 775174

Description:
  One of the most extraordinary and fascinating attractions in the south-east of
  England which draws you back into an age when life was totally different. Amble
  through an enchanting medieval hall house, recreated shopping streets, a
  Victorian grocery and see many exhibits spanning 100 years. Together with push
  button commentaries and hands-on activities you will immediately feel the past is
  resurrected and you are living in the Victorian era.
Ages: 5+
Subjects: Science; Technology; Art; History

Facilities: Car park; classroom; toilets; indoor/outdoor eating areas; refreshments; worksheets; disabled access limited; education video; teachers' pack; garden; activity area; play village; video show; mini-golf; exhibition marquee

Open: All year, 7 days a week, 10.00 am–6.00 pm. Times subject to change

Admission: Museum and garden: children (4–15 years) £2.15; students (16–24 years) £2.25; adults/teachers £2.75. Garden entry only: children, students and adults £1.00

Group size: Min 15; max 50

Length of visit: Up to one day

CANTERBURY CATHEDRAL

Address: Cathedral House, 11 The Precincts, Canterbury CT1 2EH
Tel: (01227) 762862   Fax: (01227) 762897

Description:
The principal church of the Anglican Communion, Canterbury Cathedral has been a haven of pilgrimage for many years and a tour around its magnificent building will reveal the history of the Cathedral, the Monastery and monks who lived there. There are also other organized attractions which include a Cathedral Trail, a Monks Trail (45 mins–1 hour), a Costume Trail and a St Augustine Trail (one day).

Ages: 5+

Subjects: History; R.E.

Facilities: Indoor eating area; guided tours; audiovisual facilities; project room; introductory slide show; toilets; audio; disabled access; car park nearby; worksheets; shop; opportunity to write with quill pens

Open: All year. Winter: Monday–Saturday, 9.00 am–5.00 pm. Summer: Monday–Saturday, 9.00 am–7.00 pm (Monday in term time closes 5.00 pm).
Crypt: Monday–Saturday, 10.00 am–4.30 pm. Sunday, 12.30 pm–2.30 pm and 4.30 pm–5.30 pm

Admission: Group rates upon application

Group size: N/A

Length of visit: N/A

CANTERBURY ROMAN MUSEUM

Address: Visitor Services, Royal Museum, High Street, Canterbury CT1 2JE
Tel: (01227) 785575   Fax: (01227) 455047

Description:
The specially constructed underground Roman Museum has been designed to provide visitors with the opportunity to explore a vast collection of Roman artefacts, and the remnants of a preserved Roman town house *in situ*.

Ages: All ages
Subjects: History; English; Science; Design & Technology; Geography; Art; Mathematics
Facilities: Guided tours; disabled access; worksheets; free teachers' pre-visits; indoor eating area; hands-on area; toilets
Open: All year: Monday–Saturday, 10.00 am–5.00 pm. June–October: Sunday, 1.30 pm–5.00 pm. Closed Good Friday and Christmas week
Admission: Free admission for teachers. Group rates for pupils upon application
Group size: Min 10; max 32
Length of visit: 45 minutes

THE CANTERBURY TALES VISITOR ATTRACTION

Address: St Margaret's Street, Canterbury CT1 2TG
Tel: (01227) 454888   Fax: (01227) 765584

Description:
An entertaining and informative exploration of Chaucer's medieval world, the ideal place for those studying English Literature, English Language, R.E. and many other National Curriculum subjects. Stories from the 14th century are read out by many famous celebrities such as Prunella Scales and Robert Powell in authentic surroundings.
Ages: All ages
Subjects: English; History; Geography; R.E.; Design & Technology
Facilities: Free teachers' pre-visit; educational resource packs; shop; refreshments; disabled access; events throughout the year such as Ghost Tours of Canterbury, a thrilling evening tour through the streets of Old Canterbury
Open: Daily. March–June and September–October, 9.30 am–5.30 pm. July–August, 9.00 am–6.00 pm. November–February: Sunday–Friday, 10.00 am–4.30 pm; Saturday, 9.30 am–5.30 pm. Closed 25 December
Admission: Special arrangements are available for UK schools who visit during term time
Group size: Min 20
Length of visit: 1 hour

CATHEDRAL AND ABBEY CHURCH OF ST ALBAN

Address: Sumpter Yard, St Albans, Hertfordshire AL1 1BY
Tel: (01727) 836223   Fax: (01727) 850944

Description:
Norman abbey church of a Benedictine monastery on the site of the execution of St Alban – Britain's first Christian martyr (c. 209). Wall paintings, audiovisual show and ecumenical shrine of St Alban (1309).

Ages: 5+

Subjects: History; R.E.; Mathematics; English; Science; Geography; Technology; Music

Facilities: Free teachers' pre-visit; teacher/resource packs; school guide; classroom; welcome talk/demonstrations; indoor/outdoor eating areas; toilets; shop; disabled access

Open: Daily throughout the school year, 9.30 am–5.00 pm

Admission: Children £1 (unguided): £1.74 (guided); adults/teachers free

Group size: Max 150

Length of visit: Half/full day

CHELMER CRUISES

Address: Paper Mill Lock, North Hill, Little Baddow, nr Chelmsford, Essex CM3 4BF
Tel: (01245) 225520

Description:
The only privately owned stretch of canal in the country, 13 miles long. Chelmer Cruises organize the 48-seat traditional styled barge, on the 200-year-old canal between Chelmsford and Heybridge.

Ages: 5+

Subjects: Science; Geography; Technology; History

Facilities: Free teachers' pre-visit; teacher/pupil resource packs; outdoor eating area; toilets on boat

Open: Daylight hours

Admission: Group rates upon application

Group size: Min 20; max 48

Length of visit: 2 hours (min.)

CHELMSFORD CATHEDRAL

Address: Bew Street, Chelmsford, Essex CM1 1AT
Tel: (01245) 263660   Fax: (01245) 496802

Description:
In 1914 the 15th-century building became a cathedral and worship has been available since Saxon times. The building has developed and now has an extension and two new organs.

Ages: 5+

Subjects: History; R.E.

Facilities: Free teachers' pre-visit; teacher/pupil resource packs; worksheets; quiz sheets; project book; school guide; welcome talk/demonstrations; indoor/ outdoor eating areas; shop; disabled access

Open: Daily throughout the year, 9.30 am–4.45 pm
Admission: Free
Group size: Min 5; max 30
Length of visit: 40 mins

CHELSEA PHYSIC GARDEN

Address: 66 Royal Hospital Road, London SW3 4HS
Tel: (0171) 352 5646   Fax: (0171) 376 3910

Description:
Founded by the Society of Apothecaries in 1673, the Chelsea Physic Garden is perfect for students of medicine, biology, botany and many other subjects to find out all about the healing properties of plants. Situated in the 3.5 acre garden there are glasshouses accommodating plants of many species. There is a carnivorous plant display, a tropical corridor which has many food plants such as papaya, ginger, sugar cane and even banana; the beds display a range of medicinal plants from around the world together with a collection of herbs and spices, and there is also a winter woodland pathway, a pond and a compost heap area to study soil formation and food chains.
Ages: All ages
Subjects: English; Science; Art; Geography; History; Information Technology; Mathematics
Facilities: Classroom; indoor/outdoor eating areas; free teachers' pre-visit; tailor-made visits; wormery; live invertebrate displays
Open: Wednesday, Thursday and Friday, 10.00 am–12 noon and/or 1.00 pm–3.00 pm
Admission: Free to state schools. Private schools are charged £1 per student and £10 for one adult. All other adults free
Group size: Max 30
Length of visit: N/A

CHESSINGTON WORLD OF ADVENTURES

Address: Chessington, Surrey KT9 2NE
Tel: Admin: (01372) 729560   Fax: (01372) 748410
Enquiries: (01372) 727227

Description:
A fun, entertaining and educational day rolled into one awaits all visitors to Chessington World of Adventures, providing the ideal opportunity to learn about many subjects on the National Curriculum. It is also ideal for older students on a business course.

Ages: All ages

Subjects: Science; English

Facilities: Car park; shop; first aid room; shop; toilets; circus; feeding times; indoor eating areas; special events; birds-in-flight display; rides; education centre; talks; disabled access; Discovery Centre; worksheets; education pack (contact administration for further information)

Open: March–November: daily, 10.00 am–5.30 pm, later in July and August

Admission: Special group rates upon application. One teacher free for every 10 pupils

Group size: N/A

Length of visit: All day

COTSWOLD WILDLIFE PARK

Address: Burford, Oxford OX10 4JW

  Tel: (01993) 823006   Fax: (01993) 823807

Description:

  Find out more about conservation and see many endangered species close to at the Cotswold Wildlife Park, set in 160 acres of beautiful gardens and parkland surrounding a listed Victorian manor house. Home to a collection of mammals, birds, reptiles, invertebrates and fish, together with trees, formal gardens and a tropical house, providing motivation for various areas of work.

Ages: 5+

Subjects: Science

Facilities: Free teachers' pre-visit; car park; classroom; resource packs; indoor/outdoor eating areas; playground; talks; shop; train ride (charged); brass rubbing; general worksheets; teachers' notes; disabled access; touch table presentation

Open: Throughout the year, daily from 10.00 am. Closed 25 December

Admission: Adults £3.30; children £2.80
Group size: Max 40
Length of visit: Each talk takes up to 30 minutes

THE CUTTY SARK

Address: King William Walk, Greenwich, London SE10 9HT
  Tel: (0181) 858 3445   Fax: (0181) 858 6976

Description:
  Climb aboard the famous *Cutty Sark* built in 1869 and now permanently
  berthed overlooking the River Thames. A fine sailing ship which has been
  meticulously restored to her former prime condition in order that visitors can
  tread the decks and have a taste of life on board one of the most famous of all
  tea clippers.
Ages: 5 +
Subjects: Science; History; Mathematics; Art; Geography; Music; English; Design &
  Technology
Facilities: Shop; eating area; guided tours; disabled access limited; teachers' pack;
  video presentation; worksheets
Open: All year, daily. Summer: April–September inclusive, 10.00 am–6.00 pm.
  Winter: 10.00 am–5.00 pm. Sunday and Good Friday, 12 noon–5.00 pm (6.00
  pm in summer). Closed 24–26 December
Admission: Group rates upon application
Group size: N/A
Length of visit: N/A

D-DAY MUSEUM AND OVERLORD EMBROIDERY

Address: Clarence Esplanade, Southsea, Hants PO5 3NT
  Tel: (01705) 827261   Fax: (01705) 875276

Description:
  The main feature of the D-Day Museum is the splendid Overlord Embroidery,
  which succinctly relives the story of the Allied invasion of Normandy in 1944.
  Inspired by the Bayeux Tapestry, it took 5 years to complete and is the largest
  work of its kind in the world, measuring 272 feet. There are also other exhibitions
  depicting a 1940 dining room, an air raid shelter, a factory scene, and an opportunity to see many reconstructed wartime themes.
Ages: 5 +
Subjects: History
Facilities: Free teachers' pre-visit; toilets; disabled access; shop; teachers' resource
  pack; refreshments; audiovisual facilities; exhibitions; car park

Open: Daily. Closed Monday, November–March, also 24–26 December
Admission: Free
Group size: Max 60
Length of visit: Up to 2 hours

THE DICKENS HOUSE MUSEUM

Address: 48 Doughty Street, London WC1N 2LF
 Tel: (0171) 405 2127   Fax: (0171) 831 5175

Description:
 Charles Dickens lived at 48 Doughty Street from April 1837 to December 1839, an important 2 years of his life during which he penned some of his finest works, such as *Pickwick Papers* and a large part of *Nicholas Nickleby*, for which he became renowned as one of the greatest writers of all time. Today his home is a museum in which you can see the study in which he worked; the drawing-room in which family guests were greeted and a range of his personal documents.
Ages: 5+
Subjects: English; History
Facilities: Talk available if required; worksheets for KS1, 2, 3; shop; museum guidebook
Open: Throughout the year. Monday–Friday, 9.45 am–5.00 pm. Saturday 10.00 am–5.00 pm. Closed on Sunday
Admission: Group rates 10+ children (under 15 years) £1.50; students (15+ years) £2.50
Group size: Min 10
Length of visit: ½ a day

DOVER CASTLE

Address: Dover, Kent CT16 1HU
 Tel: (01304) 201628   Fax: (01304) 214739

Description:
 Situated on a prime location on the White Cliffs of Dover, the proud and majestic fortress commands a panoramic view out over the English Channel. It was built during Henry II's reign, was added on to by King John, and was finally completed by Henry VIII – when it was called the Key of England. Henry strengthened the outer walls and added further defensive and domestic buildings, including a new hall, chambers, kitchen and chapel. In the 18th century and the Napoleonic era the outerwork was remodelled and the underground passage changed and extended.
Ages: 5+

Subjects: History; Geography; Music; Art; English; Technology

Facilities: Free teachers' pre-visit; disabled access; education room; car park; teachers' resource pack; themed activity area; shop; toilets; refreshments; indoor/outdoor eating areas

Open: 1 April–30 September, 10.00 am–6.00 pm. 1 October–31 March, 10.00 am–4.00 pm. Closed 24–26 December and 1 January

Admission: Group rates upon application

Group size: Max 120

Length of visit: N/A

DRUSILLAS PARK

Address: Alfriston, Polegate, East Sussex BN26 5QS

Tel: (01323) 870656   Fax: (01323) 870846

Description:

Known as 'The Best Small Zoo in England', Drusillas Park is where visitors can get as close as possible to animals. There is an opportunity to study Native American Indians; explore a rainforest; see animal homes and their families; learn the importance of nutrition in feeding animals; watch animal movements; and explore different cultures with the help of various exhibits and displays.

Ages: All ages

Subjects: English; Geography; Music; Mathematics; History; Science; Art; Design & Technology

Facilities: Toilets; car park; education resources; free teachers' pre-visit; under-cover picnic area; discovery centre; education offices; tailored sessions; disabled access; train and playland for children up to 12 years; refreshments; shop; special events; worksheets; education room

Open: Summer, 10.00 am–5.00 pm. Winter, 10.00 am–4.00 pm. Closed 24–26 December

Admission: Children £3.50 plus a choice of worksheets. 50p extra per child for educational sessions. One teacher free for every seven children. Extra adults £3.50

Group size: Min 15

Length of visit: N/A

ENGLISH HERITAGE PROPERTIES

Before making a visit to any of the English Heritage listed buildings in London contact them for further information: English Heritage, Historic Properties London, Room 402, 429 Oxford Street, London W1R 2HD (tel: 0171 973 3499; fax: 0171 973 3470).

Chiswick House
Down House
Eltham Palace
Jewel Tower, Westminster
Kenwood
Marble Hill House
Ranger's House
Westminster Abbey Chapter House, Pyx Chamber. and Abbey Museum

For those in the South East, contact: English Heritage, Historic Properties South East, 1 High Street, Tonbridge, Kent TN9 1SG (tel: 01732 778027; fax: 01732 778001).

Appuldurcombe House
Battle Abbey and site of the Battle Hastings
Bayham Old Abbey
Bishop's Waltham Palace
Calshot Castle
Camber Castle
Carisbrooke Castle
Deal Castle
Dover Castle Wartime Tunnels
Dymchurch Martello Tower
Farnham Castle Keep
Fort Brockhurst
Hurst Castle
Lullingstone Roman Villa
Maison Dieu
Medieval Merchant's House
Milton Chantry
Old Soar Manor
Osborne House
Pevensey Castle
Portchester Castle
Richborough Castle
Rochester Castle
Royal Garrison Church
St Augustine's Abbey
St John's Commandery Swingfield
Temple Manor
Tichfield Abbey
Upnor Castle

Walmer Castle and Gardens
Wolvesey Castle
Yarmouth Castle

FARMING WORLD

Address: Nash Court, Boughton, Faversham, Kent ME13 9SW
Tel: (01227) 751144   Fax: (01795) 522330

Description:
Situated in the centre of the Kent countryside, Farming World is a family-run attraction with over 40 different breeds of farm animals and birds, including rare, traditional and commercial ones. There is also a breeding programme where baby animals can be seen, together with a small museum housing agricultural memorabilia providing an insight into farming methods of the past 150 years.

Ages: All ages

Subjects: Geography; History; Science

Facilities: Teachers' packs; classroom; guided tours/talks; free teachers' pre-visit; disabled access; shop; refreshments; car park; indoor/outdoor eating areas; adventure playground; horse and cart or tractor rides (small cost); specially designed garden with emphasis on sensory plants chosen for touch and smell (ideal for children with special needs); bird of prey centre; walled garden; special events

Open: Daily, 1 March–1 November, 9.30 am–5.30 pm. Other times by appointment

Admission: Group rates available upon application

Group size: Min 20

Length of visit: Up to one day

FISHBOURNE ROMAN PALACE

Address: Salthill Road, Fishbourne, Chichester, West Sussex PO19 3QR
Tel: (01243) 785859   Fax: (01243) 539266

Description:
Discovered in 1960, Fishbourne Roman Palace has emerged as one of the most fascinating archaeological finds this century, exposing the remains of a military supply base constructed around the time of the Roman invasion in AD 43 together with other civilian buildings. With the help of plans, photographs, models and everyday items that were discovered, the story of the site is told in the museum and an audiovisual programme adds the human touch, exposing the amazing tale through the voices of those who may have lived, worked or dug the site.

Ages: 5+

Subjects: History; Art

Facilities: Car park; free teachers' pre-visit; talk; guided tour; outdoor/indoor eating areas; audiovisual facilities; workshops (extra charges); shop; disabled access

Open: All year. 7 February–12 December daily, 10.00 am–5.00 pm. March–July, September–October, 10.00 am–5.00 pm. August, 10.00 am–6.00 pm. February, November–December, 10.00 am–4.00 pm. The remainder of the year Saturdays and Sundays, 10.00 am–4.00 pm

Admission: Group rates of 20+: children £2.00; adults/teachers £3.20

Group size: Max 40

Length of visit: N/A

FOREDOWN TOWER VISITOR'S CENTRE AND CAMERA OBSCURA

Address: Foredown Tower, Foredown Road, Portslade, East Sussex BN41 2EW
Tel: (01273) 292092   Fax: (01273) 292092

Description:
The only working camera obscura in the south east of England is located on the Sussex Downs. Once an Edwardian water tower, the viewing gallery offers delightful views over the surrounding countryside and the Channel together with a weather station, exhibition galleries and displays, and interactive computers.

Ages: 5+

Subjects: Art; Science; History

Facilities: Car park; toilets; disabled access limited; refreshments; slide shows; shop; exhibition

Open: All year. 1 January–31 March and 1 October–24 December: Thursday–Sunday, 10.00 am–dusk. 1 April–30 September: daily, 10.00 am–5.30 pm. Closed 24 December–1 January. Schools by arrangement

Admission: Groups of 20+: children 75p; adults/teachers £1.50

Group size: Min 20

Length of visit: N/A

FORT AMHERST HERITAGE PARK AND CAVERNS

Address: Dock Road, Chatham, Kent
Tel: (01634) 847747

Description:
Built in 1756 to protect the Royal Naval Dockyard, there are a variety of complex underground tunnels and chambers. Renovation work was carried out between 1802 and 1811 by French prisoners who set to extending shelters, barracks and underground stores. Fort Amherst is Britain's most complete Georgian/

Napoleonic fortress and restoration of underground tunnels and is the most exciting project of its kind in the South East.

Ages: All ages

Subjects: History

Facilities: Free teachers' pre-visit; car park; visitors centre; refreshments; guided tours; educational pack; study rooms; uniforms for hire; exhibition; special events

Open: All year. Summer, 10.30 am–4.30 pm. Winter, 10.30 am–4.00 pm. Closed Christmas

Admission: Children £2.00. One teacher free for every 10 pupils

Group size: N/A

Length of visit: N/A

GEFFRYE MUSEUM

Address: Kingsland Road, London E2 8EA

Tel: (0171) 739 9893   Fax: (0171) 729 5647

Description:

One of London's best-loved museums depicting the changing style of the English domestic interior from the 1600s to the present time, this is the only one of its kind in the United Kingdom. Each of the rooms reflect the values and social habits which have played an important role in the style of interiors over the past 400 years.

Ages: All ages

Subjects: English; Science; Mathematics; Art; History; Design & Technology; Music

Facilities: Free teachers' pre-visit; indoor eating area; shop; disabled access; lecture hall; sound guide; library; exhibitions; herb garden; workshops

Open: Tuesday–Saturday, 10.00 am–5.00 pm. Sundays and Bank Holiday Mondays, 2.00 pm–5.00 pm. Closed Mondays (unless Bank Holidays), Good Fridays, 24–26 December and 1 January

Admission: Free

Group size: N/A

Length of visit: N/A

THE GOLDEN HINDE

Address: St Mary Overie Dock, Cathedral Street, London SE1 DG

Tel: Bookings: (0541) 505041   Fax: (01722) 333343

Ship: (0171) 403 0123

Description:

A full-size reconstruction of the 16th-century *Golden Hinde* warship in which Sir Francis Drake circumnavigated the world between 1577 and 1580 has been turned into a floating museum in which children and adults can experience living history. Crew members are dressed in genuine costumes of the time and there are five decks of artefacts and exhibits to explore, which, together with the creaks and smells of this amazing ship, will transport you back to Elizabethan times. Apart from students enjoying day visits there are two types of overnight stays, one of which involves families and the other in which children aged 6–12 years make an imaginary voyage aboard the ship. There are also holiday workshops, which are run throughout half terms and all main school holidays.

Ages: All ages

Subjects: History; Drama

Facilities: Free teachers' pre-visit; teachers' packs; educational tours; storytelling sessions; workshops; tours can be tailored to suit; overnight stays

Open: Throughout the year, seven days a week. Check on opening times

Admission: Adults £2.30; children £1.50; students up to 16 £1.50

Group size: Advisable to check

Length of visit: 2 hours

GROOMBRIDGE PLACE GARDENS AND THE ENCHANTED FOREST

Address: Groombridge, nr Royal Tunbridge Wells, Kent TN3 9QG
   Tel: (01892) 861444   Fax: (01892) 863996

Description:
   Mystery, excitement and fascination, there is something for everyone at Groombridge Place, which has an amazing history spanning over 10 centuries, and although the castle was largely destroyed during the Civil War the estate was rebuilt in 1660 by Philip Packer. The ancient mounds surrounding the old castle gardens, the jousting field and the ancient streamed moat still survive intact today. There is the Conan Doyle Museum in the old dairy which accommodates an exciting collection of memorabilia in memory of Sir Arthur Conan Doyle; the Raptor Centre, the largest conservation centre for birds of prey in the South East, where sick and injured birds are cared for before being released back into the wild, and regular flying demonstrations.

Ages: All ages

Subjects: History; Science

Facilities: Car park, toilets; secret garden; sculptured garden; enchanted forest; refreshments; free teachers' pre-visit; maze; bird of prey flying display; Romany camp; shop; canal boat rides; programme of special events; woodland walks; ride on canal boat; play area; guided tours

Open: Good Friday– 25 October: daily, 10.00 am–6.00 pm

Admission: Special rates for groups, telephone (01892) 861444

Group size: Min 20
Length of visit: N/A

GUNNERSBURY PARK MUSEUM

Address: Gunnersbury Park, London W3 8LQ
   Tel: (0181) 992 1612   Fax: (0181) 752 0686

Description:
   Experience the life of the gentry with a visit to the former residence of the Rothschilds where you will find, in their sumptuously decorated rooms, some of the finest collections of all times illustrative of Victorian life. The exhibitions include items from childhood, fashion, transport and domestic life. There are regal carriages, a costume gallery with displays from various periods and many changing displays about the history. And don't leave without visiting the reconstructed Victoria Kitchen which cleverly displays how a large house was run.

Ages: All ages
Subjects: Science; History; English
Facilities: Toilets; car park; disabled access; outdoor eating area; refreshments (during summer daily; winter at weekends); education packs (charged); special events; playground; boating lake; workshops
Open: Museum: April–October, 1.00 pm–5.00 pm (weekends and Bank Holidays 1.00 pm–6.00 pm); November–March, 1.00 pm–4.00 pm (weekends and Bank Holidays 1.00 pm–5.00 pm). Victorian Kitchen: April–October, weekends and Bank Holidays only, 1.00 pm–6.00 pm
Admission: Group rates upon application
Group size: N/A
Length of visit: N/A

HAMPTON COURT PALACE

Address: Hampton Court Palace, Surrey KT8 9AU
   Tel: (0181) 781 9554

Description:
   Experience 500 years of British history inside England's finest Royal Palace. Visit the Tudor kitchens, the State apartments, the Chapel Royal and the Great Hall. There are fine exhibits of paintings, furnishing, tapestries and furniture created by international craftsmen, providing a wealth of historical interest.

Ages: 5+
Subjects: History; Art; Music; English; R.E.
Facilities: Shops; indoor/outdoor eating areas; free teachers' pre-visit; disabled access; teachers' packs; educational resources; guided/audio tours; slide lectures

Open: Daily. Mid-March–mid-October, 9.30 am–6.00 pm (Mondays, 10.15 am–6.00 pm). Mid-October–mid-March, 9.30 am–4.30 pm (Mondays, 10.15 am–4.30 pm). Closed 24–26 December

Admission: Group rates upon application

Group size: Min 25; max 35

Length of visit: N/A

HASTINGS MUSEUM AND ART GALLERY

Address: Cambridge Road, Hastings, East Sussex TN34 1ET
Tel: (01424) 781155

Description:
Superb opportunity to see a number of exhibitions all under one roof: the Dinosaur Gallery with fossils of crocodiles, turtles, and other animals and plants of the cretaceous period transformed into lifelike models; the Wildlife Gallery, which illustrates birds and animals in a reconstruction of settings found around Hastings; and there are also displays on local ironworking, ceramics and paintings. Throughout the year there are regular changing exhibitions.

Ages: 5+

Subjects: English; Science; Geography; Technology; History; Art; R.E.

Facilities: Toilets; educational material

Open: Throughout the year. Monday–Friday, 10.00 am–5.00 pm. Saturday, 10.00 am–1.00 pm and 2.00 pm–5.00 pm. Sunday, 3.00 pm–5.00 pm. Closed Good Friday and 25–26 December

Admission: Free

Group size: N/A

Length of visit: N/A

HASTINGS SEA LIFE CENTRE

Address: Rock-A-Nore Road, Hastings, East Sussex TN34 3DW
Tel: (01424) 718776   Fax: (01424) 718757

Description:
Home to a number of marine species, Hastings Sea Life Centre makes for a thoroughly enjoyable day out. Walk underwater and confront a barrage of marine life, all colours and sizes; follow the early life cycle of many fish; and there is also the opportunity to pick up sturdy rock pool creatures such as crabs or starfish under the watchful eye of a Hastings Sea Life Centre expert.

Ages: 5+

Subjects: Science; Geography

Facilities: Shop; free teachers' pre-visit; toilets; disabled access; refreshments; guided tours; teachers' packs and workbooks available for KS1 and KS2
Open: Throughout the year from 10.00 am. Contact for winter opening times
Admission: Group rates upon application
Group size: Min 10
Length of visit: 1½–2 hours

HATFIELD HOUSE

Address: Hatfield House, Hatfield, Hertfordshire AL9 5NQ
Tel: (01707) 262823   Fax: (01707) 275719

Description:
Since the 17th century this house has been home to the Earls and Marquesses of Salisbury and it contains famous portraits, fine furniture, armour, tapestries, and possessions belonging to Elizabeth I. There are marked nature trails, several exhibitions, one initiated by the British Model Soldier Society with over 3,000 models, and a reconstruction of a William IV kitchen.
Ages: 5–18
Subjects: Science; Geography; History; Mathematics
Facilities: Free teachers' pre-visit; guided tour; car park; indoor/outdoor eating areas; toilets, shop; disabled access
Open: Contact for details
Admission: House, park, gardens, exhibition: children £2.90; adults/teachers £4.60. Park, gardens, exhibition: children £2.10; adult/teachers £2.80. One teacher free for every 15 children
Group size: Min 20
Length of visit: 3 hours

HEATHROW AIRPORT

Address: Heathrow, London
Tel: (0181) 745 6655

Description:
Pay a visit behind the scenes at the world's busiest international airport and see a Boeing 777 Cockpit mock-up; there are interactive displays and other activities to take part in, enabling students to learn more about airports while also achieving National Curriculum targets.
Ages: All ages
Subjects: Geography
Facilities: Worksheets; free audiovisual guides; car park; refreshments

Open: All year. Monday–Friday, 10.00 am–7.00 pm. Saturday–Sunday, 10.00 am–
5.00 pm
Admission: Group rates upon application
Group size: N/A
Length of visit: N/A

HERSTMONCEUX SCIENCE CENTRE

Address: Hailsham, East Sussex BN27 1RP
Tel/fax: (01323) 832731

Description:
One of a new type of discovery centre where visitors can experience science
through hands-on activities. Each exhibit offers something to do and its
connection with astronomy makes it even more exciting, especially as it occupies
buildings that until very recently were part of the Royal Greenwich Observatory.
With telescopes and domes still in place it has a very special atmosphere.
Ages: 7–12
Subjects: Science; Design & Technology
Facilities: Car park; hands-on sessions; telescope tours; indoor/outdoor eating
areas; shop; café; free teachers' pre-visit; disabled access
Open: Throughout the year, 10.00 am–6.00 pm
Admission: Groups visits are £2.50 per pupil for a hands-on session. A Telescope
Tour is an additional 80p per pupil. Teachers are free up to a maximum of 1 per 8
pupils
Group size: Max 150
Length of visit: 90 minutes for the entire visit

THE HISTORIC DOCKYARD

Address: Chatham, Kent ME4 4TE
Tel: (01634) 812551   Fax: (01634) 826918

Description:
A living, working, 18th-century museum contained within seven galleries, bringing
together over four centuries of shipping of a traditional river dockyard from the age
of sail. The galleries which include a working ropery, a Victorian sloop and
submarine, both under restoration, and over 60 maritime-related crafts.
Ages: 5+
Subjects: History; Geography; Art; Technology; English
Facilities: Indoor/outdoor eating areas; toilets; classrooms; free teachers' pre-visit;
information pack; education officer; car park; regular events; guided tours; workshops; exhibition; demonstrations; audiovisual facilities; shops

Open: Daily Easter–October. Advisable to check for times
Admission: Pupils Historic Dockyard £2.00; Submarine Ocelot £1.50. Walk through £1.00. One teacher free for every 10 pupils. Extra adults charged at pupil rates
Group size: Advisable to check
Length of visit: Full guided tour approximately 45 minutes. Walk through 20 minutes

---

HOWLETTS AND PORT LYMPNE WILD ANIMAL PARK

Address: Education Office, Howletts Wild Animal Park, Bekesbourne, nr Canterbury, Kent CT4 5EL
Tel: (01227) 721286   Fax: (01227) 721853

Description:
In 300 acres of parkland Howletts and Port Lympne Wild Animal Park have some of the most fascinating animals to be seen: western lowland gorillas, African elephants, water buffalo, prides of Atlas lions and many rare and endangered animals. For over 30 years the Animal Park has skilfully bred many endangered and rare animals with the intention of giving them back to the wild. There is also a splendid manor house standing in 15 acres of gardens which offers a look back to the early years of the 20th century. A visit to the park will provide students with an invaluable insight into the natural world and the importance of its preservation.

Ages: All ages
Subjects: English; Science; Mathematics; History; Design & Technology; Geography; R.E.
Facilities: Car park; education packs; animal fact sheets; educational sessions; talks; free teachers' pre-visit; education room; toilets; safari shuttle service; shop; video shows; restaurant; refreshments; feeding times for the animals; landscaped gardens; outdoor eating area; disabled access
Open: Throughout the year. Summer, 10.00 am–7.00 pm. Winter, 10.00 am–5.00 pm. Closed Christmas Day
Admission: Children (4–16 years) £3.00; students (17+ years) £4.00; adults/teachers £5.50. One teacher free for every 10 pupils. Extra adults £5.50
Group size: N/A
Length of visit: Up to 1 day

IMPERIAL WAR MUSEUM

Address: Cabinet War Rooms, Clive Steps, King Charles Street, London SW1A 2AQ
Tel: (0171) 930 6961   Fax: (0171) 839 5897

Description:
Step back into wartime London and visit the Cabinet War Rooms which protected the Government throughout the worst aid raids of World War II. These rooms were the very core of Britain's war efforts. Since 1945 it has been preserved and it makes an exciting and fascinating learning activity for all pupils studying World War II.

Ages: 5+

Subjects: History; English; Art; Mathematics; Technology

Facilities: Free teachers' pre-visit; workshops; study sessions; exhibitions; guided tour; free education pack; activity sheets; tailor-made sessions; audio guide; illustrated talks; shop; indoor eating area; disabled access

Open: Throughout the year, daily, 9.30 am–5.15 pm (10.00 am–5.15 pm in winter). Closed 24–26 December

Admission: Children (up to 18 years) £1.60 each; students (18+ years) £2.60 each. One teacher free for every 10 pupils. Additional adults £3.30 each

Group size: Max 50

Length of visit: N/A

KELVEDON HATCH SECRET EX-GOVERNMENT UNDERGROUND BUNKER

Address: Kelvedon Hall Lane, Kelvedon Hatch, Brentwood, Essex CM15 0LB
Tel: (01277) 364883   Fax: (01277) 372562

Description:
Ideal for students studying World War II and equally for many other topics on the curricula, the opportunity to see an underground bunker buried 100 ft underground complete with a BBC studio, canteen, dormitories, plant room, communications and scientific room.

Ages: 5–16

Subjects: Mathematics; Science; Geography; History

Facilities: Teacher/pupil resource packs; classroom, guided tour; demonstrations; car park; indoor/outdoor eating areas; toilets; shop

Open: Throughout the year. Monday–Friday, 10.00 am–4.00 pm. Weekends, 10.00 am–5.00 pm. Closed November–March, Monday–Wednesday

Admission: Children and teachers £2.70 each

Group size: Min 10

Length of visit: 1½ hours

KENNET HORSE BOAT COMPANY

Address: 32 West Mills, Newbury, Berkshire RG14 5HU
Tel: (01635) 44154   Fax: (01635) 43636

Description:
A fascinating look at the history of canal life along the Kennett Valley, providing visitors with an insight into canal life, the role the locks have to play and how they operate, the flora and fauna in and around the canal itself, together with a look at the historical role the canal had. Spanning 87 miles with 102 locks, the Kennet and Avon Canal stretches between Newbury and Hungerford and runs into the Thames at Reading, through Berkshire, Wiltshire and West Somerset to Bath, into the River Avon and joins the Bristol Channel at Bristol Docks.

Ages: 5–11
Subjects: Science; History; Technology
Facilities: Refreshments; shop; toilet; disabled access
Open: Easter–end of September, daily. First trip 10.00 am or by arrangement
Admission: Based on larger groups, 1½-hour tour £105.00, 2-hour tour £130.00. Price for smaller groups on application
Group size: Max 75
Length of visit: Up to 2 hours

LEEDS CASTLE

Address: The Sales Office, Leeds Castle, Maidstone, Kent ME17 1PL
Tel: (01622) 765400   Fax: (01622) 735616

Description:
Built on two islands in the middle of a natural lake, Leeds Castle is England's oldest and most romantic stately home and houses a collection of tapestries, furnishings and paintings. Surrounded by 500 acres of parkland, there is a duckery, greenhouses, Museum of Dog Collars, an aviary, a maze and an underground grotto to explore.

Ages: 5–15
Subjects: History; Art; Science; R.E.; Music; Mathematics; English; Technology; Geography
Facilities: Free teachers' pre-visit; car park; toilets; educational packs; indoor/ outdoor eating area; shop; disabled access; ancient watermill; Barbican; maze; aviary
Open: March–October: Park and Gardens, 10.00 am–5.00 pm; Castle, 11.00 am–5.30 pm. November–February: Park and Gardens, 10.00 am–3.00 pm; Castle, 10.15 pm–3.30 pm. Private tours can be pre-booked for educational parties outside these hours. Closed 25 December, 27 June and 4 July prior to open air concerts
Admission: Group rates available upon application

Group size: Min 20
Length of visit: N/A

LEGOLAND WINDSOR

Address: Winkfield Road, Windsor, Berkshire SL4 4AY
   Tel: (01753) 626100   Fax: (01753) 626200

Description:
   Legoland Windsor is a totally different theme park located in 150 acres of parkland with over 40 different rides, shows and attractions, many of which relate to the National Curriculum. Legoland cleverly combines pleasure with education where pupils can explore and experience a number of subjects out of school surroundings, and take part in workshops which are designed to help promote thought and reaction in a fun way.
Ages: 5+
Subjects: English; Science; Design & Technology; Information Technology
Facilities: Car park; indoor/outdoor eating areas; toilets; disabled access; shop; free teachers' pre-visit; resource packs; live shows; workshops; miniland; gardens; special events
Open: Advisable to check
Admission: Group rates available on application. One teacher free for every 10 pupils
Group size: N/A
Length of visit: 6–7 hours

THE LONDON DUNGEON

Address: 28/34 Tooley Street, London SE1 2SZ
   Tel: (0171) 403 7221   Fax: (0171) 378 1529

Description:
   Deep beneath the paving stones of Southwark lies the world's most terrifying museum of horror – explore the Theatre of the Guillotine when the French Revolution turned public execution into entertainment for the audience; listen as the judge condemns you and then climb aboard the executioner's barge for a trip through Traitors' Gate to meet your punishment (a new £3.5m development). Those brave enough may even step back to the fateful night of 31 August 1888 and pursue the steps of Jack the Ripper. The London Dungeon cleverly recreates pieces of history that are often best buried … .
Ages: 5+ (not for young children)
Subjects: History
Facilities: Education pack available; guidebooks

Open: Throughout the year from 10.00 am. Closed Christmas Day
Admission: Group rates for 20+ children (5–14 years) £4.50; students (15–18 years) £5.50; adults/teachers £6.50. One adult free for every 10 paying children
Group size: Min 20
Length of visit: N/A

MILL GREEN MUSEUM AND MILL

Address: Mill Green, Hatfield, Hertfordshire AL9 5PD
Tel: (01707) 271362   Fax: (01707) 272511

Description:
Working water-powered corn mill with a local history museum in the adjoining Mill House. Temporary exhibitions and craft exhibitions.
Ages: 5–18
Subjects: Technology; Science
Facilities: Free teachers' pre-visit; teacher/pupil resource packs; worksheets; quiz sheets; project books/guided tour; car park; outdoor eating area; toilets; shop; disabled access
Open: Throughout the year, Tuesday–Friday, 10.00 am–5.00 pm
Admission: Free
Group size: N/A
Length of visit: Up to 2 hours

MUSEUM OF KENT LIFE

Address: Lock Lane, Sandling, Maidstone, Kent ME14 3AU
Tel: (01622) 763936   Fax: (01622) 662024

Description:
An award-winning museum where pupils can experience the sights, smells and tastes of rustic Kent life; see Britain's legendary working oast house, enjoy the many exhibitions; meet the animals in the livestock centre and birds in the aviary; browse around the kitchen garden, orchard and herb garden; visit the 19th-century granary.
Ages: 5–16
Subjects: English; Mathematics; Science; Technology
Facilities: Free teachers' pre-visit; worksheets; classroom; outdoor/indoor eating areas; shop; toilets; craft demonstrations (charge); children's playground; special events
Open: Throughout the year, 10.00 am–5.30 pm
Admission: Summer: April–October, children £1.75; one teacher free for every five pupils. Winter: November–March, children £1.50; one teacher free for every five

pupils. Additional adults are charged at the group rate of £3.55. The same rates apply for special schools but one teacher is free for every two pupils
Group size: Max 30
Length of visit: Up to 4 hours

NATIONAL TRUST PROPERTIES

The National Trust's Southern Region covers Hampshire, the Isle of Wight, south-western Greater London, Surrey and West Sussex. For further information contact: National Trust Regional Office, Polesden Lacey, Dorking, Surrey RH5 6BD (tel: 01372 453401).

Black Down
Box Hill
Cissbury Ring
Clandon Park
Dapdune Wharf
Devil's Dyke
Frensham Little Pond
Ham House
Harting Down
Hindhead Commons
Leith Hill
The Needles Battery
Nymans Garden
Petworth House
Polesden Lacey
Slindon Estate
Snuff Mill Environmental Centre
Standen
Uppark
Winchester City Mill
Witley Common Information Centre

The National Trust Thames and Chilterns Region covers Bedfordshire, Berkshire, Buckinghamshire, Hertfordshire, Oxfordshire and Greater London north of the Thames. For further information contact: National Trust Regional Office, Hughenden Manor, High Wycombe, Buckinghamshire, HP14 4LA (tel: 01494 528051).

The Ashridge Estate
Claydon House

Hughenden Manor
Osterley Park
Stowe Landscape Gardens
Sutton House

The National Trust Kent and East Sussex Regions cover East Sussex, Kent and south-east Greater London. For further information contact: National Trust Regional Office, The Estate Office, Scotney Castle, Lamberhurst, Tunbridge Wells, Kent TN3 8JN (tel: 01892 890651).

Alfriston Clergy House
Beachy Head
Chartwell
Emmetts Garden
Frog Firle Farm
Ightham Mote

NATURAL HISTORY MUSEUM

Address: Cumberland House, Eastern Parade, Southsea, Portsmouth, Hants PO4 9RF
Tel: (01705) 827261   Fax: (01705) 875276

Description:
An enthralling look at the geological formation of the area around Portsmouth as it was hundreds of millions of years ago, following through to the wildlife of the present day. There is an extensive freshwater aquarium, a geology gallery, a butterfly exhibition, an Ice Age display and other attractions, depending on when visited.

Ages: All ages
Subjects: Science; Geography
Facilities: Free teachers' pre-visit; shop; disabled access limited; refreshments
Open: Throughout the year. Closed 24–26 December
Admission: April–September: children £1.20; adults/teachers £1.70. October–March: children 75p; adults/teachers £1.30
Group size: Max 30
Length of visit: 1 hour

NEWHAVEN FORT

Address: Fort Road, Newhaven, East Sussex BN9 9ND
   Tel: (01273) 517622   Fax: (01273) 512059

Description:
   Built in 1860 to discourage invaders, Newhaven Fort provides an unusual and exciting day out where visitors can step back in time to see authentic displays and exhibitions of war-torn Britain; discover the underground tunnels; see amazing exhibits reflecting the history of the fort and the D-Day landing; witness practical demonstrations, see gas masks and even try on military and civil defence helmets.

Ages: 7+

Subjects: History; Geography

Facilities: Car park; indoor/outdoor eating areas; toilets; introductory talk; shop; teachers' pre-visit; classroom; hands-on sessions; play area for younger children; disabled access limited; information pack; audio tape; quiz trail

Open: Daily, April–November, 10.30 am–6.00 pm. By appointment all year

Admission: Children £1.50. Accompanying adults free

Group size: Max 175

Length of visit: 3 hours

THE OXFORD STORY EXHIBITION

Address: 6 Broad Street, Oxford OX1 3AJ
   Tel: (01865) 790055   Fax: (01865) 791716

Description:
   Celebrate 800 years of university life with a visit to the Oxford Story Exhibition, which recounts the story of one of the world's greatest universities. See many famous graduates brought to life. Sit in a carriage and be transported around the various exhibits with an accompanying commentary revealing all its fascinating history.

Ages: All ages

Subjects: History

Facilities: Free teachers' pre-visit; teachers' pack; disabled access limited; worksheets; shop; special events

Open: Daily. April, May, June, 9.30 am–5.00 pm; July and August, 9.00 am–6.00 pm; September and October, 9.30 am–5.00 pm; November–March, 10.00 am–4.30 pm. Saturday and Sunday, 10.00 am–5.00 pm. Closed Christmas Day

Admission: Group concessions available for groups of 20+

Group size: Min 10

Length of visit: N/A

PARADISE FAMILY LEISURE PARK

Address: Avis Road, Newhaven, Sussex BN9 0DH
Tel: (01273) 512123   Fax: (01273) 616005

Description:
Discover how earthquakes and volcanoes work, experience the fun of life-sized dinosaurs and meet Veloairaptor, a vicious dinosaur which lived 150 million years ago. There is the Newhaven Botanic Garden which accommodates a selection of flowering plants from all over the world; and in the grounds of Paradise Garden you can see in miniature, handcrafted Sussex landmarks which cleverly reveal the history of Sussex with its railways, castles and waterways of days gone by.

Ages: 5+

Subjects: Science

Facilities: Car park; disabled access; refreshments; outdoor eating area; shop; exhibitions; play area; radio-controlled boats and trucks; rides; museum; worksheets; teachers' notes; function room; information pack available; Maritime Museum; miniature railway and other attractions

Open: Throughout the year

Admission: Group rates upon application

Group size: Min 10

Length of visit: N/A

PARK LODGE FARM CENTRE

Address: c/o Hillingdon Direct Services, Estates and Valuation Division, Civic Centre, Uxbridge
Tel: (01895) 250111

Description:
A fully equipped farm demonstrating dairy farming to school parties with special facilities including a rotary milking parlour with gallery viewing area, a calf rearing unit and a flock of 180 sheep. There are two farm trails and regular milking sessions which take place at 2.30 pm daily.

Ages: 5+

Subjects: Science

Facilities: Car park; free teachers' pre-visit; introductory talk; toilets; disabled access; classroom

Open: Weekdays during term time, 10.00 am–4.00 pm

Admission: Free

Group size: N/A

Length of visit: 2 hours

PAULTONS PARK

Address: Ower, Romsey, Hampshire S051 6AL
   Tel: (01703) 814442   Fax: (01703) 813025

Description:
   Learn about wildlife, understand the life of the Romanys and explore village life through demonstration trade workshops from the turn of the century. Study animals in as near as possible their natural habitats and see a collection of 250 species of birds and wildfowl from all over the world, including the hornbill collection, one of the largest in the country.

Ages: All ages

Subjects: Science; English; History; Geography; Art; Information Technology; Mathematics; P.E.; Music

Facilities: Car park; teachers' information pack; shop; first aid centre; toilets; worksheets; indoor/outdoor eating area; refreshments; disabled access; rides; magic forest; live entertainment; maze; free teachers' pre-visit; exhibitions; pets corner; Land of Dinosaurs

Open: 15 March–2 November: daily, 10.00 am–6.30 pm. Earlier closing spring and autumn. For other opening times please telephone

Admission: Special discounts available for groups of 15 or more visiting on weekdays during term time

Group size: N/A

Length of visit: N/A

PENHURST PLACE AND GARDENS

Address: Penhurst, Tonbridge, Kent TN11 8DG
   Tel: (01892) 870307   Fax: (01892) 870866

Description:
   One of England's finest and most complete 14th-century manor houses. An excellent example of architecture containing state rooms filled with an amazing collection of tapestries, paintings and furniture. There is also a toy museum creating memories of nurseries in bygone days.

Ages: 5+

Subjects: History; Art

Facilities: Free teachers' pre-visit; education resource pack; school room; guided tours; indoor/outdoor eating areas; restaurant; school room; disabled access; car park; adventure playground

Open: End March–1 November. House and grounds are open 7 days a week. Grounds: 11.00 am–6.00 pm. House: 12 noon–5.30 pm. Weekdays in October entry to the house is by guided tours only. Tours are hourly

Admission: Groups based on a minimum of 20
 Guided house tours: Children £3.00; adults/teachers £5.70
 Guided garden tours: Children £4.00; adults/teachers £6.50
 Combined guided tours: Children £4.00; adults/teachers £6.50
 Non-guided group visit: Children £2.80; adults/teachers £5.10
Group size: Min 20; max 110
Length of visit: Guided tour of the house – 45 minutes. Guided tour of the gardens
 75–90 minutes. Combined tour can be arranged

PRESTON MANOR

Address: Preston Park, Brighton BN1 6SD
 Tel: (01273) 292770   Fax: (01273) 292871

Description:
 Demonstrating the atmosphere of an Edwardian gentry home both 'upstairs' and
 'downstairs', Preston Manor house has over 20 rooms to explore, including the
 servants' quarters, kitchens and butler's pantry, together with lots of other memorabilia providing an interesting insight into Edwardian life.
Ages: 5+
Subjects: History
Facilities: Free teachers' packs; car park; disabled access limited; sales outlet at
 entrance desk; outdoor eating area; lunch room available; Victorian servants'
 role play for children aged 7–11 years studying the Victorians; hands-on sessions;
 guided tour; activity sheets
Open: Monday, 1.00 pm–5.00 pm. Tuesday–Saturday, 10.00 am–5.00 pm. Sunday,
 2.00 pm–5.00 pm. Closed Monday mornings (except Bank Holidays), Good
 Friday, 25–26 December. May be subject to variation
Admission: Group rates upon application
Group size: Min 20
Length of visit: N/A

ROMNEY, HYTHE AND DYMCHURCH RAILWAY

Address: New Romney, Kent TN28 8PL
 Tel: (01797) 362353

Description:
 Climb aboard the world's smallest public railway as it winds its way from the
 delightful Cinque Port of Hythe via Dymchurch and New Romney to the light-
 houses at Dungeness. Since it opened in 1927 the railway has become firmly
 established as a favourite destination for both school and youth groups looking for
 a different kind of educational visit. On this line you will find all the facilities
 required to operate a busy railway such as: sheds, signal boxes and coach-

building works. The most famous collection of miniature steam and diesel loco-
motives in the world are all gathered here.

Ages: All ages

Subjects: History

Facilities: Free videotape loan; worksheets; museum; children's play area; refreshments; outdoor eating area at New Romney and Dungeness; disabled access; toy
and model museum at Romney station (charge); car park; special events; toilets;
shop

Open: Apply for opening times

Admission: Group rates upon application. One teacher free with every 10 pupils

Group size: N/A

Length of visit: 1–6 hours

ROYAL ENGINEERS MUSEUM

Address: Prince Arthur Road, Gillingham, Kent ME4 4UG
Tel: (01634) 406397

Description:
Visitors are able to experience the sounds and sights of the Engineers on active
service; see exciting and dramatic displays of both historic and modern
equipment; enjoy the fascinating unique collection of costumes and relics from
all over the world and visit the medal gallery.

Ages: 5+

Subjects: History; Geography; Technology

Facilities: Free teachers' pre-visit; introductory talk; shop; outdoor/indoor eating
areas; refreshments; car park; disabled access; toilets; classroom available; shop;
videos; guided tours; guidebooks available; library

Open: Monday–Thursday, 10.00 am–5.00 pm. Saturday and Sunday, 11.30 am–
5.00 pm. Museum is open by appointment on Fridays for private tours. Closed
25–26 December, 1 January and Good Friday

Admission: Group rates upon application

Group size: N/A

Length of visit: 1½– 4 hours

THE ROYAL MARINES MUSEUM

Address: Southsea, Hampshire PO4 9PX
Tel: (01705) 819385   Fax: (01705) 838420

Description:
The Royal Marines Museum chronicles the lives of men and women who served
in the corps from 1664 to present times, showing how the people lived, worked

and died. In order to bring the reality to life the museum uses a hands-on and investigative approach and covers 18th-century history including the American War of Independence; 19th-century history including the Napoleonic Wars and Empire Wars; World Wars I and II; and international conflict – Korea, terrorism, the Falklands and UN operations.

Ages: 5+

Subjects: History; English; Mathematics; CDT and Art; Geography; Music; P.E.

Facilities: Disabled access; free teachers' pre-visit; car park; outdoor/indoor eating area; toilets; education centre; shop; library; photographic archive collection; introductory talks; handling sessions; interactive computer-based learning; displays; tailored sessions available

Open: Whitsun–August, 10.00 am–5.00 pm. September–Whitsun, 10.00 am–4.30 pm

Admission: Children 75p. One teacher free with every eight pupils. Additional adults £3.75

Group size: Caters for 30 pupils although larger numbers considered

Length of visit: 1½–2 hours

ROYAL NAVY SUBMARINE MUSEUM

Address: Haslar Jetty Road, Gosport, Hampshire PO12 2AS
Tel: (01705) 510354/765250   Fax: (01705) 511349

Description:
Learn all about the history of the Royal Navy Submarine Service from 1901 to the present day; follow the history of the submarine from Alexander the Great to the present day; climb aboard a real submarine and find out what life was really like under the sea through the personal effects of the crews. A fascinating day, a fascinating experience.

Ages: 5+

Subjects: Science; History; Geography

Facilities: Car park; shop; refreshments; outdoor eating area; guided tour; disabled access; audiovisual facilities; exhibitions; free teachers' pre-visit; education pack; tailor-made sessions; resource equipment

Open: Daily. April–October, 10.00 am–5.30 pm. November–March, 1.00 pm–4.30 pm. Closed 24 December–1 January

Admission: Children £1.50. One teacher free for every 15 pupils. Extra adults £2.50

Group size: Min 15

Length of visit: 2–3 hours

THE ROYAL PAVILION

Address: The Royal Pavilion, Brighton, East Sussex BN1 1EE
Tel: (01273) 292822   Fax: (01273) 292871

Description:
Over 200 years of history are contained within the doors of the famous seaside residence which was built for King George IV and is rated as being one of the most beautiful buildings in the British Isles. Initially a farmhouse, it was turned into a neo-classical villa in 1787. The interior is magnificent with exquisite displays of superb craftsmanship; the Music Room with its domed ceiling of gilded scallop shells and hand-knotted carpet and the huge crystal chandelier in the Banqueting Hall bring history to life.

Ages: 5+
Subjects: History; Art; Music
Facilities: Guided tours; shop; disabled access; tea-rooms; specialist tours relating to all levels of National Curriculum; introductory talk; toilets
Open: 1 October–31 May, 10.00 am–5.00 pm. 1 June–30 September, 10.00 am–6.00 pm
Admission: Group rates upon application
Group size: Min 20
Length of visit: N/A

RSPB NATURE RESERVE AT DUNGENESS

Address: RSPB South East England Office, 2nd Floor, Frederick House, 42 Frederick Place, Brighton, East Sussex BN1 1AT
Tel: (01273) 775333   Fax: (01273) 220236

Description:
The oldest RSPB Nature Reserve in Britain and the largest shingle area in Europe, Dungeness is located on the southern coastline of Kent and carefully managed for conservation. Of the 430 types of plants, 1,500 identified invertebrate species and thousands of birds, many can only be found at Dungeness, which makes it an ideal location for teaching programmes in all key stages.

Ages: 5+
Subjects: Technology; Mathematics; Art; Geography; Science
Facilities: Tailor-made courses to suit requirements; free teachers' pre-visit; disabled access; visitor centre
Open: Contact for times
Admission: Depends on key stage and subject, whether half or full day. Contact for further rates
Group size: N/A
Length of visit: N/A

RYE AUDIO TOURS

Armed with a personal stereo and headphone visitors are taken on an investigation into the old part of Rye beginning outside the Heritage Centre. Lasting 44 minutes the tape can also be hired overnight and the commentary is in English.

RYE HERITAGE CENTRE

Address: Strand Quay, Rye, East Sussex TN31 7AY
Tel: (01797) 226696   Fax: (01797) 223460

Description:
Over 700 years of the history of Rye is located in a theatre room on the ground floor of the Heritage Centre. There is a 1 in 100 scale model of Rye and within it dramatic events are re-enacted; royal visits, murders, smuggling, etc. The accompanying commentaries last 20 minutes and are available in English, French, German and Spanish. Situated on the upper floor is a free storyboard exhibition covering different areas of Rye, the Cinque Ports, Camber Castle, architecture, artists, shipbuilding, etc.

Ages: All ages
Subjects: History; Art
Facilities: Maps; disabled access limited; shop
Open: Daily, mid-March–end of October, 9.00 am–5.30 pm
Admission: Contact for different rates
Group size: Min 10
Length of visit: N/A

SHIPWRECK HERITAGE CENTRE

Address: Rock-a-Nore Road, Hastings, East Sussex TN34 3DW
Tel: (01424) 437452

Description:
An exhibition celebrating 3,000 years of shipwrecks along the English Channel. There is an exciting audiovisual show, push-button video of underwater treasures and the chance to hear tell the story of the *Amsterdam,* which was beached in a gale in 1749.

Ages: 8–16
Subjects: Mathematics; English; Science; Geography; Technology; History; Art
Facilities: Toilets; shop; guidebook; educational material; disabled access
Open: Daily, April–October, 10.30 am–5.00 pm. Other times by appointment
Admission: Group rates upon application
Group size: N/A
Length of visit: 1 hour

THE SHUTTLEWORTH COLLECTION

Address: Old Warden Aerodrome, nr Biggleswade, Bedfordshire SG18 9EP
Tel: (01767) 627288   Fax: (01767) 627745

Description:
A traditional grass aerodrome accommodating a world-famous collection of aircraft, veteran and vintage cars, motorcycles, cycles and a coach room of horse-drawn vehicles, many of which are the only ones of their kind.

Ages: 5+

Subjects: Technology; History; Science; Art

Facilities: Free teachers' pre-visit; worksheets; quiz sheets; project books; classroom; talk/demonstrations; car park; indoor/outdoor eating areas; toilets; shop; disabled access

Open: Daily. November–March, 10.00 am–3.00 pm. April–October, 10.00 am–4.00 pm

Admission: Children £1.50; adults/teachers £3.00. One teacher free for every 10 pupils

Group size: Min 20; max 70

Length of visit: N/A

A SMUGGLER'S ADVENTURE IN ST CLEMENT'S CAVES

Address: West Hill, Hastings, East Sussex TN34 3HY
Tel: (01424) 422964   Fax: (01424) 721483

Description:
Explore the labyrinth of tunnels, caves and secret passages of St Clement's Caves hidden within the West Hill of Hastings. The smuggler's life is resurrected in a themed experience which includes a museum of smuggling, video theatre and a subterranean walk. Over 50 life-sized figures' scenes are activated by push buttons and lighting and there are a few extra surprises.

Ages: 8–16 years

Subjects: English; Science; Geography; History

Facilities: Shop; guidebook; teachers' pack

Open: Daily. Easter–end September, 10.00 am–5.30 pm. End September–Easter, 11.00 am–4.30 pm. Closed 25–26 December

Admission: Group rates upon application

Group size: Min 10

Length of visit: 45 minutes–1 hour

THE SOUTH OF ENGLAND RARE BREED CENTRE

Address: Highlands Farm, Woodchurch, Ashford, Kent TN26 3RJ
   Tel: (01233) 861493   Fax: (01233) 861457

Description:
   With over 500 animals, learning is a truly unique experience at the Rare Breeds
   Centre. You can meet a collection of unusual animals: goats with tall horns; sheep
   with curly fleece and cows with handlebar horns.

Ages: All ages

Subjects: English; Science; Mathematics; Geography

Facilities: Worksheets; indoor/outdoor eating areas; shop; car park; disabled
   access; tractor and trailer rides; playground; padding pool and sandpit for the
   under-5s; children's barn; woodland walks; regular events

Open: Throughout the year. Daily, 1 April–30 September, 10.30 am–5.30 pm. 1
   October–31 March, 10.30 am–4.30 pm. Closed 24–25 December and Mondays
   in winter

Admission: Group rates upon application.

Group size: N/A

Length of visit: N/A

SOUTHSEA CASTLE

Address: Clarence Esplanade, Southsea, Hants PO5 3QL
   Tel: (01705) 827261   Fax: (01705) 875276

Description:
   Built between 1544 and 1545 to protect Portsmouth against invasion from the
   French, the most significant addition to Southsea Castle was an underground tunnel
   around the moat which you can still enter. An amazing castle with an amazing history.

Ages: All ages

Subjects: History

Facilities: Teachers' resource pack; disabled access; exhibitions; car park; shop

Open: Daily, April–October, 10.00 am–5.30 pm. November–March: Saturday and
   Sunday, 10.00 am–4.30 pm. School holidays and pre-booked groups 10.00 am–
   4.30 pm daily

Admission: Group rates upon application

Group size: Max 60

Length of visit: 1–1½ hours

SUSSEX WILDLIFE TRUSTS

Address: Woods Mill, Henfield, West Sussex BN5 9SD
   Tel: (01273) 492630   Fax: (01273) 494500

Description:
   The 15-acre nature reserve covers a variety of habitats including freshwater meadow with woodland and hedgerows. There is an 18th-century watermill which houses environmental displays and audiovisual facilities. Ideal for students following environmental or/and conservation studies.

Ages: All ages

Subjects: Science; Geography; Mathematics; English

Facilities: Car park; indoor/outdoor eating areas; free teachers' pre-visit; disabled access; classroom; exhibitions; take appropriate footwear

Open: Visits take place during spring, summer and autumn terms between 10.00 am and 3.00 pm

Admission: Spring term: £3.00 per pupil per day; summer and autumn terms: £3.50 per pupil per day

Group size: Tuesdays and Thursdays max 70. Wednesday max 35 (due to staff availability)

Length of visit: Full day

THORPE PARK

Address: Staines Road, Chertsey, Surrey KT16 8PN
   Tel: (0990) 880880   Fax: (0990) 880889

Description:
   A visit to Thorpe Park, one of the country's premier leisure parks, brings the classroom to life and is somewhere where children can make sense of complex theorems and principles, where they can touch and see many breeds of animals, study farm crafts, explore nature and wildlife and have an enjoyable time.

Ages: All ages

Subjects: Science; History; Technology; Mathematics

Facilities: Car park; toilets; disabled access; indoor/outdoor eating areas; refreshments; shop; worksheets; Thorpe Park waterbus; theatre; rides and attractions

Open: Contact for opening times

Admission: Group rates upon application

Group size: N/A

Length of visit: Up to a full day

TONBRIDGE CASTLE

Address: Castle Street, Tonbridge, Kent TN9 1BG
Tel: (01732) 770929

Description:
Step back 900 years into historic Tonbridge Castle and learn about castle life in the 13th century via interactive displays and life-sized figures. Find out how the castle faced bitter sieges and how the Pope excommunicated the castle's inhabitants. Visit the basement stores and the armoury, climb up to the battlements and imagine the castle under attack. The visit can be divided into three parts: a guided tour or personal audio tour; use of Education Facility complete with various medieval activities with a member of staff provided; various activities.

Ages: All ages
Subjects: History
Facilities: Car park; free teachers' pre-visit; audio tour; worksheets; teachers' pack
Open: Throughout the year. Daily, Monday–Saturday, 9.00 am–5.00 pm. Sunday and Bank Holidays from 10.30 am–5.00 pm. October–Easter Saturday and Sunday, 9.00 am–4.00 pm. Closed 25–27 December and 1 January
Admission: Group rates upon application. Groups of 10+ 10 per cent discount
Group size: N/A
Length of visit: At least 2 hours

THE TWICKENHAM EXPERIENCE

Address: Rugby Football Union, Rugby Road, Twickenham, Middlesex TW1 1DZ
Tel: (0181) 892 2000   Fax: (0181) 892 9816

Description:
Rugby is one of the fastest growing competitive sports in the world and Twickenham, home of the England Rugby Union, is one of the world's grandest rugby stadiums, seating 75,000 spectators. Opened in 1996, the Museum of Rugby brings the history of the sport to life with the help of displays providing visitors with a fascinating glimpse behind the scenes, a chance to visit the dressing rooms and players' tunnels, and to have an overall view of the stadium where some of the most exciting matches have been played. School tours can be organized to meet the National Curriculum.

Ages: All ages
Subjects: History; P.E.
Facilities: Refreshments; tour; shop; museum, quiz worksheets; audiovisual interactive computer technology
Open: Throughout the year. Tuesday–Saturday, 10.30 am–5.00 pm. Sunday, 2.00 pm–5.00 pm. Open Bank Holidays. Closed Monday, Good Friday, 25–26 December

Admission: For groups of 15+ there is a 10 per cent discount
Group size: Min 15
Length of visit: N/A

VERULAMIUM MUSEUM

Address: St Michael's, St Albans, Hertfordshire AL3 4SW
   Tel: (01727) 819341   Fax: (01727) 859919

Description:
   Depicting everyday life in Roman Britain with recreated rooms, hands-on
   discovery areas, excavation video and mosaics, Verulamium Museum is the
   perfect venue, located on the site of one of the major cities of Roman Britain.
Age: 5+
Subjects: Technology; History; Art
Facilities: Free teachers' pre-visit; teacher/pupil resource packs, worksheets, quiz
   sheets, project books; welcome talk, guided tour; car park; outdoor eating area;
   toilets; shop; disabled access
Open: Throughout the year. Monday–Saturday, 10.00 am–5.00 pm. Sunday, 2.00
   pm– 5.00 pm
Admission: Children and teachers £1.55
Group size: Min 12; max 60
Length of visit: 1–1½ hours

VICTORIA AND ALBERT MUSEUM

Address: Cromwell Road, South Kensington, London SW7 2RL
   Tel: (0171) 938 8638

Description:
   The Victoria and Albert Museum is a classic example of Victorian architecture and
   decoration, accommodating works of art, craft and design from all around the world
   with a range of opportunities to link in with the National Curriculum at all key stages.
Ages: All ages
Subjects: Art; Technology; History; Mathematics; English; R.E.; Science
Facilities: Shop; toilets; refreshments; disabled access; eating area; lunch room;
   free teachers' pre-visit; temporary displays; worksheets
Open: Tuesday–Sunday from 10.00 am–5.50 pm. Closed 24–26 December. Various
   galleries are open at differing times and therefore it is advisable to check
   beforehand
Admission: Free for those aged under 18. Entry is also free to everyone from 4.30
   pm–5.50 pm daily
Group size: N/A
Length of visit: N/A

THE WEALD AND DOWNLAND OPEN AIR MUSEUM

Address: Singleton, Chichester, Sussex PO18 OEU
Tel: (01243) 811348   Fax: (01243) 811475

Description:
Situated in 50 acres of Sussex countryside the museum accommodates a plethora of historic buildings rescued from destruction, farm buildings and workshops, farms and houses dating from medieval times.
Ages: All ages
Subjects: History; Geography; Science; Mathematics: Art; Music; English; Design & Technology
Facilities: Car park; indoor/outdoor eating areas; shop; classroom; disabled access most places; free teachers' pre-visit; exhibitions; various museum services; tour guides available; workshops
Open: Daily. 1 March–31 October, Monday–Sunday, 10.30 am–5.00 pm. 1 November–28 February, Wednesdays, Saturdays, Sundays and Bank Holidays, 11.00 am–4.00 pm
Admission: Group rates upon application
Group size: Max 30–40
Length of visit: Half day

WEMBLEY STADIUM LIMITED

Address: Wembley HA9 0DW
Tel: (0181) 902 8833   Fax: (0181) 900 1055

Description:
Wembley is the world's most famous stadium and is unique in the history of sport and entertainment. The tour highlights cover the past, present and into the future and include a walk around the complex and a look behind the scenes with an audiovisual presentation orchestrated by Des Lynam. The tour takes you into the event control rooms, television studio, England changing room and the players' tunnel. Furthermore you can also run up the 39 steps to receive 'The Cup' to the roar of the crowd, and those who feel regal can sit in the royal box.
Ages: All ages
Subjects: History; P.E.; Music
Facilities: Car park; shop; refreshments; visit on land train around Wembley; guided tour; audiovisual presentation
Open: Summer: tours operate between 10.00 am and 4.00 pm. Winter: tours operate between 10.00 am and 3.00 pm. Not available when major events are taking place and closed 25–26 December

Admission: Groups and school bookings 20+: children (15 years and under) £4.45; students (with presentation of student card) £5.25; adults/teachers £6.45. Pre-paid bookings of 20+ will receive one free ticket for every 10 pupils. One teacher free per every 10 pupils

Group size: N/A

Length of visit: 2 hours +

WHITE CLIFFS EXPERIENCE

Address: Market Square, Dover, Kent CT16 1PB

Tel: (01304) 210101   Fax: (01304) 212057

Description:

An opportunity to experience history in an interactive, educational, fun way at the White Cliffs Experience. The Experience concentrates mainly on World War II and the Romans, together with leisure and tourism in Dover.

Ages: 5–18

Subjects: History; Geography; French

Facilities: Free teachers' pre-visit; talks; resource packs; information sheets; education room; indoor/outdoor eating areas; slide presentations; audiovisual facilities; shop; special events
Open: Throughout the year – advisable to check
Admission: Group rates upon application. Teachers and accompanying adults are admitted free
Group size: N/A
Length of visit: 2 hours

THE WIMBLEDON LAWN TENNIS MUSEUM

Address: Church Road, Wimbledon, London SW19 5AE
Tel: (0181) 946 6131   Fax: (0181) 944 6497

Description:
All aspiring tennis stars and even those not interested in the game will find a visit to Wimbledon Lawn Tennis Museum an enlightening experience. Find out how the gentle game of lawn tennis has grown beyond anyone's expectations to become a multi-million-dollar professional sport played all over the world. The museum has a fascinating collections of paintings, ornaments, jewellery and costume and of course tennis rackets, but no visit would be complete without a look over the famous Centre Court which will enable you to catch up on some of those special moments from past Championships.
Ages: All ages
Subjects: History; P.E.
Facilities: Car park; refreshments; disabled access; special exhibitions; videos; quizzes; library (by appointment)
Open: Throughout the year Tuesday–Saturday, 10.30 am–5.00 pm. Sunday, 2.00 pm–5.00 pm
Admission: Children (under 16 years) £1.50; adults/teachers £2.50. Pre-booked groups of 20 receive a 10 per cent discount
Group size: N/A
Length of visit: N/A

WOBURN ABBEY

Address: Woburn Abbey, Woburn, Bedfordshire MK43 0TP
Tel: (01525) 290666   Fax: (01525) 290271

Description:
Home of the Duke of Bedford for over 350 years, Woburn Abbey holds an important collection of art work with paintings created by world famous artists

and also furniture and porcelain. It is located within a 3,000-acre park with nine species of deer. A joint visit can be arranged with nearby Woburn Safari Park.

Ages: 7–18

Subjects: History; Art

Facilities: Free teachers' pre-visit; teacher/pupil resource packs; guided tour; car park; outdoor eating area; toilet; shop; disabled facilities.

Open: Daily, 11.00 am–4.00 pm

Admission: Pupils (7–16 years) £2.50. One teacher free per 15 pupils, extra adults £2 each

Group size: N/A

Length of visit: 1½–2 hours

WOBURN SAFARI PARK

Address: Woburn, Bedfordshire MK43 0TP

Tel: (01525) 290407   Fax: (01525) 290489

Description:

A superb drive-through safari park with sea lions, elephants, parrots and bird of prey demonstrations. There is an interactive computer centre, a walk-through aviary, an indoor adventure playground and lots more.

Ages: 5–16

Subjects: Science

Facilities: Free teachers' pre-visit; teacher/pupil resource packs; guided tour; classroom; car park; outdoor eating area; toilets; shop; disabled access; worksheets/ teacher notes for Wild Watch computer centre; Adventure Ark

Open: Daily, March–October, from 10.00 am–5.00 pm

Admission: Children £3.50; adults/teachers £4.50. One teacher free for every 10 children. All attractions included in the entry price

Group size: N/A

Length of visit: 4 hours +

8 | Wales

ANGLESEY SEA ZOO

Address: Isle of Anglesey, Brynsiencyn, North Wales LL61 6TQ
Tel: (01248) 430411   Fax: (01248) 430213

Description:
Combine pleasure with education at Anglesey Sea Zoo, where you will see many fascinating wonders of the ocean depths, including conger eels, sea bass, baby lobsters and many other creatures, making it ideal as a cross-curricula resource.

Ages: All ages

Subjects: English; Science; Mathematics; History; P.E.; Art; Technology; Music; R.E.; Geography; Languages

Facilities: Guided tours (charge); video; 'A' level worksheets; resource centre; disabled access; shop; restaurant/outdoor eating area; adventure playground; car park

Open: Daily. March–October, 10.00 am–5.00 pm. November–February, 11.00 am–3.00 pm

Admission: Group rates for 12+ children £2.85. One teacher free for every 10 pupils

Group size: N/A

Length of visit: N/A

BIG PIT

Address: Blaenafon, Torfaen NP4 9XP
Tel: (01495) 790311   Fax: (01495) 792618

Description:
The Big Pit is the only place in Wales where visitors can descend 300 feet underground into the original workings of a coal mine. Armed with a helmet and cap lamp visitors are transported down the 90-metre shaft in the pit cage and they can

then explore the underground roadways, stables and engine houses created by past generations of mine workers. When back on the surface explore the colliery buildings and learn more about the story of coal from the exhibitions and mining galleries.

Ages: 7+

Subjects: History; Geography; Science

Facilities: Study pack; guided tour; disabled access; shop; exhibitions; outdoor eating area; car park; refreshments

Open: Daily, 1 March–31 November, 9.30 am–5.00 pm. Tours regularly throughout the day, starting at 10.00 am

Admission: Group rates of 10+ children (5–18 years) £3.25; students (over 18 years) £3.75. Adults/teachers £4.50. One teacher free for every 10 pupils

Group size: For underground visits parties are divided into groups of 17

Length of visit: Up to 3 hours

BODELWYDDAN CASTLE

Address: Bodelwyddan, Denbighshire LL18 5YA
Tel: (01745) 584060   Fax: (01745) 584563

Description:
A splendid Victorian house and estate accommodating the finest collection of 19th-century portraits outside London. The Castle's hands-on galleries have some fascinating optical illusions and tricks to try which even mystified the Victorians.

Ages: All ages

Subjects: Art; Design & Technology; History

Facilities: Teachers' notes; quiz sheets; free teachers' pre-visit; education room; workshops; outdoor eating area; parkland; children's playground; tours; slide presentations; disabled access; car park

Open: Throughout the year. Easter–1 November: daily, 10.00 am–5.00 pm except Fridays. (Open every day during July and August.) 2 November–Easter, 11.00 am–4.00 pm but closed Monday and Fridays

Admission: £1.50 to pre-booked school groups. One free adult with every 10 pupils

Group size: N/A

Length of visit: 2 hours

CADW

Welsh Historic Monuments undertakes the statutory responsibilities of the Secretary of State for Wales for the conservation and preservation of ancient monuments and buildings of historic significance throughout Wales. Covering

6,000 years of heritage, they represent some of the most famous monuments in Wales, ranging from Roman forts, medieval abbeys and castles to monuments of the 19th century. For further information about those sites under the jurisdiction of Cadw contact: Cadw Welsh Historic Monuments, Crown Building, Cathays Park, Cardiff CF1 3NQ (tel: 01222 500200; fax: 01222 826375).

Attractions in South and West Wales

Blaenafon Ironworks
Caerleon Roman Baths and Amphitheatre
Caerphilly Castle
Carreg Gennen Castle
Castell Coch
Chepstow Castle
Cilgerran Castle
Coity Castle
Kidwelly Castle
Lamphey Bishop's Palace
Laugharne Castle
Llawhaden Castle
Neath Castle
Oxwich Castle
Raglan Castle
St David's Bishop's Palace
Strata Florida
Tally Abbey
Tintern Abbey
Tretower Court and Castle
Weobly Castle
White Castle

Attractions to visit in North and Mid-Wales

Beaumaris Castle
Caernafon Castle
Conwy Castle
Criccieth Castle
Cymber Abbey
Denbigh Castle and Town Walls
Dolbadarn Castle
Dolwyddelan Castle
Dyfi Furnace
Flint Castle

Gwydir Uchaf Chapel
Harlech Castle
Rhuddlan Castle
Rug Chapel and Llangar Church
Valle Crucis Abbey

CARDIFF CASTLE

Address: Castle Street, Cardiff CF1 2RB
Tel: (01222) 878100/878102   Fax: (01222) 231417

Description:
With a colourful history spanning nearly 2,000 years the Castle is one of Cardiff's premier attractions, where visitors may explore Roman remains, two regimental museums and a Norman keep.
Ages: All ages
Subjects: History; Art
Facilities: Guided tours of castle apartments; shop; toilets; tearoom; eight acres of land to explore
Open: Throughout the year. Extended tours can be arranged for pre-booked parties
Admission: Group rates upon application
Group size: N/A
Length of visit: N/A

CELTICA

Address: Y Plas, Ffordd, Aberystwyth, Machynlleth, Powys SY20 8ER
Tel: (01654) 702702   Fax: (01654) 703604

Description:
A unique heritage centre introducing the history and culture of the Celts, past, present and future, with the sights and sounds of Celtic life brought to life in an audiovisual experience.
Ages: All ages
Subjects: History
Facilities: Audiovisual facilities; exhibitions; children's play area; shop; refreshments; car park; guided tours; classroom; disabled access; toilets; workshops; interpretative centre
Open: Daily. January–December, 10.00 am–6.00 pm
Admission: Group rates upon application
Group size: N/A
Length of visit: N/A

CENTRE FOR ALTERNATIVE TECHNOLOGY

Address: Machynlleth, Powys SY20 9AZ
Tel: (01654) 703743   Fax: (01654) 702782

Description:
Information and entertainment await all who visit Europe's leading eco-centre, with exciting activities covering 7 acres: the best insulated house in the United Kingdom, energy displays, and creatures who lurk underground. Ride the water-powered cliff railway from Easter to the end of October; make a huge splash at the Wave Power Display and see Britain's largest solar roof.

Ages: All ages

Subjects: Science; Design & Technology; Mathematics

Facilities: Guided tours; worksheets; disabled access; indoor/outdoor eating areas; shop; adventure playground; gardens; transport maze; car park; exhibitions; workshops; toilets; question/answer sessions

Open: Most days of the year. April–October, 10.00 am–6.00 pm (dusk if earlier). November–March, check for opening times. Closed Christmas and three weeks in January

Admission: Group rates upon application

Group size: N/A

Length of visit: Up to one day

DAN-YR-OGOF SHOWCAVES

Address: Glyntawe, Abercrave, Upper Swansea Valley SA9 1GJ
Tel: (01639) 730284   Fax: (01639) 730293

Description:
Wales' best kept secret for over 315 million years has been revealed – the most magical showcaves complex in Western Europe. Children can learn all about life in the Iron Age, confront prehistoric creatures and meet up with the 'talking' sheepdog who will take visitors back in time to when shire-horses were the local mode of transport.

Ages: All ages

Subjects: History; English; Art; Drama; Geography; Music; Design & Technology; Science

Facilities: Information centre; museum; free teachers' pre-visit; theatre; dry-ski sessions; Dinosaur Park; Shire-horse Centre; outdoor eating area; refreshments; toilets; car park; shop; video centre; disabled access limited – advisable to check; teacher pack in Welsh or English

Open: Daily, Easter–end October from 10.00 am (winter openings times on request)

Admission: Group rates apply to 15+ children (4–16 years) £3.00. Adults/teachers £4.50. One adult free for every 10 pupils
Group size: N/A
Length of visit: N/A

ELAN VALLEY VISITOR CENTRE

Address: Rhayader, Powys LD6 5HP
Tel: (01597) 810390   Fax: (01597) 811276

Description:
There is a mixed assortment of learning experiences at the Elan Valley Visitor Centre – the opportunity to study rivers, learn about Birmingham's Victorian water supply, tour the reservoirs, explore the woodland, forest and meadows, and then combine it with a look at the many geological features.
Ages: All ages
Subjects: Science; History
Facilities: Classroom; exhibitions; shop; refreshments; car park
Open: Throughout the year, 9.00 am–5.00 pm
Admission: Free
Group size: N/A
Length of visit: N/A

FIRST HYDRO

Address: Dinorwig Power Station, Llanberis, Gwynedd LL55
Tel: (01286) 870166   Fax: (01286) 872486

Description:
Journey into the centre of the earth to Dinorwig Pumped Storage Power Station, where your experience of a lifetime will commence. Experience an exciting vision, sound and effects show, ride the tour bus through 16 kilometres of tunnels and see one of the world's largest excavated caverns, which accommodates sufficient electricity for the entire of Wales for up to 5 hours.
Ages: All ages
Subjects: Science
Facilities: Multimedia show; guided tour of Dinorwig Pumped Storage Power Station inside the mountain; disabled access; car park; café; shop; toilets; exhibitions and various events
Open: January–Easter, Thursday–Sunday. Easter–Christmas, daily. April–September, 9.30 am–5.30 pm. October–March, 10.30 am–4.30 pm
Admission: Electric Mountain Centre – free. Electric Mountain Tour – £2.00 per person, maximum 50

Group size: Max 50 for tour
Length of visit: N/A

KING ARTHUR'S LABYRINTH

Address: Corris, Machynlleth, Powys SY20 9RF
  Tel: (01654) 761584   Fax: (01654) 761575

Description:
  Since its opening in 1994 King Arthur's Labyrinth has created great interest. The 45-minute underground boat trip takes visitors deep into the spectacular caverns where fascinating stories of King Arthur are told accompanied by dramatic sound and lighting effects. An ideal resource for younger and even older students who are studying social studies and English literature.

Ages: All ages
Subjects: Science; History; Art; English
Facilities: Free teachers' pre-visit; activity pack; café; children's play area; outdoor eating area; workshops; car park; shop; toilets; warm clothing advised
Open: Daily, April–October, 10.00 am–5.00 pm. Winter opening by arrangement.
Admission: Rates for groups of 15+: children £2.45; teachers £3.45
Group size: Groups of 20 into the Labyrinth leave every 15 minutes
Length of visit: 45 minutes

LLANCCIACH FAWRE LIVING HISTORY MUSEUM

Address: Nelson, Treharris CF46 6ER
  Tel: (01443) 412248   Fax: (01443) 412688

Description:
  An example of 17th-century life awaits you inside this living history museum and when you step inside the manor house you are welcomed by the servants of Colonel Pritchard, dressed in authentic period costume of the era and speaking in the style of the 17th century as they guide you around the manor's beautiful rooms, revealing tales of life in a typical Civil War gentry household.

Ages: All ages
Subjects: History
Facilities: Car park; exhibition; restaurant; shop; toilets; guided tour; welcome host; disabled access
Open: Daily. January–December, 10.00 am–5.00 pm. Weekends, 10.00 am–6.00 pm. October–March Sundays, 12 noon–6.00 pm
Admission: Upon application
Group size: N/A
Length of visit: N/A

LLECHWEDD SLATE CAVERNS

Address: Blaenau Ffestiniog, Gwynedd LL41 3NB
  Tel: (01766) 830306   Fax: (01766) 831260

Description:
  A look at Victorian village life when mining was the main occupation will entertain and fascinate everyone, whatever the age, especially when you see the authentic village complete with a range of businesses, providing an extensive overall understanding of the slate industry, environment, community and culture via tours and exhibitions. The Deep Mine visit provides an alternative view of slate mining where visitors are transported down a 300 foot underground incline into the lower depths of the mine.
Ages: All ages
Subjects: History; Geography
Facilities: Free teachers' pre-visit; education packs; outdoor/indoor eating areas; disabled access; tramway tour; workshop; shop; guidebook; activity pack; exhibitions
Open: Throughout the year, 7 days a week from 10.00 am
Admission: For groups of 20+ there is a reduction in the fare for underground tours. All pupils in a school party are charged at a child rate, with teachers and helpers free. The child rate applies to pupils from 5–15 years; adult rates apply from 16 years +
Group size: N/A
Length of visit: N/A

MUSEUM OF WELSH LIFE

Address: St Fagans, Cardiff CF5 6XB
  Tel: (01222) 569441   Fax: (01222) 578413

Description:
  An open-air museum recreating Welsh life from the Celtic village of 2,000 years ago to a 20th-century miner's cottage; experience a typical Victorian schoolroom and browse around a 19th-century farmyard.
Ages: 5+
Subjects: Technology; Science; History
Facilities: Workshops; wooded walks; events; exhibitions; shop; children's play area; car park; loans service
Open: Daily. July–September, 10.00 am–6.00 pm. October–June, 10.00 am–5.00 pm. Closed 24–25 December

Admission: Group rates upon application
Group size: Max 100
Length of visit: N/A

MUSEUM OF THE WELSH WOOLLEN INDUSTRY

Address: Dre-fach, Felindre, Llandysul, Ceredigion SA44 5UP
Tel: (01559) 370929   Fax: (01559) 371592

Description:
The story of wool together with the ancient skills of weaving are displayed inside this fascinating museum, where you will find centuries-old techniques and technology alongside a busy working woollen mill still producing for the modern market.

Ages: All ages
Subjects: Design & Technology; History
Facilities: Working woollen mill; factory trails; indoor/outdoor eating area; refreshments; shop; changing exhibitions; car park
Open: Daily. April–September: Monday–Saturday, 10.00 am–5.00 pm. October–March: Monday–Friday, 10.00 am–5.00 pm
Admission: Free to Welsh schools whose Unitary Authority subscribe to the museum's school service or any school that has subscribed to this service on an individual basis. Non-subscribing educational establishments, 80p per person. One teacher free with every 10 pupils under 8 years; one teacher free for every 15 pupils over 8 years.
Group size: Max 60
Length of visit: 1 hour

NATIONAL MUSEUM AND GALLERY

Address: Cathays Park, Cardiff CF1 3NP
Tel: (01222) 397951   Fax: (01222) 373219

Description:
Exciting displays of art, science and natural history are all housed together in the National Museum and Gallery. There is also an exhibition on the creation of Wales, animated Ice Age creatures, plus wildlife and woodland displays.

Ages: All ages
Subjects: Science; Art
Facilities: Workshops; restaurant; shop; car park; disabled access; museum
Open: Throughout the year, Tuesday–Sunday and Bank Holiday Mondays, 10.00 am–5.00 pm. Closed 24–25 December

Admission: £1.10 per person
Group size: Max 450
Length of visit: 1 hour

NATIONAL TRUST PROPERTIES

The National Trust has a number of properties in Wales. For further information contact: North Wales National Trust Regional Office, Trinity Square, Llandudno, Gwynedd LL30 2DE (tel: 01492 860123). For information about properties in South Wales contact: South Wales National Trust Regional Office, The King's Head, Bridge Street, Llandeilo, Carmarthenshire SA19 6BB (tel: 01558 822800).

> Aberconwy House
> Aberdulais Falls
> Bodnant Garden
> Chirk Castle
> Colby Woodland Gardens
> Conwy Suspension Bridge
> Dinefwr Park
> Dolaucoth Gold Mines
> Erddig
> Llanerchaeron
> Penrhyn Castle
> Plas Newydd
> Plas Yn Rhiw
> Powis Castle
> Tudor Merchant's House
> Ty Mawr
> Ty'n-y-Coed

PENRHYN CASTLE

Address: Bangor, Gwynedd LL57 4HN
Tel: (01248) 353084   Fax: (01248) 371281

Description:
Built between 1820 and 1840 from the profits of the local slate quarry and sugar plantations in Jamaica, Penrhyn Castle is a large neo-Norman fantasy castle and accommodates a fascinating collection of old masters together with stained glass and hand-made wallpapers. Set among 40 acres of grounds, the ancient stable block was restored in 1995 and is now home to the Industrial Railway Museum, which offers you the chance to see full-size engines and historic quarrying locomotives.

126

Ages: All ages
Subjects: History; Geography; English
Facilities: Exhibition; audio tapes; activity sheets; free teachers' pre-visit; education officer; hands-on activities; orienteering course; castle tour; adventure playground; car park; outdoor eating area; shop
Open: Daily 27 March–30 September. Closed Saturdays. 3 October–2 November, Friday and Sunday only. House: 12 noon–5.00 pm. Garden: 11.00 am–5.30 pm
Admission: Group rates upon application
Group size: N/A
Length of visit: N/A

RHONDDA HERITAGE PARK

Address: Lewis Merthyr Colliery, Coed Cae Road, Trehafod CF37 7NP
Tel: (01443) 682036   Fax: (01443) 687420

Description:
It only takes a 2-minute ride to the 'Pit' bottom for an enjoyable and memorable experience to find out what a working mine is really like. You can touch the machinery, hear and smell the changing conditions and see the shadows of men at work. Back on top in daylight there is still plenty to visit around the site.
Ages: All ages
Subjects: Geography; History; Science; English; Mathematics
Facilities: Exhibitions; multimedia displays; adventure playground; classroom; free teachers' pre-visit; visitor centre; shop reconstruction of a village street; play area; artefacts; restaurant; guided tours; disabled access; energy zone; education pack (charged); worksheets
Open: Throughout the year. Closed 25–26 December, also Mondays, October–March
Admission: School groups: £2.95 each. One adult free with every 10 pupils
Group size: No limit
Length of visit: 2–2½ hours

RHYL SEA LIFE CENTRE

Address: East Parade, Rhyl, Denbighshire LL18 3AF
Tel: (01745) 344660   Fax: (01745) 332991

Description:
Fun and education are both available for all ages at Rhyl Sea Life Centre in the first and only walk-through underwater tunnel in Wales. Discover the magical kingdom where beautiful creatures lurk; learn all about captive breeding programmes; see the touch pools and handle many types of fish; explore the dark

murky waters where catfish and octopus lurk and where the sun never penetrates and then if you are still feeling brave step into the shark encounter.

Ages: All ages

Subjects: Science; Art; Design & Technology

Facilities: Free teachers' pre-visit; teachers' notes; worksheets; disabled access; toilets; shop; special school talks; guided tour; educational park; demonstrations; presentations; refreshments; car park

Open: Throughout the year. Advisable to check for times

Admission: School parties £2.50 per student. One teacher free with every five paying pupils

Group size: Min 10

Length of visit: Up to ½ a day

ROMAN LEGIONARY MUSEUM

Address: High Street, Caerleon, Newport NP6 1AE
  Tel: (01633) 423134   Fax: (01633) 422869

Description:

In AD 75 a castle was built at Caerleon to protect the area from invasion by the Romans and today the museum reveals what made the Romans such a domineering group. You will find out how they lived, ate and slept, how they kept fit and prepared themselves for battle and what it meant to be a Roman soldier.

Ages: All ages

Subjects: History

Facilities: Shop; toilets; disabled access; children can dress up in Roman costume and take part in various activities

Open: Daily. 15 March–15 October, 10.00 am–6.00 pm. Sunday, 2.00 pm–6.00 pm. 16 October–14 March: Monday–Saturday, 10.00 am–4.30 pm; Sunday, 2.00 pm–4.30 pm

Admission: Discounts for pre-booked groups of 20+

Group size: Max 90

Length of visit: 1 hour

SEGONTIUM ROMAN MUSEUM

Address: Beddgelert Road, Caernarfon LL55 2LN
  Tel: (01286) 675625   Fax: (01286) 678416

Description:

Segontium Roman Museum portrays the story of the conquest and occupation of Wales by the Romans with exhibits from the nearby auxiliary fort of Segontium, one of the most famous in Britain.

Ages: All ages
Subjects: History; Technology
Facilities: Shop
Open: March–end of October: Monday–Saturday, 9.30 am–5.30 pm; Sunday, 2.00 pm–5.00 pm. November–February: Monday–Saturday, 9.30 am–4.00 pm; Sunday, 2.00 pm–4.00 pm. Closed 24–26 December and 1 January
Admission: Group rates on application
Group size: Max 50
Length of visit: 1 hour

TECHNIQUEST

Address: Stuart Street, Cardiff Bay, Cardiff CF1 6BW
   Tel: (01222) 475475   Fax: (01222) 482517

Description:
A science discovery centre with 160 hands-on exhibitions, a planetarium, science theatres and a discovery room. Hours of fun and also a perfect educational resource for all ages.
Ages: All ages
Subjects: Science
Facilities: Car park; indoor eating area; guided tours; toilets; welcome host; disabled access
Open: Throughout the year. January–December: Monday–Friday, 9.30 am–4.30 pm; weekends, 10.30 am–5.00 pm
Admission: Upon application
Group size: N/A
Length of visit: N/A

TURNER HOUSE GALLERY

Address: Plymouth Road, Penarth CF64 3DM
Tel: (01222) 708870

Description:
The Gallery provides visitors with a varied and changing programme of pictures and *objets d'art* from the museum's extensive collection. It also is used regularly for travelling exhibitions and displays of work by local art societies.
Ages: 11+
Subjects: History; Art; Technology
Open: Advisable to check beforehand
Admission: Group discounts for pre-booked parties of 20+
Group size: Max 60
Length of visit: 1 hour

WELSH SLATE MUSEUM

Address: Gilfach Ddu, Padarn Country Park, Llanberis LL55 4TY
Tel: (01286) 870630   Fax: (01286) 871906

Description:
Amidst a beautiful landscape, the Welsh Slate Museum is a living, working site. It includes a quarry workshop still in frequent use, one of the world's largest working waterwheels, a narrow gauge steam locomotive, a forge and locomotive shed.

Ages: All ages

Subjects: History

Facilities: Museum shop; picnic area; refreshments; car park; temporary exhibitions throughout the year; craftsmen at work dressing slates throughout the season

Open: Easter–30 September: daily, 9.30 am–5.30 pm. October–Easter: Monday–Friday, 10.00 am–4.00 pm

Admission: Discounted rates for booked groups of 20+

Group size: Max 60

Length of visit: 1 hour

9 | The Midlands

THE AEROSPACE MUSEUM

Address: Cosford, Shifnal, Shropshire TF11 8UP
   Tel: (01902) 374112   Fax: (01902) 376211

Description:
   One of the largest aviation collections in Britain, accommodating military and civil transport aircraft, including several unique examples of World War II British, American, German and Japanese aircraft, and post-war RAF aircraft.
Ages: All ages
Subjects: History; Science; Mathematics; English; Geography; Art
Facilities: Education room; activity material; indoor eating area; guided tours; artefacts; hands-on activities; education officer
Open: Daily, 10.00 am–6.00 pm (last admission 4.00 pm). Closed 25–26 December, 1 January
Admission: Children £3. One teacher free for every 10 children. Additional adults £3
Group size: N/A
Length of visit: 2 hours

AVONCRAFT MUSEUM OF HISTORIC BUILDINGS

Address: Stoke Heath, Bromsgrove, Worcestershire
   Tel: (01527) 831886   Fax: (01527) 876934

Description:
   A collection of ancient buildings which include a windmill, industrial workshops, an ice-house, a church, timber-framed houses and an earth closet, all cleverly rebuilt on the 15-acre open-air site at Stoke Heath, illustrating over 600 years of English history.
Ages: All ages
Subjects: History
Facilities: Free teachers' pre-visit; indoor/outdoor eating areas; car park; toilets; shop; classroom; disabled access; activity workshops; various literature resources

Open: Contact for times
Admission: Children £1.50
Group size: Min 15
Length of visit: 2½–4 hours

BLACK COUNTRY LIVING MUSEUM

Address: Tipton Road, Dudley, West Midlands DY1 4SQ
Tel: (0121) 520 8054   Fax: (0121) 557 4242

Description:

An open-air museum with authentic shops, houses and workshops recreated to depict life around the turn of the century. There is an underground coal mine, canal boats, tram rides, Victorian schoolroom, steam engine and old-time fairground rides, plus exhibitions and demonstrations illustrating chainmaking and glass cutting.

Ages: All ages

Subjects: History; Technology

Facilities: Car parking; toilets; indoor/outdoor eating areas; guides; exhibitions; disabled access; free teachers' pre-visit; shop; teacher resource books; activity guides

Open: Daily, March–October, 10.00 am–5.00 pm. November–February: closed Monday and Tuesday; open Wednesday–Sunday, 10.00 am–4.00 pm

Admission: Group rates upon application

Group size: Min 20

Length of visit: 4 hours

BOSWORTH BATTLEFIELD VISITOR CENTRE AND COUNTRY PARK

Address: Ambion Hill, Sutton, Cheney, nr Market Bosworth, Leicestershire CV13 0AD
Tel: (01455) 290429   Fax: (01455) 292841

Description:

Location of the Battle of Bosworth (1485). Inside the Visitor Centre are exhibitions of ancient life, the actual history of the battle and models illustrating armour that was worn at the time. There is a special battle trail that you can follow and relive the moment when the battle was in full force.

Ages: 7+

Subjects: History

Facilities: Free teachers' pre-visit; car park; shop; guides; indoor/outdoor eating areas; toilets; disabled access (may have problems with the battle trail)

Open: Throughout the year, daily from 10.00 am

Admission: Children £1.20; adults/teachers £1.90. One adult free with every 10 children

Group size: Min 20; max 150
Length of visit: Indoors 1½ hours. Outdoors 1 hour

BROADWAY TOWER COUNTRY PARK LIMITED

Address: Broadway, Worcestershire WR12 7LB
  Tel: (01386) 852390   Fax: (01386) 858829

Description:
  History and Science are just two of the subjects which can be studied in this superb resource centre but there are opportunities for many others, as can be found when you prepare for a visit. There are exhibitions on the history of the Tower and the immediate surrounding area; the chance to study the earth's features or learn more about William Morris and the Pre-Raphaelites – contact for teaching packs. Lots of outdoor activities are also available, including nature trails, animal enclosures, an adventure playground and a ball-game area.
Ages: 4–13
Subjects: History; Science
Facilities: Car park; shop; toilets; disabled access limited; free teachers' pre-visit; indoor/outdoor eating area; adventure playground
Open: Contact for opening times
Admission: Children £1.65; adults/teachers £2.25
Group size: Min 15
Length of visit: Indoors: 30 mins–1 hour. Outdoors: 30 mins–2 hours

CADBURY WORLD

Address: PO Box 1958, Linden Road, Bourneville, Birmingham B30 2LD
  Tel: (0121) 451 4159 to book visits
    (0121) 456 2000, Ext. 3555 for advice on talks

Description:
  Step inside Cadbury World to find out how chocolate was first made by hand, trace the history of cocoa through Aztec times and the development of eating chocolate in Victorian time up until the present day. There are lots of attractions and exciting exhibitions, with the opportunity to see how advertising and packaging have developed and the chance to watch how famous chocolate bars are made.
Ages: 5+
Subjects: History; Design & Technology
Facilities: Car park; indoor/outdoor picnic areas; shop; toilets; educational resource packs; disabled access (excluding Packaging Plant); free teachers' pre-visit; outdoor play area

133

Open: Daily, February–October. November–February, 4 days a week – Wednesday, Thursday, Saturday and Sunday
Admission: Group rates upon application
Group size: Min 20; max 60
Length of visit: 1½–4 hours

CHATSWORTH

Address: Chatsworth, Bakewell, Derbyshire DE45 1PP
Tel: (01246) 582204   Fax: (01246) 583536

Description:
Home of the Cavendish family for nearly 450 years, Chatsworth represents the wealth, power and personal tastes of 11 generations. The house accommodates one of the most important private art collections in the world, including Gainsboroughs and Rembrandts; the garden, with a fascinating maze to get lost inside, covers over 100 acres. There is a farmyard exhibition initially created to explain the life cycles of various farm animals, and an adventure playground with attractions for both young and older age groups.

Ages: All ages
Subjects: History; Art; Science; Technology
Facilities: Free teachers' pre-visit; car park; indoor eating area; restaurant; guided tours; teachers' packs; education room; shop; disabled access limited; introductory presentation
Open: House: daily, 18 March–1 November, 11.00 am–5.30 pm. Garden: 11.00 am–6.00 pm. June, July and August open from 10.30 am. Alternative arrangements can be made
Admission: Group rates upon application
Group size: N/A
Length of visit: 1¼ hours

CLEARWELL CAVES

Address: Ancient Iron Mines, Clearwell, nr Coleford, Royal Forest of Dean, Gloucestershire GL16 8JR
Tel: (01594) 832535

Description:
For over 2,500 years iron ore has been mined in these caves. And now there is an invitation for visitors to descend 100 feet beneath the surface to the working mine and find out how miners survived. For those brave enough there is an opportunity to go even deeper. All visits can be adapted to suit particular subjects.

Ages: All ages

Subjects: History
Facilities: Indoor eating area; toilets; car park; guides; shop; disabled access not suitable for wheelchair users; free teachers' pre-visit
Open: All year
Admission: Children (under 16 years) £2.00; adults/teachers £3.00. Group concessions available
Group size: N/A
Length of visit: Indoors: 1–2 hours. Outdoors: 35 mins–1 hour

COTSWOLD FARM PARK

Address: Rare Breeds Survival Centre, Guiting Power, nr Stow-on-the-Wold, Cheltenham, Gloucestershire GL54 5UG
Tel: (01451) 850307   Fax: (01451) 850423

Description:
Established in 1971, the home of rare breeds conservation is located on a 1,600-acre working farm with over 50 rare breeds of British farm livestock, making it an ideal resource centre for all ages. Visits can be adapted to suit different themes. The lambing season is from March to April and shearing takes place in June.
Ages: All ages
Subjects: History
Facilities: Car park; indoor/outdoor eating areas; teachers' resource pack with worksheets; disabled access; shop; pets corner, adventure playground; free teachers' pre-visit; project room; outdoor eating area
Open: Daily, 22 March–28 September, 10.30 am–5.00 pm (6.00 pm Sundays, Bank Holidays and daily in July and August)
Admission: Group rates upon application
Group size: N/A
Length of visit: 2 hours–1 day

DRAYTON MANOR THEME PARK

Address: Nr Tamworth, Staffordshire B78 3TW
Tel: (01827) 287979

Description:
Where else can learning be so much fun than at one of the country's top family theme parks set in 250 acres of parkland and lakes? Educational facilities include a nature trail, a farm and a look into the insect kingdom, and entertainment is provided with over 50 rides and attractions, many of which involve high-tech features. Ideal for students undertaking a business or leisure and tourism course.

Ages: All ages
Subjects: English; Design & Technology; Mathematics; Art; Science
Facilities: Project room; free teachers' pre-visit; shop; car park; worksheets; conservation centre; museums; rides and attractions; disabled access (minimum of 20 for group discount); toilets
Open: Contact for current opening times
Admission: Group rates upon application. One adult free for every 10 pupils
Group size: Min 20; no upper limit
Length of visit: N/A

DUDLEY ZOO AND CASTLE

Address: 2 The Broadway, Dudley, West Midlands DY1 4QB
Tel: (01384) 215300   Fax: (01384) 456048

Description:
An educational and entertaining day can be spent at Dudley Zoo and Castle, providing visitors with an opportunity to see an amazing array of zoo animals with tours and activity sessions relating to many areas of the National Curriculum.
Ages: All ages up to 18 years
Subjects: History
Facilities: Undercover visitor centre in castle; indoor/outdoor eating areas; toilets; car park; project room; shop; free teachers' pre-visit; disabled access; guides; adventure playground; teachers' guides; work booklets; guidebooks
Open: Throughout the year from 10.00 am
Admission: Group rates upon application
Group size: Min 15
Length of visit: Half a day +

ENGLISH HERITAGE PROPERTIES

See listings under East Anglia.

HARVINGTON HALL

Address: Harvington, Kidderminster, Worcestershire DY10 4LR
Tel: (01562) 777846   Fax: (01562) 777190

Description:
Experience life in Tudor times with a visit around the house and grounds of Harvington Hall, which clearly displays the religious tensions of the period. There are wall decorations of the era and the priests' hides enable visitors to understand the problems that faced Roman Catholics during the Elizabethan period.

Ages: 8+

Subjects: History; Art

Facilities: Car park; free teachers' pre-visit; shop; indoor eating area; toilets; disabled access; guided tours; worksheets

Open: Throughout the year. Monday–Friday and Sundays, 9.30 am–5.00 pm

Admission: Children £2.00. One adult free for every 10 pupils

Group size: Min 10; max 200

Length of visit: Indoors: 1¼ hours–2 hours. Outdoors: no limit

THE IRONBRIDGE GORGE MUSEUMS TRUSTS

Address: Ironbridge, Telford, Shropshire TF8 7AW

  Tel: (01952) 433970/433522   Fax: (01952) 433204

Description:

Spread over an area of 6 square miles, the Ironbridge Gorge Museums are more extensive than one would imagine and support is offered to teachers with subjects covered by the National Curriculum. The individual museums offer a number of workshops throughout the year and children always find them a worthwhile, informative and entertaining visit. The museums include:

Blists Hill Open Air Museum – A recreated Victorian town set in 1900.

Time required – 2½ hours

Museum of Iron – An early 19th-century surveyor takes you on a tour of Coalbrookdale Company Works and there is an exhibition of industrial art on the second floor.

Time required – 1 hour

Darby Furnace – Authentic Abraham Darby I's blast furnace.

Time required – 20–30 minutes

Quaker Houses – Rosehill House decorated in early Victorian style and Dale House decorated in the late 18th-century style, both former homes of the Darby family.

Time required – 1½ hours

Ironbridge Visitor Centre – Step back in history to find out the story of the Ironbridge Gorge and also the role it plays today as a World Heritage Centre.

Time required – 1 hour

Iron Bridge – Possibly the most famous symbol of the Industrial Revolution, built in 1779.

Time required – 30 minutes

Coalport China Museum – Follow social history through the 18th and 19th centuries and exhibitions of Coalport China and the manufacturing processes.

Time required – 2 hours

Jackfield Tile Museum – There is a geology gallery and also exhibitions of tiles from the Victoria era, with period rooms; discover the Great Rock Sandwich, which was a company making tiles.
Time required – 1½ hours
Broseley Pipeworks Clay Tobacco Pipe Museum – Exhibits displaying the foundations of the Victorian Broseley Pipe Industry and the manufacturing processes involved. Groups of 50 at any one time.
Time required – 1 hour
Ages: All ages
Subjects: History; Science; Art; Design & Technology; Geography
Facilities: Depending on which museum you intend visiting, it is advisable to contact the museum beforehand. However, generally they include: free teachers' pre-visit; introductory video loan; classroom; workshops; car park; toilets; outdoor eating areas; some museums also have indoor eating areas; individual requests geared to specific projects catered for; disabled access (advisable to check)
Open: Contact for opening times
Admission: Group rates upon application
Group size: Min 10; max 500
Length of visits: See individual museum

LUDLOW CASTLE

Address: Castle Square, Ludlow, Shropshire
Tel: (01584) 873355/873947

Description:
Once a fine Norman castle occupied by Edward V and later Catherine of Aragon, the remains of this prestigious building are extensive, with the castle ruins including the nave of the chapel, which has decorative Norman doorways. There are several other ancient buildings of historical and architectural interest.
Ages: 4–18+
Subjects: Architecture
Facilities: Free teachers' pre-visit; car park; shop; guides; outdoor eating area; toilets; audiotape guide; guidebook
Open: Throughout the year, daily. February–April and October–December, 10.30 am–4.00 pm. May–September, 10.30 am–5.00 pm. Closed January
Admission: Contact for rates. Reduction for groups of more than 10
Group size: Min 10
Length of visit: 1–3 hours

MUSEUM OF ADVERTISING AND PACKAGING

Address: Albert Warehouse, Gloucester Docks, Gloucester GL1 2EH
Tel: (01452) 302309   Fax: (01452) 308507

Description:
Over 30 years of research is brought together in Britain's very first Museum of Advertising and Packaging. The variety of exhibitions on display provide an invaluable insight into the British way of life and social history over the past 130 years.
Ages: 10–16
Subjects: History; Technology; English; Science; Art
Facilities: Free teachers' pre-visit; indoor/outdoor eating areas; shop; disabled access limited; project room; school pack available
Open: Contact for opening times
Admission: Children 80p provided that they are in groups
Group size: Max 50
Length of visit: 1½–2½ hours

MUSEUM OF BRITISH ROAD TRANSPORT

Address: St Agnes Lane, Hales Street, Coventry CV1 1PN
Tel: (01203) 832425   Fax: (01203) 832465

Description:
Accommodating an amazing 150 motor cars, 75 motorcycles and 200 bicycles, the museum has the most extensive collection of vehicles to be found in Europe. See the first motorcars, follow the story of Edwardian motoring and the mode of transport used by members of royalty; pursue the fascinating story of 'Thrust 2', the fastest car on earth via the magic of the latest audiovisual techniques. There is also an opportunity to experience the devastation of the Coventry Blitz.
Ages: All ages
Subjects: History
Facilities: Education room; shop; café; disabled access; toilets; library; hands-on activities
Open: Throughout the year, daily, 10.00 am– 4.30 pm
Admission: Contact for rates
Group size: N/A
Length of visit: 1½–4 hours

THE NATIONAL TRAMWAY MUSEUM

Address: Crich, Matlock, Derbyshire DE4 5DP
Tel: (01773) 852565   Fax: (01773) 852236

Description:
For a special day out visit the National Tramway Museum in the heart of Derbyshire, where visitors can learn about the past, present and future in the world of trams and see for themselves a colourful selection which have been carefully restored to their former pristine condition. The National Tramway Museum preserves an important piece of history that may have disappeared for ever.

Ages: 5+
Subjects: History
Facilities: Car park; free teachers' pre-visit; teachers' packs; disabled access with a specially adapted tram for people with mobility problems; video theatre; exhibitions; tram depots; unlimited vintage electric tram rides; outdoor eating areas; playground
Open: 1 April–end of October, daily, 10.00 am–5.30 pm; 6.30 pm Saturdays, Sundays and Bank Holidays, June–August. Winter Sundays only (apart from school and pre-booked parties), 11.00 am–3.00 pm
Admission: Special rates for groups on application
Group size: N/A
Length of visit: 3 hours

NATIONAL TRUST PROPERTIES

The National Trust's East Midlands region covers Derbyshire, Leicestershire, Lincolnshire, Northamptonshire, Nottinghamshire, South Humberside and the Peak District National Park. For further information contact: National Trust Regional Office, Clumber Park Stableyard, Worksop, Nottinghamshire S80 3BE (tel: 01909 486411).

Belton House
Calke Abbey
Canons Ashby House
Clumber Park
Hardwick Hall
Longshaw Estate
South Peak Estate – Ilam Country Park
Sudbury Hall and Museum of Childhood

The National Trust Mercia Region covers Cheshire, Greater Manchester, Merseyside, Shropshire, most of Staffordshire and part of the West Midlands. For further information contact: National Trust Regional Office, Attingham Park, Shrewsbury, Shropshire SY4 4TP (tel: 01743 709343).

Attingham Park
Dunham Massey
Formby
Little Moreton Hall
Lyme Park
Moseley Old Hall
Quarry Bank Mill
Shugborough
South Shropshire Hills
Speke Hall
Styal Country Park
Tatton Park
Wightwick Manor

THE NATIONAL WATERWAYS MUSEUM

Address: Llanthony Warehouse, Gloucester Docks, Gloucester GL1 2EH
Tel: (01452) 318054

Description:
Learn about the inland waterways of England in this fascinating museum housed in a Victorian warehouse on three floors, where the emphasis is on involvement, with many hands-on activities, including practical sessions in the workshop for primary schools. It is also an ideal resource centre for many areas of the National Curriculum and can encompass English and Mathematics, with opportunities for older students who are studying leisure and tourism, or local studies.
Ages: 5+
Subjects: Science; Mathematics; Geography; Technology; History; Music; Art; English
Facilities: Toilets; indoor eating area; project room; shop; disabled access (limited in some areas); demonstrations; recreated canal maintenance yard; boat trips; horse and cart tour of the dock with the museum shire-horse.
Open: Contact for details
Admission: Group rates upon application
Group size: No limit
Length of visit: 1½–5 hours

ROCKINGHAM CASTLE

Address: Rockingham Castle, Market Harborough, Leicestershire
Tel: (01536) 770240   Fax: (01536) 771692

Description:
Over 90 years of history can be found at Rockingham Castle, located on a prime hilltop site taking in over five counties. The Castle played an important role in the Civil War and in its heyday was a Victorian mansion.

Ages: All ages

Subjects: History; Art

Facilities: Free teachers' pre-visit; education pack; indoor/outdoor eating areas; gardens; shop; refreshments; hands-on experience; exhibitions; specialized visits

Open: Groups and schools any day by appointment

Admission: Group rates upon application

Group size: N/A

Length of visit: N/A

THE SHREWSBURY QUEST

Address: 193 Abbey Foregate, Shrewsbury, Shropshire SY2 6AH
Tel: (01743) 366355   Fax: (01743) 244342

Description:
An amazing visitor attraction which takes you back to the dramatic and fascinating times of the 12th century, this was actually recreated on part of Shrewsbury Abbey's original grounds and the Quest is based on the real history and monastic life of ancient Shrewsbury. Wander around the 12th-century herb gardens; try your hand at calligraphy; and discover the workshop of Brother Cadfael, famous sleuth from *The Chronicles of Brother Cadfael* and TV series *Cadfael*.

Ages: 5+

Subjects: History; English; R.E.

Facilities: Free teachers' pre-visit; indoor eating area; project room; car park; adventure playground; shop; teachers' resource pack on the castle (charged); interactive exhibition; slide show; worksheets; toilets

Open: All year. Monday–Saturday, 10.00 am–4.30 pm. Sunday, 2.00 pm– 4.30 pm

Admission: Children 60p. One teacher free for every five pupils

Group size: Limited to 20 children. Larger numbers need to make arrangements when booking

Length of visit: 2–3 hours

THE SHUGBOROUGH ESTATE

Address: Milford, nr Stafford, Staffordshire ST17 0XB
Tel: (01889) 881388   Fax: (01889) 881323

Description:
The 900-acre estate of the Earls of Lichfield is home to a mansion containing a collection of paintings, French furniture and silverware. In the stableblock the servants' quarters can be found together with the original kitchens, brewhouse, laundry and coach-houses. The Park is a rare breeds centre with bread ovens and a corn mill. Throughout the year there are general tours and demonstrations.

Ages: 4–18
Subjects: Art
Facilities: Car park; project room; free teachers' pre-visit; guided tours (charged); shop; disabled access; taped tours around mansion; talks if required; working demonstrations (charged); toilets
Open: Throughout the year, Monday–Friday, 10.30 am–4.00 pm
Admission: Group rates upon application
Group size: No limit
Length of visit: 2–5 hours

STRATFORD-UPON-AVON BUTTERFLY FARM

Address: Tramway Walk, Swan's Nest Lane, Stratford-upon-Avon, Warwickshire CV37 7LS
Tel: (01789) 299288

Description:
This is Europe's most extensive live butterfly and insect display, with many colourful butterflies flying free in exotic surroundings. Amble through Insect City with its vast collection of minibeasts to amaze and astound you. There is a full tour, which can be tailored to explore such areas as life cycles, colour, rainforest, etc.

Ages: All ages
Subjects: Science
Facilities: Tour; educational room available for packed lunch if raining; refreshments
Open: Throughout the year, daily. Advisable to check on times
Admission: Group rates upon application
Group size: Max 100
Length of visit: 1½ –2½ hours

STRATFORD SHIRE-HORSE CENTRE

Address: Clifford Road, Stratford-upon-Avon, Warwickshire CV37 8HW
Tel/fax: (01789) 415274

Description:
The centre provides ideal opportunities to study a range of curriculum-based topics, in particular for classes studying science, life and living processes. It also provides an opportunity to see and learn more about the fascinating shire-horses and other rare breeds of farm animals.
Ages: 5–16
Subjects: Science
Facilities: Free teachers' pre-visit; indoor eating area; guides; shop; project room; disabled access; car park; toilets
Open: All year, daily, 10.00 am–5.00 pm
Admission: Children £2.70; adults/teachers £3.00. One adult free for every 10 pupils
Group size: Max 350 per day
Length of visit: 3–5 hours

THE TALES OF ROBIN HOOD

Address: 30–38 Maid Marian Way, Nottingham NG1 6GF
Tel: (0115) 948 3284   Fax: (0115) 950 1536

Description:
Craftsmen have cleverly created an ancient Nottingham town just as Robin Hood would have found it and the story of this notorious outlaw who robbed the rich and gave to the poor has been recreated in three dimensions using the most modern audiovisual technology to transport visitors back over 700 years of history. After the adventure, pupils are able to try archery, watch an exciting audiovisual presentation on the legend of Robin Hood or meander around the ancient market-place and imagine for themselves what life must have been like then.
Ages: 5–15
Subjects: History; Technology; English; R.E.
Facilities: Educational pack; storytelling sessions; education room; café; disabled access; exhibitions; audiovisual facilities; attractions
Open: Throughout the year, seven days a week. Summer: 10.00 am–6.00 pm. Winter: 10.00 am–5.00 pm. Closed 25–26 December
Admission: School parties £2.75 per child. One adult free with every 10 pupils
Group size: N/A
Length of visit: N/A

TAMWORTH CASTLE

Address: The Holloway, Tamworth, Staffordshire B79 7LR
Tel: (01827) 63563

Description:
Fifteen rooms fully furnished and covering 800 years of history are contained within one of the very few Norman motte and bailey shell keep castles still in existence. Special features include the ghost of St Editha in the haunted bedroom, the speaking Norman knight and the Baron Marmion. Tamworth Castle offers an ideal opportunity to study local history and architecture.

Ages: 5–16
Subjects: History
Facilities: Free teachers' pre-visit; shop; teachers' resource pack; exhibition; disabled access; car park; adventure playground; slide show; guided tour; worksheets
Open: All year, daily. Monday–Saturday, 10.00 am–4.30 pm. Sunday, 2.00 pm–4.30 pm
Admission: Group rates upon application
Group size: Limited to 20. Larger groups need to make arrangements when booking
Length of visit: 2–3 hours

TWYCROSS ZOO

Address: Atherstone, Warwickshire CV9 3PX
Tel: (01827) 880250   Fax: (01827) 880700

Description:
With over 200 species of mammals, a fascinating ape collection, birds and reptiles, Twycross Zoo has lots of offer. There is a spacious parkland, a zoo centre with discovery room, hands-on specimens, exhibitions and teaching sessions tailored to individual class requirements.

Ages: 3–14 plus facilities for 'A' level students and undergraduates
Subjects: Science; Art
Facilities: Free teachers' pre-visit; indoor/outdoor eating area; shop; first aid room; educational talks (charged); project room; adventure playground; car park; café; teacher and student literature
Open: Contact for dates
Admission: Group rates upon application
Group size: Min 25
Length of visit: Min 2 hours

WALSALL LEATHER MUSEUM

Address: Wisemore, Walsall WS2 8EQ
  Tel: (01922) 721153   Fax: (01922) 725827

Description:
  A working and living museum looking at the leather industry with reconstructed workshops demonstrating genuine leather working skills. Hands-on activities can be arranged.

Ages: 4+

Subjects: Art; Design & Technology; History

Facilities: Indoor/outdoor eating areas; guides; free teachers' pre-visit; toilets; disabled access; project room; shop; guidebook; library; videos for hire; hands-on activities

Open: November–March: Tuesday–Saturday, 10.00 am–4.00 pm; Sunday, 12 noon–4.00 pm. April–October: Tuesday–Saturday, 10.00 am–5.00 pm; Sunday, 12 noon–5.00 pm

Admission: Free

Group size: Max 45

Length of visit: N/A

WARWICK CASTLE

Address: Warwick, Warwickshire CV34 4QU
  Tel: (01926) 495421   Fax: (01926) 401692

Description:
  Owned at one time by William the Conqueror, and Richard III, Warwick Castle has also been host to Elizabeth I and Queen Victoria and is regarded as the finest medieval castle in England, combining a fascinating look at history and mystery. A visit will reveal the former home of Sir Greville. Other features are the Ghost Tour, the Dungeons and the Torture Chamber. The Great Hall has Oliver Cromwell's death mask.

Ages: 5+

Subjects: History

Facilities: Free teachers' pre-visit; outdoor eating area; guided tour; audio tour commentary in various languages for hire, also guidebooks; worksheets; teachers' notes; café; shop; toilet; disabled access; special events; gardens

Open: Daily, 10.00 am–6.00 pm. November–March until 5.00 pm. Closed 25 December

Admission: Group rates upon application

Group size: No limit

Length of visit: 3–7 hours

10 | East Anglia

ANGLESEY ABBEY AND GARDENS

Address: Lode Cambridge, Cambridgeshire CB5 9EJ
Tel/fax: (01223) 811200

Description:
A 17th-century house owned by the National Trust, which is built on the site of an Augustinian priory and contains the famous Fairhaven collection of paintings, clock and furniture. There is also an amazing 100-acre garden and arboretum.

Age: 5+
Subjects: History; Technology; Art
Facilities: Free teachers' pre-visit; welcome talk/demonstration; outdoor eating area; toilets; shop; disabled access; working watermill with milling demonstrations
Open: By arrangement
Admission: House and garden: children £2.30. Garden only £1.30. One teacher free for every 10 children
Group size: Min 15
Length of visit: 2–3 hours

BANHAM ZOO LIMITED

Address: The Grove, Banham, Norwich, Norfolk NR16 2HE
Tel: (01953) 887773   Fax: (01953) 887445

Description:
The opportunity to see a collection of some of the world's rare breeds and endangered species, including snow leopards, cheetahs, many exotic birds and a large collection of primates. There are daily animal feeding sessions and informative keeper's talks.

Ages: 5–16
Subjects: Science

Facilities: Free teachers' pre-visit; teacher and resource packs; worksheets; quiz sheets; project workbooks; classroom; qualified guide; guided tours/talks; outdoor eating area; toilets; shop
Open: Daily from 10.00 am. Closed 25–26 December
Admission: Group rates upon application
Group size: Min 15
Length of visit: 4–5 hours

BATTLE OF BRITAIN MEMORIAL VISITORS CENTRE

Address: RAF Coningsby, Lincolnshire LN4 4SY
Tel: (01526) 344041

Description:
A fascinating guided tour around the Battle of Britain Memorial Flight aircraft carried out by volunteer guides, many of whom actually had first-hand experience of the aircraft. The flight operates Spitfires, Hurricanes, a Dakota and a Lancaster Bomber.
Age: 5+
Subjects: Technology; History
Facilities: Free teachers' pre-visit; worksheets; quiz sheets; project book; guided tour; car park; outdoor eating area; toilets; shop
Open: Monday–Friday, 10.00 am–5.00 pm
Admission: Children and teachers £1.00
Group size: Min 10; max 60
Length of visit: 2 hours

BRESSINGHAM STEAM MUSEUM TRUST AND GARDENS

Address: Bressingham, Diss, Norfolk IP22 2AB
Tel: (01379) 687386   Fax: (01379) 688085

Description:
Located in 6 acres of famous gardens, an exceptional working steam museum gives the history of steam railway a totally different meaning. Complete with narrow gauge railway rides, according to availability, there is an opportunity to take a ride. With many other attractions, it is the perfect place to learn about railways in a superb and most unusual setting.
Ages: 5+
Subjects: History; Science; Technology; Art
Facilities: Refreshments; indoor/outdoor eating areas; car park; toilets; free teachers' pre-visit; shop; guided tour
Open: Easter–end October daily from 10.30 am–5.30 pm
Admission: Group rates upon application. One teacher free for every 10 children

Group size: Min 12
Length of visit: 2–3 hours

BRITISH BIRDS OF PREY AND CONSERVATION CENTRE

Address: Stonham Barns, Pettaugh Road, Stonham Aspal, Suffolk IP14 6AT
Tel: (01449) 711425

Description:
Many subjects in the National Curriculum can be studied at this centre, which is entirely dedicated to British owls and other birds of prey. There are spectacular flying displays, a bird hospital, weatherings, aviaries where you can browse around and see the birds at close hand, plus an information centre, lecture area and other facilities.
Ages: 5+
Subjects: English; Science; Geography; Technology; Art
Facilities: Free teachers' pre-visit; teacher/pupil resource packs; worksheets; quiz sheets; project books; welcome talk/demonstration; guided tour; outdoor eating area; toilets; shop; disabled access
Open: All year, 10.00 am–5.00 pm. Closed Christmas and New Year holidays
Admission: Children £2.00; adults/teachers free
Group size: Min 20; max 100
Length of visit: 1–2 hours

BROADS TOURS LTD

Address: The Bridge, Wrexham, Norfolk NR12 8RX
Tel: (01603) 782207   Fax: (01603) 784272

Description:
Trips along the Norfolk Broads provide the ideal opportunity to find out more about the Broadland area plus its surrounding flora and fauna. Trips can last up to three-and-a-half hours and can be arranged to individual requirements.
Ages: 5+
Subjects: English; Science; Geography; Technology; History
Facilities: Worksheets; quiz sheets; project books; teacher/pupil resource books; qualified guide; classroom on boat; welcome talk/demonstration; guided tour; toilets; shop; pond dipping; bird watching; plant identification
Open: March–October: Monday–Friday, 9.00 am–5.30 pm
Admission: Group rates upon application
Group size: Min 12; max 36
Length of visit: Half/full day

BURE VALLEY RAILWAY

Address: Aylsham Station, Norwich Road, Aylsham, Norfolk NR11 6BW
Tel: (01263) 733858   Fax: (01263) 733814

Description:
From the busy town of Aylsham to Wroxham, Norfolk's premier tourist narrow-gauge railway runs through 9 miles of delightful Norfolk countryside, providing an ideal opportunity to see the countryside and learn more about the workings of this ancient mode of transport. During the summer months there is a boat train.
Ages: 5–16
Subjects: Science; Technology; Geography
Facilities: Teacher/pupil resource packs; guided tour; indoor/outdoor eating areas; toilets; shop; disabled access
Open: During term time only. Contact for details
Admission: Children £2.00; adults/teachers £6.90. One teacher free for every 10 children
Group size: Min 20; max 200
Length of visit: 1½–2½ hours

BURGHLEY HOUSE

Address: Stamford, Lincolnshire PE9 3JY
Tel: (01780) 752451   Fax: (01780) 480125

Description:
There are 18 state rooms in this fine Elizabethan home which accommodates a collection of fine art, furniture, porcelain and textiles. It was built in 1587 by William Cecil, 1st Lord Burghley, Lord Treasurer to Queen Elizabeth I.
Ages: 5–18
Subjects: History; Art
Facilities: Free teachers' pre-visit; guided tours; outdoor eating area; toilets; shop
Open: Contact for details
Admission: Group rates upon application
Group size: Min 15
Length of visit: 2–3 hours

THE BUTTERFLY AND FALCONRY PARK

Address: Long Sutton, Lincolnshire PE12 9LE
Tel: (01406) 363833/363209   Fax: (01406) 363182

Description:
Hundreds of exotic butterflies can be seen flying around in a tropical setting at Britain's only Butterfly and Falconry Park. There are regular flying displays of owls,

East Anglia

hawks, falcons, vultures, and there is a newly opened Reptile Land and Pheasants of the World Park.

Ages: 5–16

Subjects: English; Science; Geography

Facilities: Free teachers' pre-visit; teacher/pupil resource packs; worksheets; quiz sheets; project books; qualified guide; car park; outdoor/indoor eating areas; toilets; shop; disabled access; adventure playground; pets corner

Open: 20 March–end October

Admission: Children £2.20; adults/teachers £2.60. One teacher free for every 10 pupils

Group size: Min 12; max 300

Length of visit: 4–5 hours

CAITHNESS CRYSTAL

Address: 10–12 Paxman Road, Hardwick Industrial Estate, King's Lynn, Norfolk PE30 4NE

Tel: (01553) 765111   Fax: (01553) 767628

Description:

Glassmaking is an art in itself and a tour around Caithness Crystal will leave you feeling totally overawed by the sheer craftsmanship as you watch the craftspeople transform sand into amazing pieces of glassware using only the heat of a furnace and a skill of the hand and eye.

Ages: 5+

Subjects: Science; Technology; Art

Facilities: Free teachers' pre-visit; worksheets; quiz sheets; project books; car park; toilets; shop; free glassmaking video loan

Open: Throughout the year, Monday–Friday, 9.15 am–4.00 pm

Admission: Free

Group size: Min 2; max 54

Length of visit: 1¼ hours

CHRISTCHURCH MANSION AND WOLSEY ART GALLERY

Address: Christchurch Park, Ipswich, Suffolk IP4 2BE

Tel: (01473) 253246   Fax: (01473) 210328

Description:

A 16th-century house with period rooms housing a fine collection of furniture, ceramics and famous works of art by artists including Gainsborough and Constable. Interesting exhibition in the Wolsey Gallery.

Ages: 5+

151

Subjects: History; Art

Facilities: Free teachers' pre-visit; teacher/pupil resource packs; worksheets; quiz sheets; guided tour; toilets; shop; disabled access; education programme

Open: Throughout the year. Tuesday–Saturday from 10.00 am–5.00 pm, Sunday from 2.30 pm–4.00 pm and Monday from 10.00 am–5.00 pm. In winter it closes at dusk

Admission: Group rates upon application

Group size: Max 25 primary school-age children

Length of visit: 2½ hours

COCKLEY CLEY ICENI VILLAGE AND MUSEUMS

Address: The Estate Office, Cockley Cley Hall, Swaffham, Norfolk PE37 8AG
Tel: (01760) 724588   Fax: (01760) 721339

Description:

The genuine reproduction of an Iceni settlement dating back to the 1st century AD is undoubtedly the major attraction at Cockley Cley. There is also a nature trail, farm and carriage implement collection, a museum, a Saxon church and a 17th-century cottage.

Ages: 5–16

Subjects: History

Facilities: Free teachers' pre-visit; teacher/pupil resource packs; classroom; guided tour; indoor/outdoor eating areas; car park; toilets; shop; disabled access

Open: Daily, 1 April–31 October, 9.30 am–5.30 pm

Admission: Children £1.30; adults/teachers £2.80

Group size: Min 10; max 100

Length of visit: 2–4 hours

OLIVER CROMWELL'S HOUSE

Address: 29 St Mary's Street, Ely, Cambridgeshire CB7 4HF
Tel: (01353) 662062   Fax: (01353) 668518

Description:

In 1636 Oliver Cromwell inherited this house, where he lived for 10 years. It includes a visitor centre, a tourist information centre, films, displays, period rooms, a Civil War exhibition and even a haunted bedroom.

Ages: 7–18

Subjects: Geography; History

Facilities: Free teachers' pre-visit; teacher/pupil resource packs; school guide/talks; guided tours; car park; shop; disabled access

Open: Tour times: summer, 10.00 am–6.00 pm; winter, 10.00 am–5.15 pm
Admission: Children £1.00; adults/teachers free
Group size: Min 10
Length of visit: ¾ hour

EASTON FARM PARK

Address: Easton, Woodbridge, Suffolk IP13 0EQ
   Tel: (01728) 746475   Fax: (01728) 747861

Description:
   Located near the Deben river is a Victorian model farm with a collection of farm animals, many of which are rare breeds. There is also a modern dairy where visitors can watch the cows being milked and a working blacksmith's forge, and there are lots of other activities to take part in.
Ages: 5+
Subjects: English; Science; Geography; Technology; History; Art
Facilities: Free teachers' pre-visit; teacher/pupil resource pack; worksheets; quiz sheets; project books; welcome talk; guided tour; car park; indoor/outdoor areas; toilets; shop; disabled access
Open: Daily, 23 March–30 September, 10.30 am–6.00 pm. Closed Mondays except Bank Holidays and in July, August
Admission: Children £2.00; adults/teachers £3.50. One free adult with every 10 children
Group size: Min 20
Length of visit: 3–4 hours

ELTON HALL

Address: Elton, Peterborough, Cambridgeshire PE8 6SH
   Tel: (01832) 280468   Fax: (01832) 280584

Description:
   For over 300 years this fine hall was home to the Proby family and it contains a combination of Gothic, medieval and classical styles of furniture with paintings by Gainsborough, Constable and other famous artists. You can also see Henry VIII's prayer book.
Ages: 11–18
Subjects: English; History; Art
Facilities: Worksheets; quiz sheets; project books; car park; indoor eating area; toilets; shop
Open: April–September. Advisable to check on times
Admission: Children and teachers £2.00 each

Group size: Min 20; max 50
Length of visit: 1 hour

ELY CATHEDRAL

Address: The Chapter House, The College, Ely, Cambridgeshire CB7 4DL
Tel: (01353) 667735   Fax: (01353) 665658

Description:
This is an outstanding example of Norman architecture with the Octagon and Lantern tower well worth viewing, together with the Lady Chapel and collection of medieval domestic buildings surrounding the Cathedral.

Age: 5+

Subjects: Mathematics; Science; Geography; History; Art; Music; R.E.

Facilities: Free teachers' pre-visit; teacher/pupil resource packs; worksheets; quiz sheet or project books; schools guide; classroom; welcome talk/demonstration; car park; outdoor eating area; disabled access; study centre

Open: Summer: 7.00 am–7.00 pm. Winter: Monday–Saturday, 7.30 am–6.00 pm; Sunday, 7.30 am–5.00 pm.

Admission: £10 per class

Group visit: Max 100

Length of visit: 1 hour–1 day

ENGLISH HERITAGE

Before making a visit to any of the English heritage listed buildings in the Midlands contact them for further information: English Heritage Historic Properties Midlands, Hazelrigg House, 33 Marefair, Northampton NN1 1SR (tel: 01604 730325; fax: 01604 730321).

Ashby de la Zouch Castle
Audley End House and Park
Berkhamsted Castle
Berney Arms Windmill
Bolsover Castle
Boscobel House and the Royal Oak
Buildwas Abbey
Bushmead Priory
Castle Acre Priory
Castle Rising Castle
Chichele College
De Grey Mausoleum
Denny Abbey

Duxford Chapel
Framlingham Castle
Gainsborough Old Hall
Goodrich Castle
Grime's Graves
Halesown Abbey
Hardwick Old Hall
Haughmond Abbey
Isleham Priory Church
Kenilworth Castle
Kirby Hall
Kirby Muxloe Castle
Leigh Court Barn
Lilleshall Abbey
Lincoln Bishop's Old Palace
Longthorpe Tower
Lyddington Bede House
Mistley Towers
Mortimer's Cross Water Mill
Old Gorhambury House
Old Merchant's House Row 111 House and Greyfriars' Cloisters
Orford Castle
Prior's Hall Barn
Rufford Abbey
Rushton Triangular Lodge
Saxstead Green Post Mill
Stokesay Castle
Tilbury Fort
Wall Roman Site (Letocetum)
Wenlock Priory
Wingfield Manor
Witley Court
Wrest Park Gardens
Wroxeter Roman City

FITZWILLIAM MUSEUM

Address: Trumpington Street, Cambridge CB2 1RB
Tel: (01223) 332993   Fax: (01223) 332923

Description:
Many subjects on the National Curriculum can be studied at this outstanding museum, which houses one of the UK's finest collections of antiquities (including

Greek and Egyptian), armour, furniture, ceramics, pottery, paintings, prints, sculpture and much more. There are also temporary exhibitions.

Ages: 5–18

Subjects: English; Science: Technology; History; Art; R.E.

Facilities: Free teachers' pre-visit; teacher/pupil resource packs; worksheets; quiz sheets; project books; school guide; outdoor eating area; toilets; shop; education service

Open: Tuesday–Friday, 10.00 am–5.00 pm

Admission: Free

Group size: Min 15; max 45

Length of visit: 2 hours

FLAG FEN BRONZE AGE EXCAVATIONS

Address: Fourth Drove, Fengate, Peterborough, Cambridgeshire PE1 5UR
  Tel: (01733) 313414   Fax: (01733) 349957

Description:

An unusual site which cleverly combines working excavations with a semi-floating visitor centre. Visitors can see reconstructed round-houses, the Museum of the Bronze Age, an award-winning Preservation Hall and primitive animals.

Ages: 5–18

Subjects: Science; Geography; Technology; History; R.E.

Facilities: Free teachers' pre-visit; teacher/pupil resource packs; worksheets; quiz sheets; project books; classroom; guided tours; car park; outdoor eating area; toilets; shop; videos; environmental talks

Open: Daily, 10.00 am– 4.00 pm

Admission: Children £1.75; adults/teachers and helpers free

Group size: Min 10

Length of visit: 3–4 hours

GAINSBOROUGH'S HOUSE

Address: 46 Gainsborough Street, Sudbury, Suffolk CO10 6EU
  Tel: (01787) 372958   Fax: (01787) 376991

Description:

A Georgian-fronted town house with attractive walled garden, birthplace of Thomas Gainsborough (1727–1788), where you will find a fascinating collection of the artist's fine work. There is also 18th-century furniture and memorabilia.

Ages: 5+

Subjects: English; History; Art

Facilities: Free teachers' pre-visit; teacher/pupil resource packs; worksheets; quiz sheets; project books; schools guide; welcome talk/demonstrations; car park; toilets; shop

Open: Tuesday–Saturday, 10.00 am–5.00 pm. Sunday, 2.00 pm–5.00 pm. Closes at 4.00 pm, November–March

Admission: Children £1.00; teachers and helpers free

Group size: Max 30

Length of visit: 1–2 hours

HAMERTON WILDLIFE PARK

Address: Hamerton, Huntingdon, Cambridgeshire PE17 5RE
Tel: (01832) 293362   Fax: (01832) 293677

Description:
Covering 15 acres in delightful Cambridgeshire countryside, this wildlife park is home to over 100 species of creatures from around the world, including marmosets, lemurs and meerkats. There is a new children's zoo, making a visit an enlightening experience in an environment where pupils can learn about animals and their natural habitats.

Ages: 5–11

Subjects: Science

Facilities: Free teachers' pre-visit; teacher/pupil resource packs; worksheets; quiz sheets; project books; school guide; welcome talk/demonstrations; car park; indoor/outdoor eating areas; toilets; shop

Open: Daily, 10.30 am–3.00 pm

Admission: Children £2.00; adults/teachers £3.20. One adult free with every eight pupils

Group size: Min 15

Length of visit: 4 hours

HERMITAGE HALL

Address: Bridge Farm, Downham Market, Norfolk PE38 0AU
Tel: (01366) 383185   Fax: (01366) 386519

Description:
Enjoy a trip back in time and take a guided tour around Hermitage Hall, the Armstrong Siddeley Car Museum and the Chapel, and visit the Dickens World of Christmas. There is also a brass rubbing at the centre.

Ages: 5+

Subjects: History

Facilities: Free teachers' pre-visit; welcome talk/demonstration; guided tour; car park; indoor/outdoor eating areas; toilets; shop

Open: Normal school hours by appointment
Admission: Children £3.00; adults/teachers £3.50
Group size: Min 15; max 60
Length of visit: 1½ hours

HOLKHAM HALL AND BYGONES MUSEUM

Address: Holkham, Wells-next-the-Sea, Norfolk NR23 1AB
   Tel: (01328) 710227   Fax: (01328) 711707

Description:
   Holkham Hall is located in a 3,000-acre deer park on the North Norfolk coast
   and is one of Britain's most majestic stately homes. The Bygones Museum is
   accommodated in the original stables with over 4,000 items of memorabilia,
   from modes of transport to kitchens. There is also a History of Farm exhibition, a
   19th-century walled garden, lake cruises and other attractions.

Ages: 5–16
Subjects: History
Facilities: Free teachers' pre-visit; qualified guide; car park; indoor/outdoor eating
   areas; toilets; shop
Open: 25 May–30 September: Sunday–Thursday, 1.30 pm–5.00 pm. Easter, May
   and Summer Bank Holidays: Sunday and Monday, 11.30 am–5.00 pm
Admission: Hall or Museum: groups of 20–39 children £1.80; groups of 40+
   children £1.60. All inclusive groups of 20–39 children £2.70; groups of 40+
   children £3.40. Adults/teachers free
Group size: Min 20
Length of visit: Hall: 1 hour. Bygones Museum: 1 hour

IMPERIAL WAR MUSEUM

Address: Duxford Airfield, Duxford, Cambridge, Cambridgeshire CB2 4QR
   Tel: (01223) 835000   Fax: (01223) 837267

Description:
   Located on an historic wartime airfield, this is Europe's top aviation museum,
   with over 140 historic aircraft from World War I to the present time, all under
   cover. There are also military vehicles and an assortment of exhibitions.

Ages: 8+
Subjects: Science; Technology; History
Facilities: Free teachers' pre-visit; teacher/pupil resource packs; guided tour; prac-
   tical activities; classroom; welcome talk; car park; indoor/outdoor eating area;
   toilets; shop; disabled access
Open: Summer, 10.00 am–6.00 pm; winter, 10.00 am–4.00 pm
Admission: Children £2.00. One teacher free for every 10 children

Group size: N/A
Length of visit: 4–5 hours

INSPIRE HANDS-ON SCIENCE CENTRE

Address: St Michael's Church, Coslany Street, Norwich, Norfolk NR3 3DT
Tel: (01603) 612612   Fax: (01603) 616721

Description:
The only hands-on science centre in East Anglia situated in a medieval church. There are over 35 hands-on exhibits, regular exhibitions plus science show performances.
Ages: 5–16
Subjects: Science; Technology
Facilities: Free teachers' pre-visit; welcome talk/demonstrations; indoor/outdoor eating areas; shop; toilets
Open: Daily, 9.30 am–5.30 pm
Admission: Children £2.00; teachers and helpers free
Group size: Min 10; max 100
Length of visit: 1½ hours

LINCOLN CASTLE

Address: Castle Hill, Lincoln, Lincolnshire LN1 3AA
Tel: (01522) 511068   Fax: (01522) 512150

Description:
An exciting visit to this 900-year-old castle built in 1068 by William the Conqueror will help add a whole new dimension to history and many other National Curriculum lessons. Still maintaining many authentic features which include wall walks and towers offering visitors breathtaking views over the countryside, there is also the Prison Chapel, itself a unique building. The castle still contains the Lincoln Magna Carta, one of the only three originals still remaining.
Ages: 5+
Subjects: Mathematics; English; Science; Geography; Technology; History; R.E.; Art
Facilities: Free teachers' pre-visit; worksheets; quiz sheets; workbooks; classroom; guide; car park; indoor/outdoor eating areas; shop; disabled access limited; toilets
Open: Monday–Saturday, 9.30 am–5.30 pm. Sunday, 11.00 am–5.30 pm. Closes 4.00 pm in the winter
Admission: Children £1.00. One teacher free for every 10 children
Group size: Min 20
Length of visit: 2–3 hours

THE LONG SHOP MUSEUM

Address: Main Street, Leiston, Suffolk IP16 4ES
Tel: (01728) 832189

Description:
Explore the fascinating world of steam with a visit to the Long Shop Museum, built in 1852 as one of the first production-line engineering halls in the world. Discover the magic of steam and see the moving engine and rollers where they were built. A superb award-winning museum with three exhibition halls, full of items from the age of steam.

Ages: 7–18
Subjects: History; Science; Design & Technology
Facilities: Free teachers' pre-visit; teacher/pupil resource packs; outdoor eating area; toilets; shop; disabled access; education officer
Open: Contact for details
Admission: Children 50p
Group size: Min 10; max 50
Length of visit: 1½ hours

LOWESTOFT MARITIME HERITAGE MUSEUM

Address: Sparrows Nest Park, Whapload Road, Lowestoft, Suffolk N32 1XG
Tel: (01502) 511260

Description:
Find out more about the history of Lowestoft fishing fleets with exhibitions of lifeboat evolution, a copy of a drifter's cabin, and pictures and tools relating to the town's fishing industry in the 1920s.

Ages: 5–18
Subjects: History
Facilities: Free teachers' pre-visit; teacher/pupil resource packs; guided tour; car park; outdoor eating area; toilets; shop; disabled access
Open: All year, 10.00 am–4.30 pm
Admission: Children and adult/teachers 25p
Group size: Min 8; max 70
Length of visit: ¾ hour–1 hour

MABLETHORPE ANIMAL GARDENS

Address: North End, Mablethorpe, Lincolnshire LN12 1QG
Tel: (01507) 473346

Description:
The past wildlife of Lincolnshire blends with the present in a delightful visit to Mablethorpe Animal Gardens. There is a seal and sea-bird hospital; a special barn owl feature. Marvel at the new lynx caves and Ice Age display which are actually inhabited by Northern Lynx. There are also snowy owls and Arctic foxes to be seen.

Ages: 5–11

Subjects: Science

Facilities: Free teachers' pre-visit; worksheets; quiz sheets; project books; guided tour; classroom; teacher/pupil resource packs; car parking; outdoor/indoor eating area; toilets; shop; disabled access

Open: Easter–last Sunday in October, daily from 10.00 am

Admission: Children £1.00; adults/teachers £2.00. One teacher free for every 10 pupils

Group size: Min 10

Length of visit: 1–4 hours

MANNINGTON AND WOLTERTON ESTATE

Address: Mannington, Norwich, Norfolk NR11 7BB
Tel: (01263) 584175   Fax: (01263) 716214

Description:
The 18th-century Wolterton Park was built for Prime Minister Sir Robert Walpole's brother Horatio, 1st Lord Walpole, and is still owned by the Walpole family. There are delightful country walks, and a famous heritage rose collection.

Ages: 5–18

Subjects: History

Facilities: Free teachers' pre-visit; classroom; welcome talk/demonstrations; guided tour; car park; indoor/outdoor eating areas; toilets; shop

Open: By arrangement

Admission: Upon application

Group size: N/A

Length of visit: 2 hours

MANOR HOUSE MUSEUM

Address: Honey Hill, Bury St Edmunds, Suffolk IP33 1LF
   Tel: (01284) 757072   Fax: (01284) 757079

Description:
   An amazing opportunity for young and older students studying History and Art to
   see the types of textiles worn in the past. Exhibited in excellent surroundings and
   interpreted via the latest technology, this cleverly restored Georgian mansion
   makes learning an exciting experience and accommodates a varied collection of
   items from the past.

Ages: 5–18

Subjects: Science; Technology; History; Art

Facilities: Free teachers' pre-visit; teacher/pupil resource packs; worksheets; quiz
   sheets; project books; qualified tour; classroom; welcome talk/demonstrations;
   car park; indoor/outdoor eating area; toilets; shop; disabled access

Open: Monday–Saturday, 10.00 am–5.00 pm. Sunday, 2.00 pm–5.00 pm

Admission: Children £1.20; adults/teachers free

Group size: Min 15

Length of visit: 1 hour

MOYSE'S HALL MUSEUM

Address: Cornhill, Bury St.Edmunds, Suffolk IP33 1DX
   Tel: (01284) 757488   Fax: (01284) 757079

Description:
   Visit Moyse's Hall, an unrivalled example of Norman domestic architecture,
   where you will see a collection of Roman and medieval artefacts, and relics of the
   Red Barn Murder.

Ages: 5+

Subjects: History

Facilities: Free teachers' pre-visit; worksheets; quiz sheets; project books; welcome
   talk/demonstration; guided tours; car park; shop; disabled access

Open: Monday–Saturday, 10.00 am–5.00 pm. Sunday, 2.00 pm–5.00 pm

Admission: Children 50p; adults/teachers free

Group size: Min 10; max 60

Length of visit: 1 hour +

THE MUCKLEBURGH COLLECTION

Address: Weybourne Military Camp, Weybourne, nr Holt, Norfolk NR24 7EG
Tel: (01263) 588210   Fax: (01263) 588425

Description:
An exciting experience to actually see over 3,000 exhibits of militaria, including armoured cars and aircraft and 16 working tanks under one roof at the largest privately owned museum of its type in Europe. There is also a chance to see the Gamma Goat, take a coastal ride and inspect the Harrier GR3.
Ages: 7–18
Subjects: History; Geography; English; Technology
Facilities: Free teachers' pre-visit; teacher/pupil resource packs; worksheets; quiz sheets; project books; welcome talk/demonstration; guided tours; car park; outdoor eating area; toilets; shop; disabled access
Open: Daily, 10.00 am–5.00 pm
Admission: Children £1.50. One teacher free for every 10 children. Additional adults £3.00
Group size: Min 10; max 85
Length of visit: 2½ hours

MUSEUM OF EAST ANGLIAN LIFE

Address: Stowmarket, Suffolk IP14 1DL
Tel: (01449) 612229

Description:
An exciting open-air museum with various collections of regional social, industrial and agricultural history. Listed buildings, working steam traction engines and animals.
Ages: 5–16
Subjects: Science; Geography; Design & Technology; History; Art; English; Mathematics
Facilities: Free teachers' pre-visit; teacher/pupil resource packs; worksheets; quiz sheets; project books; classroom; car park; indoor/outdoor eating areas; toilets; shop
Open: Daily, 10.00 am–5.00 pm
Admission: Children £1.50. One teacher free for every eight children. Additional adults £3.35
Group size: Min 10; max 120
Length of visit: 3–6 hours

NATIONAL HORSE-RACING MUSEUM

Address: 99 High Street, Newmarket, Suffolk CB8 8JL
Tel: (01638) 667333   Fax: (01638) 665600

Description:
You don't have to be a lover of horses to enjoy a visit to this museum, where you will find a collection of paintings and memorabilia telling the story of racing from the times of Charles II to more recent times and more familiar horse riders such as Lester Piggott. There is also an invitation to put on the racing silks and, for those brave enough, an opportunity to ride the mechanical horses in the hands-on gallery.

Ages: 5+

Subjects: English; Science; Technology; History; Art

Facilities: Free teachers' pre-visit; teacher/pupil resource packs; worksheets; quiz sheets; project books; classroom; guided tours; car park; indoor/outdoor eating areas; toilets; shop

Open: By appointment

Admission: Children 90p; adults/teachers free

Group size: Min 10; max 40

Length of visit: 1 hour–day

NATIONAL TRUST PROPERTIES

The National Trust's East Anglia region covers Cambridgeshire, Essex, Norfolk and Suffolk. For further information contact: National Trust Regional Office, Blickling, Norwich NR11 6NF (tel: 01263 733471).

Blakeney Point
Blickling Hall
Dunwich Heath
Felbrigg Hall
Hatfield Forest
Houghton Mill
Ickworth House, Park and Garden
Wicken Fen
Wimpole Hall and Home Farm

NATURELAND SEAL SANCTUARY

Address: North Parade, Skegness, Lincolnshire PE25 1DB
Tel: (01754) 764345   Fax: (01754) 764345

Description:
A famous sanctuary for rescuing and rearing abandoned seal pups and returning them to the wild. See the collection of penguins, tropical butterflies (April–October), an aquarium, pets corner and reptiles, and watch the seals and penguins being fed. There are also opportunities to do animal brass rubbings.
Ages: 5–11
Subjects: Science; Art
Facilities: Free teachers' pre-visit; worksheets; quiz sheets; project workbooks; teacher/pupil resource packs; car park; outdoor eating area; toilets; shop
Open: Daily, 10.00 am–5.00 pm
Admission: Children £1.70; adults/teachers £2.70. One teacher free for every 10 children. Special rates for animal brass rubbings
Group size: Min 20
Length of visit: Up to 2 hours

NENE VALLEY RAILWAY

Address: Wansford Station, Stibbington, Peterborough, Cambridgeshire PE8 6LR
Tel: (01780) 784444   Fax: (01780) 784440

Description:
Proving that learning can be fun, enjoy a 7½-mile trip on a preserved railway running along the banks of the River Nene. The railway's headquarters and engine shed are located at Wansford, offering an ideal opportunity to see how a steam railway actually works.
Ages: 5–11
Subjects: Geography; Technology; History
Facilities: Free teachers' pre-visit; teacher/pupil resource packs; worksheets; quiz sheets; project books; guided tour/demonstrations; car park; outdoor eating area; toilets; shop; disabled access
Open: Wednesdays from May to July (scheduled). Other times by appointment
Admission: Children £4.50; adults/teachers £3.00
Group size: Min 40; max 800
Length of visit: 2½ hours

THE NORFOLK RARE BREEDS CENTRE

Address: Decoy Road, Ormesby St Michael, Great Yarmouth, Norfolk NR29 3LY
  Tel: (01493) 732990   Fax: (01493) 732990

Description:
  Browse around the museum, follow the rare breeds trail and see baby chickens
  hatching at this exciting rare breed centre which has won the EDP business award
  for the best industry education link. There is also a nature trail, pond dipping,
  donkey rides and videos.

Ages: 5–18

Subjects: Mathematics; English; Science; Geography; Technology; History

Facilities: Free teachers' pre-visit; worksheets; quiz books; project workbook;
  guided tour; welcome talk/demonstrations; car park; indoor/outdoor eating area;
  toilets; shop; disabled access

Open: Daily, 10.00 am–5.00 pm. Other times can be arranged

Admission: Children £1.25; adults/teachers £2.25. One teacher free for every 10
  children

Group size: Any number

Length of visit: Up to one day

NORWICH CASTLE MUSEUM

Address: Castle Meadow, Norwich, Norfolk NR1 3JU
  Tel: (01603) 223624   Fax: (01603) 765651

Description:
  Tour the dungeon and battlements, see the world's most extensive collection of
  teapots, view an art collection, visit the Egyptian mummies and see the glittering
  Celtic gold – all of this and much more to be enjoyed with a visit to this ancient
  Royal Castle.

Ages: 5+

Subjects: English; Science; Geography; Technology; History; Art

Facilities: Free teachers' pre-visit; teacher/pupil resource packs; worksheets; quiz
  sheets; project books; school guide; welcome talk/demonstrations; guided tour;
  car park; indoor/outdoor eating areas; toilets; shop; disabled access; handling
  sessions and workshops

Open: Monday–Saturday, 10.00 am–5.00 pm. Sunday, from 2.00 pm–5.00 pm

Admission: Winter: children £1.00; students £1.50. Summer (July, August,
  September): children £1.50; students £2.10. Adults/teachers free

Group size: Upon application

Length of visit: Up to 4 hours

166

NORWICH CATHEDRAL

Address: 62 The Close, Norwich NR1 4EH
Tel: (01603) 620864   Fax: (01603) 766032

Description:
A Norman Cathedral of amazing architectural interest and beauty which includes the largest monastic cloisters in England, the ancient Saxon Bishop's Throne and a unique nave roof.

Ages: 5–18

Subjects: History; Mathematics; English; Science; Technology; Art; Music; R.E.

Facilities: Free teachers' pre-visit; teacher/pupil resource packs; guided tour; welcome talk/demonstrations; car park; outdoor eating area; toilets; shop; disabled access

Open: Daily, 9.00 am–6.00 pm (tours 10.00 am–4.00 pm)

Admission: Free

Group size: Guided tours, one guide for every 30 pupils

Length of visit: 1 hour–1 day

PENSTHORPE WATERFOWL PARK

Address: Fakenham, Norwich NR21 0NL
Tel: (01328) 851465   Fax: (01328) 855905

Description:
One of the largest collections of exotic/endangered waterbirds can be found living in 200 acres of beautiful countryside alongside woodland, meadow and waterside walks. There are wildlife exhibitions and a heated indoor observation gallery, enabling visitors to see some of the more exotic birds first hand.

Ages: 5–16

Subjects: English; Science; Geography; Mathematics; Art; History

Facilities: Free teachers' pre-visit; teacher/pupil resource packs; worksheets; quiz sheets; project books; guide; classroom; welcome talk; car park; outdoor eating area; shop; toilets; disabled access

Open: Throughout the year from 10.00 am

Admission: Group rates upon application. One teacher free for every 10 children

Group size: Min 15

Length of visit: 3–4 hours

PLEASUREWOOD HILLS FAMILY THEME PARK

Address: Corton, Lowestoft, Suffolk NR32 5DZ
Tel: (01502) 586000   Fax: (01502) 567393

Description:
Over 50 rides, attractions and sideshows where many aspects of the National Curriculum can be studied and enjoyed. An ideal learning adventure for older students, where they can learn more about the leisure industry and find out how much fairground rides have changed over the years while exploring modern safety methods.

Ages: All ages

Subjects: Mathematics; English; Science; Geography; Technology; History

Facilities: Free teachers' pre-visit; teacher/pupil resource packs; worksheets; classroom; welcome talk; car park; indoor/outdoor eating areas; toilets; disabled access; shop

Open: Throughout the year, 10.00 am–5.00 pm or 6.00 pm, depending on season

Admission: Group rates upon application

Group size: Min 20

Length of visit: 5 hours

RAILWORLD

Address: Oundle Road, Peterborough, Cambridgeshire PE2 9NR
Tel: (01733) 344240   Fax: (01733) 344240

Description:
Enter the future with a visit to Railworld. Find out what the future holds for worldwide railway, look at hovertrains and take environmental challenges. There is a fascinating Age of Steam Exhibition together with hands-on displays.

Ages: 5+

Subjects: Science; Geography; Technology; History

Facilities: Free teachers' pre-visit; teacher/pupil resource packs; worksheets; quiz sheets; project books; classroom; guided tour/talks; car park; indoor/outdoor eating areas; toilets

Open: Daily, 11.00 am–4.00 pm. Other times by arrangement

Admission: Children 75p; teachers/helpers £1.50

Group size: Min 15

Length of visit: 1 hour

RUTLAND WATER

Address: Anglian Water Bird-watching Centre, Rutland Water Nature Reserve, Egleton, Oakham, Rutland LE15 8BT
Tel: (01572) 770651   Fax: (01572) 756611

Description:
Covering 3,100 acres, Rutland Water is the largest man-made lake in Western Europe and makes for a fascinating visit. There is a guided tour around the Butterfly and Aquatic Centre; a sunken church; Barnsdale Draught Garden; the bird-watching centre and cycle hire plus the opportunity to take a ride in the 110-seat passenger cruiser around the lake.

Ages: 5+

Subjects: Science; Geography; Technology; History

Facilities: Free teachers' pre-visit; teacher/pupil resource packs; quiz sheets; project books; school guide; classroom; welcome talk; car park; outdoor eating area; toilets; shop; disabled access

Open: Daily, 9.00 am–5.00 pm

Admission: Group rates upon application

Group size: Min 20; max 30

Length of visit: Up to 4 hours

SIZEWELL POWER STATION VISITOR CENTRE

Address: Sizewell, nr Leiston, Suffolk IP16 4UR
Tel: (01728) 642139

Description:
Something for everyone at this purpose-built exhibition centre, where you will witness and hear the hi-tech world of power generation explained through multi-media shows and interactive displays.

Ages: 5+

Subjects: Science; Geography; Technology

Facilities: Free teachers' pre-visit; teacher/pupil resource packs; worksheets; quiz sheets; project books; classroom; welcome talk/demonstrations; guided tours; car park; indoor/outdoor eating areas; toilets; shop; disabled access

Open: Daily, 10.00 am–4.00 pm. Closed Christmas and New Year

Admission: Free

Group visit: Min 1; max 40

Length of visit: 3–5 hours

THETFORD FOREST PARK

Address: High Lodge Visitor Centre Forest Enterprise, Santon Downham, Brandon, Suffolk IP27 0TJ
Tel: (01842) 810271   Fax: (01842) 811309

Description:
Thetford Forest Park is Britain's largest lowland pine forest and the visitor centre is located deep in the forest, providing well-marked cycle and walk trails, enabling pupils to learn more about the flora and fauna of the area and also to study the many types of wildlife living in the forest.

Ages: 5+

Subjects: Mathematics; English; Science; Geography; Technology; History; P.E.; Art; Music

Facilities: Free teachers' pre-visit; teacher/pupil resource packs; worksheets; quiz sheets; project workbooks; guided tour; classroom; car park; welcome talk; outdoor eating area; toilets; shop; disabled access; cycle hire; play area; adventure ropes course; maze

Open: Daily, 10.00 am–5.00 pm

Admission: Depends on chosen activities

Group size: Max 30

Length of visit: 5 hours

THE THURSFORD COLLECTION

Address: Thursford, Fakenham, Norfolk NR21 0AS
Tel: (01328) 878477   Fax: (01328) 878415

Description:
Lots to both see and do at the Wurlitzer show – music from nine mechanical organs, an elaborate fairground, dance organs, amazing old road engines and entertaining rides.

Ages: 5+

Subjects: Science; History; Art; Music

Facilities: Free teachers' pre-visit; teacher/pupil resource packs; worksheets; quiz sheets; project books; car park; indoor/outdoor eating areas; toilets; shop; disabled access

Open: Daily, 12.30 pm–5.00 pm

Admission: Children £2.00; adults/teachers £3.55

Group size: Min 15

Length of visit: 2½ hours

TOLLY COBBOLD AND THE BREWERY TAP

Address: Cliff Road, Ipswich, Suffolk IP3 0AZ
Tel: (01473) 231723   Fax: (01473) 281508

Description:
An entertaining experience for any student studying science, catering, history or engineering, with the opportunity to take a tour around an authentic Victorian brewery.

Age: 14+

Subjects: Science; History; Technology

Facilities: Free teachers' pre-visit; teacher/pupil resource packs; classroom; guided tour; car park; toilets; shop

Open: Daily, 10.00 am–8.00 pm. Closed 24–25 December and 1 January

Admission: Children £2.75; adults/teachers free

Group size: Min 15; max 50

Length of visit: 2 hours

TROPICAL BUTTERFLY GARDENS

Address: Long Street, Great Ellingham, Norfolk NR17 1AW
Tel: (01953) 453175

Description:
The perfect location for pupils studying any form of wildlife, environmental issues or conservation. A landscaped 2,400 square foot tropical garden which is actually modelled on a rainforest, where visitors can stroll between waterfalls and pools surrounded by some of the most exciting tropical plants in the world, together with a colourful selection of free-flying exotic butterflies and birds. There is a 15-acre conservation area and walk which is perfect for pond discoveries and wildlife studies.

Ages: 5–11

Subjects: Mathematics; Science; Geography

Facilities: Free teachers' pre-visit; teacher/pupil resource packs, worksheets, quiz sheets, projects books; guided tours; welcome talk; car park; outdoor eating area; toilets; shop; disabled access

Open: Monday–Friday, 9.00 am–6.00 pm

Admission: Children and adults/teachers £1.35 each

Group size: Min 15; max 90

Length of visit: Full day

WINGFIELD OLD COLLEGE AND GARDENS

Address: Wingfield, Eye, Suffolk IP21 5RA
Tel: (01379) 384888   Fax: (01379) 384034

Description:
A delightful family home with walled gardens, offering the best heritage and arts experience in Suffolk. There is an old kitchen, exhibitions and garden sculpture together with permanent collections of textiles and ceramics, etc.
Ages: 7–16
Subjects: Science; Geography; History; Art; R.E.
Facilities: Free teachers' pre-visit; classroom; guided tour; car park; indoor/outdoor eating areas; shop; toilets; video presentation
Open: By arrangement
Admission: Children £1.00; adults/teachers £2.00
Group size: Min 20; max 60
Length of visit: 1½ hours

11 | The North West

ANIMAL WORLD, BUTTERFLY HOUSE AND MOSS BANK PARK

Address: Moss Bank Park, Moss Bank Way, Bolton
Tel: (01204) 846157

Description:
A popular park with a variety of attractions to suit all ages. Formerly the site of the Ainsworth family's bleaching business, the only surviving building of the original estate is the Tower, which is located in the Animal World. Inside the Butterfly House, opened in 1996, there are free-flying butterflies and moths in an authentic tropical environment. There are also other collections, including stick insects, spiders and reptiles, while Animal World features a collection of small animals and tropical birds.

Ages: All ages
Subjects: Science
Facilities: Refreshments; toilets; car park; disabled access; guided tours
Open: Daily. April–October, 10.00 am–5.00 pm. November–March, 10.00 am–4.00 pm
Admission: Free
Group size: N/A
Length of visit: 2 hours

APPLEBY CASTLE LIMITED

Address: Appleby-in-Westmorland, Cumbria CA16 6XH
Tel: (017683) 51402   Fax: (017683) 51082

Description:
Appleby Castle played an important role in defending this part of England from Scottish invasion and although the town was attacked and burned in 1314, the Castle was able to escape without incurring very much damage. Explore the Keep, known as Caesar's Tower, one of the best preserved buildings of its type in

England, visit Lady Anne's Bee House, which is thought to be a private haven. The impressive oak panelling and other internal adornments are thought to date from the 17th century. Outside it is surrounded by 25 acres of parkland.

Ages: 5+

Subjects: History

Facilities: Teachers' worksheets; outdoor eating areas; children's animal garden; deer park; refreshments; shop; brass rubbing and medieval activity centre; rare breeds of animals; conservation centre; nature trail; special events; car park

Open: Saturday and Sunday only until end of May, 10.00 am–5.30 pm. After Spring Bank Holiday open every day

Admission: Children £1.25; adults/teachers £2.50 excluding Great Hall. One teacher free for every 15 pupils.

Group size: Max 30

Length of visit: 2 hours

AQUARIUM OF THE LAKES

Address: Lakeside, Newby Bridge, Cumbria LA12 9AS
Tel: (015395) 30153   Fax: (015395) 30152

Description:
Visit the UK's largest collection of freshwater fish, where you can see over 30 displays under one roof; explore the underwater tunnel which enables visitors to enjoy a bird's eye view of life beneath the lake and take the chance to see a river bank at night.

Ages: All ages

Subjects: Science; Geography

Facilities: Free teachers' pre-visit; tailored resource packs; free introductory talk if required; combined steam train and boat journeys; disabled access; car park; worksheets; shop

Open: 7 days a week, from 9.00 am–5.00 pm. Closed 25 December

Admission: Children £2.50; adults/teachers free. Additional adults £2.50. Group concessions available

Group size: Min 15

Length of visit: 1–1½ hours

BARTON AERODROME

Address: Liverpool Road, Eccles, Salford M30
Tel: (0161) 789 4785

Description:
Barton Aerodrome, built in 1928, was Britain's first municipal airport. With its 1930 control tower and hangar (both listed buildings), it still retains the atmos-

phere of the golden age of pioneering aviation. It is also home to the country's oldest flying club, Lancashire Aero, established in 1922.

Ages: All ages
Subjects: History
Facilities: Visitor centre; guided tours; car park; refreshments
Open: Throughout the year the airfield is open daily from 9.00 am to sunset. The Visitor Centre is open from 11.00 am to 5.00 pm at weekends
Admission: Free
Group size: Min 15
Length of visit: Up to 2 hours

THE BEACON

Address: West Strand, Whitehaven, Cumbria CA28 7LY
Tel: (01946) 592302   Fax: (01946) 599025

Description:
With the help of modern technology find out more about the past, present and future of Whitehaven's industrial, social and maritime heritage. Four exhibitions: Harbour Gallery; Whitehaven Looking Out; Whitehaven Looking In; Met. Office Weather Gallery. There is also an annual programme of changing exhibitions and events.

Ages: All ages
Subjects: History; Science; Geography; Design & Technology
Facilities: Free teachers' pre-visit; education packs; loans service; themed activities; activity sheets; role-play; lecture service; education room; indoor eating area; library; shop
Open: Throughout the year, Tuesday–Sunday; Bank Holiday Mondays and Mondays in school holidays. Easter–October, 10.00 am–5.30 pm. November–March, 10.00 am–4.30 pm
Admission: Group rates: 15+ children £1.50. One teacher free for every 10 pupils. Additional adults £3.30
Group size: Min 15; max 50 for talks, 25 for activities
Length of visit: 2 hours

BOLTON MUSEUM, ART GALLERY AND AQUARIUM

Address: Le Mans Crescent, Bolton BL1 1SE
Tel: (01204) 522311, Ext. 2191   Fax: (01204) 391352

Description:
Whether you are studying Art, Conservation, Science or any other similar subject on the National Curriculum, Bolton Museum, Art Gallery and Aquarium has something for everyone: a collection of Egyptian antiquities; a changing

programme of exhibitions and a collection of British art from the 18th century in the art gallery; a wildlife gallery with an activity centre, and due to their involvement in the breeding of endangered species, also an aquarium.

Ages: 5+

Subjects: Art; History; Science

Facilities: Workshops; loans service; information sheets; disabled access; shop; guided tours

Open: Throughout the year. Monday, Tuesday, Thursday and Friday, 9.30 am–5.30 pm. Saturday, 10.00 am–5.00 pm. Closed Wednesday, Sundays and Bank Holidays.

Admission: Free

Group size: N/A

Length of visit: 2 hours

CATALYST: THE MUSEUM OF THE CHEMICAL INDUSTRY

Address: Gossage Building, Mersey Road, Widnes WA8 0DF
Tel: (0151) 420 1121   Fax: (0151) 495 2020

Description:

Suitable for all ages from primary to degree level, Science, Mathematics and Geography are just three of the many subjects which come alive at the Catalyst, the only museum in the world which explores Science and Technology behind the chemical industry, offering a unique interactive experience linked directly to the National Curriculum. There are over 100 exhibits, reconstructed scenes and multimedia programmes, plus four exhibition galleries – Scientific, Observatory, Birth of an Industry and Chemicals for Life. There are also workshops and theme weeks held throughout the year – an experience not to be missed.

Ages: All ages

Subjects: Mathematics; Science; Technology; Geography; Humanities; History

Facilities: Lunchroom; education centre; workshop studios; refreshments; car park; shop; science trail; special events; topic trails; education team; free teachers' pre-visit; toilets; cloakroom

Open: Throughout the year. Tuesday–Friday and Bank Holiday Mondays, 10.00 am–5.00 pm. Saturday and Sunday, 11.00 am–5.00 pm. In addition, open on Mondays for events and some theme weeks

Admission: Children £2.35. One adult free for every seven pupils of primary school age or 10 pupils of secondary school age. Additional adults £3.55. Hands-on workshops are £25 per session for a class up to 35. Theme weeks and events cost 50p per child in addition to the entrance fee

Group size: N/A

Length of visit: N/A

CHESTER ZOO

Address: The Group Sales Office, Chester Zoo, Caughall Road, Upton, Chester CH2 1LH
Tel: (01244) 380280   Fax: (01244) 371273

Description:
You will need a full day to get the best out of this fascinating zoo which is one of Europe's leading conservation zoos, accommodating over 5,000 animals in spacious enclosures. A perfect resource centre to study Conservation, Science, English and many other cross-curriculum topics for all ages.

Ages: All ages

Subjects: Mathematics; English; Science; Art; Design & Technology

Facilities: Free teachers' pre-visit; teachers' packs; activity centre (Let's Make 30p per item); storytelling sessions (30p per child; Let's Make/Story combined 45p per child); brass rubbing (50p per item); disabled access; outdoor/indoor eating area; shop; car park; toilets

Open: Easter–autumn, check for times

Admission: Group rates upon application

Group size: Advisable to check as each activity has different numbers that can be catered for at any one time

Length of visit: N/A

THE CONSERVATION CENTRE

Address: Whitechapel, Liverpool L1 6HZ
Tel: (0151) 478 4999

Description:
Inside Merseyside's Conservation Centre, the only one in Europe to open its doors to the public, a fascinating insight into the world of museum conservators is glimpsed where many experts all in their respective fields preserve and restore everything from fine art and sculpture to archaeological artefacts. There are interactive exhibits; a studio tour to see what goes on behind the laboratories; illustrated lectures, and a variety of other attractions.

Ages: All ages

Subjects: Art; Science; History

Facilities: Refreshments; teachers' resource packs; special activities; shop; hands-on activities; disabled access

Open: Throughout the year. Monday–Saturday, 10.00 am–5.00 pm. Sunday, 12 noon–5.00 pm. Closed 23–25 December and 1 January

Admission: Group rates upon application

Group size: N/A

Length of visit: N/A

ENGLISH HERITAGE PROPERTIES

See under The North East.

GRANADA STUDIOS TOUR

Address: Water Street, Manchester M60 9EA

Tel: (0161) 833 0880 Fax: (0161) 834 3684

Description:

There are many different educational packages available at Granada, attractive to all ages within the context of the National Curriculum. Look behind the camera to learn more about the technological aspect of TV; learn about the many aspects of drama, art and associated topics; explore the sights, smells and sounds of Victorian England on the Baker Street film set, visit *Coronation Street* and have a truly memorable day.

Ages: All ages

Subjects: English; History; Design & Technology

Facilities: Education packs/teachers' notes; car park; rides; hands-on experience; audio tours; museum; various shows; disabled access; shops; café; restaurant

Open: School visits by arrangement

Admission: Group rates upon application

Group size: N/A

Length of visit: N/A

HALL I'TH 'WOOD

Address: Green Way, off Crompton Way, Bolton BL1 8UA

Tel: (01204) 301159

Description:

Step inside the home of the late-medieval merchant Samuel Crompton, inventor of the Spinning Mule, which transformed the whole cotton industry. The house is smartly decorated with English furniture from the 18th century and not only will you see the room where he invented the Mule and the violin which he played but you can also see the roof area where he hid his invention from potential machine wreckers.

Ages: All ages

Subjects: History; Art; Design & Technology

Facilities: Tour; shop; toilets; spinning demonstration; car park

Open: April–September: Tuesday–Saturday, 11.00 am–5.00 pm; Sunday, 2.00 pm–5.00 pm. Closed Mondays

Admission: Group rates upon application

Group size: Min 25; max 50
Length of visit: 1 hour

JODRELL BANK, SCIENCE CENTRE AND ARBORETUM

Address: Macclesfield, Cheshire SK11 9DL
Tel: (01477) 571339   Fax: (01477) 571695

Description:
An extensive range of displays and 'hands-on' interactive exhibitions can be explored at Jodrell Bank relating to many aspects of the National Curriculum. There are eight exhibition galleries; a Planetarium; an Arboretum with over 2,000 species of trees and shrubs; an abundance of wildlife, together with the environmental discovery centre where the main core of the centre is the Lovell Telescope.
Ages: 5+
Subjects: Science; Art; Mathematics; Design & Technology; English; History
Facilities: Free teachers' pre-visit; car park; disabled access; indoor/outdoor eating areas; shop; refreshments; information packs; resource room; special exhibitions; other activities; education officer; playground; tree trails
Open: Mid-March–October, 10.30 am–5.30 pm. November–March, 10.00 am–4.30 pm
Admission: Children £2.00; adults/teachers £4.00. Contact for group concessions. One adult free for every seven children
Group size: Min 20; max 200
Length of visit: Up to 3 hours

LANCASHIRE MINING MUSEUM

Address: Buile Hill Park, Eccles Old Road, Salford M6 8GL
Tel: (0161) 736 1832

Description:
Located in a 19th-century building set in the delightful grounds of Buile Hill Park, the Lancashire Mining Museum reveals what life was really like underground for miners at the two recreated mines. Find out also about the great triumphs and tragedies that occurred in the nearby Lancashire coalfields.
Ages: All ages
Subjects: History; Geography; Design & Technology; English; Science; Mathematics; Art
Facilities: Worksheets; teachers' notes; library; shop; disabled access; exhibition; car park
Open: Monday–Friday, 10.00 am–12.30 pm and 1.30 pm–5.00 pm. Sunday, 2.00 pm–5.00 pm. Closed Saturdays

Admission: Free
Group size: Upon application
Length of visit: N/A

MANCHESTER AIRPORT

Address: Spectators Terraces, Manchester Airport, Manchester M90 1QX
Tel: (0161) 489 2442   Fax: (0161) 436 3030

Description:
Proving that education can be exciting, Manchester Airport offers visitors an invitation to step inside their tour centre and find out about the history of air travel with the help of numerous displays by major airlines; discover facts about aviation both past and present, watch many specialist aviation videos and find out about the inner workings of the Airport. Programmes are all linked to the National Curriculum.
Ages: All ages
Subjects: Science
Facilities: Worksheets; video; tailored tours organized; disabled access limited; car park; refreshments
Open: Throughout the year, daily, 9.30 am–8.00 pm. Closed Christmas
Admission: Children (4–15 years) £2.00; adults/teachers £3.50
Group size: Max 60
Length of visit: 2 hours

MANCHESTER UNITED MUSEUM AND TOUR CENTRE

Address: Sir Matt Busby Way, Old Trafford, Manchester M16 0RA
Tel: (0161) 877 4042   Fax: (0161) 930 2902

Description:
Spend a morning on a guided tour of Britain's first purpose-built football museum, which covers the history of the club from 1878 to the present with over 1,000 exhibits. Stadium tours are also available.
Ages: All ages
Subjects: History
Facilities: Education packs; teachers' notes; disabled access; car park; refreshments; shop
Open: Throughout the year, six days a week. Closed Mondays except local school holidays and Bank Holidays
Admission: Group rates available upon application
Group size: N/A
Length of visit: N/A

MARITIME MUSEUM

Address: Custom House, St George's Quay, Lancaster LA1 1RB
Tel: (01524) 64637   Fax: (01524) 841692

Description:
Opened in 1985, the 18th-century riverside Custom House was designed by Richard Gillow, the famous furniture maker. With the help of sound reconstructions, smells, and audiovisual aids, it cleverly reveals the story of the port of Lancaster, Morecambe Bay, fishing and the Lancaster Canal.
Ages: All ages
Subjects: Science; History
Facilities: Education programme; exhibitions; shop; car park; disabled access
Open: Daily. Easter–October, 11.00 am–5.00 pm. November–Easter, 12.30 pm–4.00 pm. Closed Christmas and New Year
Admission: Group rates upon application
Group size: N/A
Length of visit: N/A

MERSEYSIDE MARITIME MUSEUM

Address: Albert Dock, Liverpool L3 4AA
Tel: (0151) 478 4499

Description:
Merseyside Maritime Museum is a major tourist attraction in Liverpool. Part of the National Museums and Galleries on Merseyside, it covers seven acres, the many exhibits reflecting the history of the merchant navy and shipping from the 13th century, plus the development of the port of Liverpool and its international links. Other galleries include Battle of the Atlantic, *Titanic* and *Lusitania,* and there is a permanent gallery looking at the slave trade.
HM Customs & Excise National Museum
Explore the fascinating world of customs & excise, which is comprised of seven sections: customs today; the Channel Tunnel; preventative role; the collection of taxes; catching the smugglers; literary links; and a hands-on hot news point.
Museum of Liverpool Life, Mann Island, Liverpool LS 4AA
Find out more about Liverpool's amazing history and its contribution to national life; how men and women endeavoured to survive through the bad times. The museum also stages temporary exhibitions and displays.
Ages: All ages
Subjects: History
Facilities: Information packs; worksheets; refreshments; play area; disabled access limited in some areas; special events; activities; shop

Open: Daily, 10.00 am–5.00 pm
Admission: Contact for group rates
Group size: Upon application
Length of visit: N/A

MIREHOUSE

Address: Keswick, Cumbria CA12 4QE
Tel/fax: (017687) 72287

Description:
Built more than 300 years ago, this fine typical English manor house set amidst the delightful Cumbrian countryside is a very popular venue for students of all ages. The house has only changed hands once, in 1688, so there are many intriguing artefacts depicting how different life used to be. A visit to the house can be combined with a nature trail through the woods, gardens and fields, where you will find a selection of wildlife and the walled garden has been replanted with bee plants. An exhibition about bee-keeping is underway.
Ages: All ages
Subjects: History; English; R.E.; Geography; P.E.; Art; Science
Facilities: Free teachers' pre-visit; worksheets; tearoom; car park; guidebook; tour; toilets; adventure playground; bee garden; mountain forest trail
Open: Daily, April–October. Gardens and tearoom: 10.00 am–5.30 pm. House: Sundays, Wednesday (also Fridays in August), 2.00 pm, last entries 4.30 pm. This is because the house is a family home. Groups are welcome any day subject to appointment
Admission: Group rates upon application
Group size: N/A
Length of visit: Tour of the house can take ¾–1½ hours +

MUNCASTER CASTLE, GARDENS AND OWL CENTRE

Address: Muncaster Castle, Ravenglass, Cumbria CA18 1RQ
Tel: (01229) 717614   Fax: (01229) 717010

Description:
Standing on the foundations of a Roman watch tower, Muncaster Castle, home of the Pennington family, has been of great importance since Roman times and has been described as a 'Gateway To Paradise'. Inside this magnificent building are seven centuries of treasure: an alabaster Lady in the Great Hall, paintings by Gainsborough and some delightful hand-crafted tapestries. There are 77 acres of gardens; the largest communal aviary in the UK; the peaceful Muncaster Parish Church (well worth a visit); a children's play area; and the Owl Centre, which has the finest collection of owls in the world.

Ages: All ages
Subjects: Geography; Art; History
Facilities: Free guided audio tour; indoor/outdoor eating areas; refreshments; car park; free teachers' pre-visit; good facilities for the less able-bodied; shop; plant centre; nature trail; orienteering course
Open: Castle: last Sunday in March until last Sunday in October, 12.30 pm–4.00 pm; closed Saturdays. Gardens and Owl Centre: daily, 11.00 am–5.00 pm. The castle may open outside these official hours by prior appointment
Admission: Castle, gardens and Owl Centre: children £2.50. Gardens and Owl Centre only: children £1.50. Prices are based on groups of 12+. One teacher is admitted free for every 15 pupils. Extra adults/teachers charged at child rate.
Group size: Upon application
Length of visit: 3 hours

THE MUSEUM OF SCIENCE AND INDUSTRY IN MANCHESTER

Address: Liverpool Road, Castlefield, Manchester MS 4FP
Tel: (0161) 833 0027   Fax: (0161) 832 1511

Description:

An amazing museum which guarantees fun and information on space; machines; pioneering power, electric energy and fascinating inventions. Everything is closely linked to the National Curriculum and various objects can be used as a stimulus for exploring a range of topics. Trace the history of Manchester; follow the story of the world's first industrial city from its Roman origins; explore the science centre and discover revelations where you will find out things are not always as they appear. See the lamps that illuminated the streets in the 1800s; follow the story of Manchester's textile industry both past and present; find out how the pioneers of the sky flew machines; and, if you are brave enough, deep in the cellars of the Museum you will find underground Manchester.

Ages: All ages
Subjects: History; Science; Art; Design & Technology; English
Facilities: Guided tours (charged); talks; tailor-made sessions; free teachers' pre-visit; classroom; disabled access; resource packs; workshops; toilets; car park; shop; refreshments; information point; library and record centre (open at certain times)
Open: Daily, 10.00 am–5.00 pm. Closed 24–26 December
Admission: Children £2.00; adults/teachers free. One adult free for every 15 children. Separate charges for workshops and guided tours
Group size: Min 10
Length of visit: N/A

NATIONAL TRUST PROPERTIES

For information about National Trust sites to visit in the north-west contact: National Trust Regional Office, The Hollens, Grasmere, Ambleside, Cumbria LA22 9QZ (tel: 01539 435599).

The Trust also run a minibus tour in the Lake District, enabling students to meet foresters, wardens, estate teams and specialists as they undertake their work in protecting the lakeside landscape. This is suitable for KS2 +. Further information can be obtained from the Regional Office.

Beatrix Potter Gallery
Gawthorpe Hall
Rufford Old Hall
Sandscale Haws Nature Reserve
Sizergh Castle
Townend
Wordsworth House

NORTH WEST WATER LTD

Address: Education Liaison Officer, Dawson House, Great Sankey, Warrington WA5 3LW
Tel: (01925) 234000

Description:
North West Water have several centres throughout the area where parties of schoolchildren can spend a day learning about a number of issues concerning water, eg water cycle, water management and the environment. They also have a mobile visitor centre which visits schools within a certain perimeter and the swim safe team co-ordinates closely with the police to provide safety presentations in schools. The centres are located at Worthington Lakes, near Wigan; Pex Hill, near Widnes; Leigh, near Manchester; Fleetwood; Brockhole at Windermere; and the North West Water/RSPB Baywatch Centre, Lytham. For further information about each centre contact (01925) 234000 or the respective sites (see below).
Ages: All ages
Subjects: Science; Geography; Design & Technology; History; Mathematics; English
Facilities: Although each site has different facilities, most provide teaching packs; videos for short-term free loan; teacher placements; work experience for 15–16-year-olds can be arranged; craft apprenticeship; training schemes

Pex Hill Environmental Education Centre

Address: Pex Hill Avenue, Cronton, Widnes, Cheshire WA8 9QW

Tel: (0151) 495 1410

Facilities: Classroom; observatory; outdoor eating area; disabled access; car park; education centre

Leigh Environmental Education Centre

Address: Hope Carr Barn, Hope Carr Lane, Leigh, Lancashire WN7 3XB

Tel: (01942) 601114

Facilities: Education centre; warden; nature reserve; observation hide; car park; disabled access; virtual reality model of the site

Worthington Lakes Environmental Education Centre

Address: Chorley Road, Standish, Wigan WN1 2XN

Tel: (01257) 425550

Facilities: Country park; disabled access; outdoor eating area; car park; nature reserve

Brockhole Environmental Education Centre

Address: The Lake District Visitor Centre, Brockhole, Windermere, Cumbria LA23 1LJ

Tel: (01539) 446601

Facilities: Classroom; disabled access; small theatre for talks; presentations; enquiry service for schools; residential field studies centre at Blencathra; exhibitions; visitor centre; outdoor eating area; walks; adventure playground

Open: Contact respective site

Admission: Contact for group rates

Group size: This depends on the individual centre

Length of visit: Dependent on the centre

ORDSALL HALL MUSEUM

Address: Ordsall Hall Museum, Taylorson Street, Ordsall, Salford M5 3EX

Tel: (0161) 872 0251

Description:

An impressive timber-framed building, the Ordsall Hall has some splendid features: the Great Hall dates back to Henry VIII's reign with the original panelling; there is a room with a ceiling of stars and some rather strange objects including a 3-legged chair. It is said that the Radclyffes, who once owned Orsdall Hall, gave Guy Fawkes refuge in their home.

Ages: All ages

Subjects: History; English; Art; Design & Technology

Facilities: Worksheets; teachers' notes; shop; car park; disabled access limited

Open: Monday–Friday, 10.00 am–12.30 pm and 1.30 pm–5.00 pm. Sunday, 2.00 pm–5.00 pm. Closed Saturday

Admission: Free
Group size: N/A
Length of visit: N/A

ROYAL MAIL

Address: Royal Mail House, Clippers Quay, Salford M5 2NW
   Tel: (0161) 869 7019   Fax: (0161) 869 7126

Description:
   English and Mathematics can be combined with an interesting tour around the
   Royal Mail Centre at Farnworth in Bolton, where you will find out what happens
   to mail from the moment it arrives at the sorting office, on its journey through the
   entire sorting system. There is an introductory video and at the end of the tour an
   opportunity to ask questions.
Ages: 7+
Subjects: English; Mathematics
Facilities: Tours can be tailored to suit particular requirements; refreshments;
   disabled access; car park
Open: Tours: Tuesday, Wednesday and Thursday at 2.00 pm and 7.00 pm
Admission: Free
Group visit: Min 6; max 25
Length of visit: 2 hours

SALFORD MUSEUM AND ART GALLERY

Address: Peel Park, The Crescent, Salford M5 4WU
   Tel: (0161) 736 2649

Description:
   Dating back to 1849, the museum which was once the first free library in the
   country now houses the world's largest public art collection by the City's most
   famous painter, L S Lowry. There is a reconstruction of a typical northern street at
   the turn of the century complete with 16 period shops and rooms and, to make it
   even more authentic, genuine sounds of the times.
Ages: All ages
Subjects: History; English; Art; Geography; Design & Technology
Facilities: Free worksheets; car park; teachers' notes; guidelines; workshops;
   hands-on activities; shop; café (packed lunches may be pre-booked); car park;
   disabled access; temporary exhibitions
Open: Throughout the year. Monday–Friday, 10.00 am–4.45 pm. Saturday and
   Sunday, 1.00 pm–5.00 pm
Admission: Free

Group size: Upon application
Length of visit: N/A

TULLIE HOUSE MUSEUM AND ART GALLERY

Address: Castle Street, Carlisle CA3 8TP
Tel: (01228) 34781

Description:
Journey back in time to experience the sights and sounds of the Roman occupation; travel through the Dark Ages to grind corn as the Celts did; visit the Middle Ages and relive the Anglo-Scottish wars; walk through a city under siege in England's Civil War; and gaze upon the night sky in the Wildlife Dome.
Ages: All ages
Subjects: History
Facilities: Free teachers' pre-visit; handling sessions; role-play; resource pack; worksheets; school loans; catering facilities; special events
Open: Monday–Saturday, 10.00 am–5.00 pm. Sunday, Boxing Day and New Year's Day, 12.00 noon–5.00 pm
Admission: £1.50 per person
Group size: Min 10; max 60
Length of visit: 2 hours

WINDERMERE STEAMBOAT MUSEUM

Address: Rayrigg Road, Windermere, Cumbria LA23 1BN
Tel: (01539) 445565   Fax: (01539) 448769

Description:
The museum is situated on a former sand wharf site and accommodates up to 15 boats, many of which are still in working order. The building includes displays of speed craft and Beatrix Potter's rowing boat, and, weather allowing, there are also historic 50-minute steamboat trips on one of the two boats.
Ages: 7+
Subjects: English; Science; History
Facilities: Free teachers' pre-visit; car park; outdoor eating area; refreshments; lecture room for hire; guide tour; boat trips on Lake Windermere; toilets; disabled access; shop; exhibitions; special events throughout the year; worksheets
Open: Daily, 23 March–1 November, 10.00 am–5.00 pm
Admission: Group rates for 12+ pupils £1.50; adults/teachers £1.50
Group size: N/A
Length of visit: 2 hours

12 Yorkshire

ALLERTON PARK

Address: Nr Knaresborough, North Yorkshire HG5 0SE
Tel: (01423) 331123   Fax: (01423) 331125

Description:
Owned in the 18th century by Prince Frederick, the Duke of York, brother to King George IV, Allerton Park is an outstanding Gothic revival stately home, possibly the best in the country.

Ages: 14+
Subjects: Technology; History; Art
Facilities: Free teachers' pre-visit; guided tour/talk; indoor/outdoor eating area; car park; disabled access
Open: Sunday afternoons and Bank Holidays, 1.00 pm–5.00 pm
Admission: Children £3.00; teachers free
Group size: Max 100
Length of visit: 1½ hours

ARCHAEOLOGICAL RESOURCE CENTRE

Address: St Saviourgate, York, North Yorkshire Y01 2NN
Tel: (01904) 543402   Fax: (01904) 543410

Description:
Situated close to the Shambles in the delightful restored church of St Saviour, the Archaeological Resource Centre brings history alive. Visitors are invited to handle genuine archaeological relics, try out ancient crafts and use the latest video and computer technology in finding out about the past.

Ages: 5+
Subjects: English; Mathematics; Science; Technology; History; Geography; Art; R.E.
Facilities: Free teachers' pre-visit; audiovisual facilities; talks; study room; disabled access limited; shop

Open: Monday–Friday, 10.00 am–4.00 pm. Saturday, 1.00 pm–4.00 pm. Closed
Sundays and 14 December–4 January
Admission: Children £2.95; adults/teachers £3.50. One adult free for every 10 pupils
Group size: Max 35
Length of visit: 1½ hours

BANKFIELD MUSEUM

Address: Akroyd Park, Boothtown Road, Halifax, West Yorkshire HX3 6HG
Tel: (01422) 354823/353334   Fax: (01422) 349020

Description:
There are a variety of temporary exhibitions and educational activities located in
a Victorian textile mill owner's house which also accommodates a collection of
international textiles plus displays of military and toys relating to the Duke of
Wellington's regiments.
Ages: 5+
Subjects: History; Geography; Science; Art; Music; English
Facilities: Indoor eating area; study room; car park; shop; guides; disabled access;
toilets
Open: Tuesday–Saturday, 10.00 am–5.00 pm. Sundays, from 2.00 pm–5.00 pm.
Closed Mondays
Admission: Group rates upon application
Group size: Upon application
Length of visit: 1–2 hours

BOLTON ABBEY ESTATE

Address: Estate Office, Bolton Abbey, Skipton, North Yorkshire BD23 6EX
Tel: Estate Office (01756) 710227   Fax: (01756) 710535
Tourism (01756) 710533

Description:
Bolton Estate is the estate of the Duke and Duchess of Devonshire and has been
the inspiration of many artists and poets over the years. The 30,000-acre estate
provides an invaluable insight into farming, forestry and conservation, and can be
adapted to facilitate various other subjects in the National Curriculum.
Ages: 8–16
Subjects: Mathematics; English; Art; Science; Design & Technology; R.E.; History;
Geography
Facilities: Free teachers' pre-visit; exhibitions; video; nature trails; teachers'
handbook; animal tracker guide; disabled access; car park; shop; outdoor eating
areas; refreshments; steam railway; classroom; guided tours; toilets

189

Open: Daily. Winter from 8.00 am; summer, 8.00 am–9.00 pm
Admission: Group rates upon application
Group size: Max 50
Length of visit: 2 hours +

BOLTON CASTLE

Address: Leyburn, North Yorkshire DL8 4ET
  Tel: (01969) 623981   Fax: (01969) 623332

Description:
  A historic castle with a colourful past partly furnished and equipped to illustrate military and domestic life from 1399 to 1647. There is a tableaux of the armourer's forge, old kitchen, Mary, Queen of Scots' bedchamber and the Monk's cell.
Ages: 5+
Subjects: English; History
Facilities: Free teachers' pre-visit; teachers' packs; guided tours/talk; worksheets; toilets; indoor/outdoor eating areas; disabled access limited; period costumes; artefacts; books; wall displays; re-enactment groups
Open: March–November, 10.00 am–5.00 pm/dusk
Admission: Children £2.00; adults/teachers free. Additional adults £3.00. Discounts available for groups of 25+
Group size: Max 50
Length of visit: 1 hour

BRADFORD INDUSTRIAL AND HORSES AT WORK MUSEUM

Address: Moorside Mills, Moorside Road, Eccleshill, Bradford BD2 3HP
  Tel: (01274) 631756, Ext. 230   Fax: (01274) 636362

Description:
  Take a nostalgic look down memory lane with a visit to this fascinating museum in Bradford where you will find steam engines, shire-horses, and a genuine spinning mill housing magnificent machinery. Inside the mill you can actually experience the sounds and smells of the engines which once powered the mills throughout Yorkshire as it changed raw wool into woven cloth.
Ages: 5+
Subjects: History; Design & Technology
Facilities: Free teachers' pre-visit; exhibitions; tailor-made programmes; talks; demonstrations; car park; workshops; disabled access; refreshments; toilets; shop
Open: Tuesday–Saturday, 10.00 am–5.00 pm. Sunday, 12 noon–5.00 pm. Closed Mondays except Bank Holidays

Admission: Group rates upon application
Group size: Upon application
Length of visit: 1–3 hours

BRONTË PARSONAGE MUSEUM

Address: Haworth, Keighley, West Yorkshire BD22 8DR
Tel: (01535) 642323   Fax: (01535) 647131

Description:
The famous Brontë family who gave so much to the literary world have left behind
not only their home but a museum with a collection of their own possessions:
furniture; their earliest literary efforts; pebbles which Anne collected from her
visits to Scarborough; and Emily's writing-desk complete with authentic contents.
Ages: All ages
Subjects: History; English; Art; Technology
Facilities: Self-guided tours; worksheets; guidebooks and leaflets; video for hire;
workshop groups; disabled access limited; educational resources; shop; library
Open: Daily. April–September, 10.00 am–5.00 pm. Wednesdays in August, 10.00
am–7.00 pm. October–March, 11.00 am–4.30 pm
Admission: Group rates upon application
Group size: Min 20
Length of visit: 45 minutes–1 hour

CALDERDALE INDUSTRIAL MUSEUM

Address: Square Road, Halifax, West Yorkshire HX1 0QG
Tel: (01422) 358087   Fax: (01422) 349310

Description:
With over 20 industries represented on four floors, over 150 years of Calderdale
industry are captured inside this working museum, enabling visitors to take a look
back in time and to explore industrialization and the role it played in people's
lives, the development of textiles and how they evolved, and different modes of
transport used; there is a unique collection of early machinery, including the
Spinning Jenny.
Ages: 5–16
Subjects: Science; History; Geography; Art; Music; English; Information Technology
Facilities: Free teachers' pre-visit; resource packs; packed lunch area; toilets; study
area; disabled access; tailor-made programmes; education programme
Open: Tuesday–Saturday, 10.00 am–5.00 pm. Sunday, 2.00 pm–5.00 pm. Closed on
Mondays excluding Bank Holidays
Admission: Group rates upon application

Group size: N/A
Length of visit: 2 hours

CASTLE HOWARD

Address: York, North Yorkshire YO6 7DA
   Tel: (01653) 648444   Fax: (01653) 648462

Description:
   Set in 1,000 acres of parkland, Castle Howard is the largest house in the north of England inhabited and cared for by the same family since it was built in 1699. It provides an ideal opportunity to find out how people lived centuries ago, with photographic exhibitions tracing the restoration work undertaken.
Ages: All ages
Subjects: English; Geography; Science; Art; P.E.; R.E.
Facilities: Free teachers' pre-visit; teachers' packs; guided tours/talks; worksheets; adventure playground; indoor eating area; disabled access; car park; shop
Open: Gardens and grounds from 10.00 am. House from 11.00 am. 13 March– 1 November
Admission: Group rates upon application. One teacher free for every 10 children
Group size: Max 50
Length of visit: Half a day

CLEETHORPES HUMBER ESTUARY DISCOVERY CENTRE

Address: c/o Leisure Services, The Knoll, Knoll Street, Cleethorpes DN35 8LN
   Tel: (01472) 323232   Fax: (01472) 323233

Description:
   Designed to arouse interest in one of Europe's most important estuaries – The Humber – the Discovery Centre provides a fascinating hands-on learning experience into wildlife and shipping. Through high-powered telescopes in the observatory, panoramic views out across the natural land can be seen.
Ages: 5+
Subjects: English; Mathematics; Science; Technology; Geography; Art; P.E.
Facilities: Free teachers' pre-visit; teachers' packs; audiovisual facilities; study room; guided tour/talk; worksheets; trails; indoor/outdoor eating areas; car park; education officer; disabled access; shop
Open: Daily, 10.00 am–5.00 pm
Admission: Group rates 10+ children: exhibition £1 each; activities 80p/hour each. One adult free for every 10 pupils. Additional adults £1.50
Group size: Max 100
Length of visit: Up to 3 hours

THE COLOUR MUSEUM

Address: Perkin House, PO Box 244, 1 Providence Street, Bradford, West Yorkshire
BD1 2PW
Tel: (01274) 390955   Fax: (01274) 392888

Description:
Divided into two main galleries, the first gallery at the Colour Museum succinctly illustrates the importance of colour in everyday life, human and animal perception, light and the spectrum, primary colours, colour illusions, colour blindness and the physical nature of colour. The second gallery deals with colour in textiles, examining natural dye colours, methods and styles of textile printing, introduction of synthetic fibres and their effects on the industry.

Ages: 7+

Subjects: Art; History

Facilities: Workshops; toilets; disabled access; audiovisual theatre; shop; video loans; activity worksheets

Open: Tuesday–Friday, 2.00 pm–5.00 pm. Saturday, 10.00 am–4.00 pm

Admission: Group rates upon application

Group size: Upon application

Length of visit: Up to 2 hours

DEEP SEA EXPERIENCE CENTRE

Address: Central Promenade, Cleethorpes, North East Lincolnshire DN35 8SE
Tel: (01472) 290220   Fax: (01472) 290220

Description:
An informative educational tour revealing amazing facts about fish, both the friendly and the unfriendly variety, their habitat off our local shores and across the world, their diets, individual breeding patterns, and the kind of water in which they live. There is also a touch pool for visually impaired students.

Ages: All ages

Subjects: Science; Technology; Art

Facilities: Free teachers' pre-visit; teachers' packs; quiz sheet; guided tours/talk; lunch area; shop; disabled access

Open: Monday–Friday, 10.00 am–5.00 pm (winter may vary)

Admission: Winter: children £1.95; adults/teachers £2.50. Summer: children £2.95; adults/teachers £3.95

Group size: Max 15

Length of visit: 2 hours

DUNCOMBE PARK

Address: Helmsley, York, North Yorkshire Y06 5EB
Tel: (01439) 770213   Fax: (01439) 771114

Description:
Home of Lord and Lady Feversham and their family since it was built in 1713, the baroque mansion provides an insight into this splendid home with its smart late-Victorian furnishings. Outside visitors can explore the captivating 35-acre 18th-century landscaped gardens with mature trees, an early 19th-century water tower, the secret garden and the temples, which are well worth investigating.

Ages: 5+

Subjects: English; Mathematics; Science; Design & Technology; Geography; Art; R.E.; History; P.E.

Facilities: Free teachers' pre-visit; education pack; worksheets; guided tours; car park; disabled access limited; education room; shop; tearoom; outdoor eating area; toilets; Woodland and Oak Wood Discovery Trails; orienteering facilities; parkland walks; National Nature Reserve; displays; Ice-House

Open: Park all year. House/garden: April–October, Monday–Friday (contact for exact times)

Admission: Children £1.70, which includes house, garden and park (group of 25 minimum, otherwise £2.00 each). Garden and park £1.20. One adult free for every seven children. Extra adults at children's rates

Group size: Upon application

Length of visit: Up to a full day

EDEN CAMP MODERN HISTORY THEME MUSEUM

Address: Malton, North Yorkshire Y017 0SD
Tel: (01653) 697777   Fax: (01653) 698243

Description:
A unique experience unlike any other, where visitors can see for themselves the heartache that war brought, encounter what it was like during the black-outs, how people dealt with rationing, how they coped during the Blitz and what life was really like for the young evacuees.

Ages: 6+

Subjects: English; Mathematics; Science; Technology; Art; P.E.; Geography; R.E.; History; Music

Facilities: Free teachers' pre-visit; teachers' packs; quiz sheet; worksheets; audio-visual facilities; education officer available; talk; classroom; trails; eating areas; disabled access; car park; exhibitions; artefacts; shop

Open: From 15 January–13 February, open Monday–Friday. From 14 February open 7 days a week, 10.00 am–5.00 pm until 23 December

Admission: Children £1.50. One teacher free for every 10 children. Additional adults £1.50

Group visit: Max 400

Length of visit: 3–4 hours

ELSECAR BARNSLEY

Address: Wath Road, Elsecar, Barnsley, South Yorkshire S74 8HJ
Tel: (01226) 740203   Fax: (01226) 350239

Description:

Located within restored Victorian industrial workshops, Elsecar Barnsley is an enterprising history and science centre with an assortment of attractions and exhibitions including: the Newcomen Beam Engine, the only one of its type in the world still in its original location; environmental science workshops; a Victorian classroom; people exhibition; craft workshops; hot-metal press and many other exhibitions all bearing some relevance to the National Curriculum.

Ages: 5+

Subjects: English; Science; Technology; History; Geography

Facilities: Free teachers' pre-visit; teachers' packs; study room; indoor/outdoor eating area; quiz sheets; trails; audiovisual facilities; guided tours/talk; worksheets; car park; toilets; disabled access; shop

Open: Daily, 10.00 am–5.00 pm. Closed 25 December–1 January

Admission: Group rates upon application

Group size: Upon application

Length of visit: Varies from ½ hour–full day

EMBSAY AND BOLTON ABBEY STEAM RAILWAY

Address: Bolton Abbey Station, Bolton Abbey, Skipton, North Yorkshire BD23 6AX
Tel: (01756) 794727   Fax: (01756) 795189

Description:

Travel by steam locomotive from the historic station at Embsay, built in 1888, along to Bolton Abbey Station past some beautiful landscape which inspired both Turner and Wordsworth. The site of Bolton Abbey Station boasts being home to a variety of rare plants and flowers and the station is a reconstruction of the original, situated only a mile and a half away from the Abbey ruins.

Ages: All ages

Subjects: Technology; History

Facilities: Shop; refreshments; disabled access; car park; toilets

Open: Contact for opening times
Admission: Group rates upon application
Group size: Upon application
Length of visit: 2 hours

ENGLISH HERITAGE PROPERTIES

Sites to visit within Yorkshire are listed under The North East.

EUREKA! THE MUSEUM FOR CHILDREN

Address: Discovery Road, Halifax, West Yorkshire HX1 2NE
Tel: (01422) 330012   Fax: (01422) 330275

Description:
A hands-on museum especially for children up to 12 years, where they can see, listen, touch, smell and role-play with over 400 exhibits. Learn more about the human body; discover the world of communications; send messages on a video-phone and fax machine; investigate living conditions in years gone by. With seven galleries and nine workshops, the museum provides endless opportunities for children to use all their senses and actively learn more about themselves and the world in general.

Ages: Up to 12 years
Subjects: English; Science; Technology; Geography; Music; Art; Mathematics
Facilities: Free teachers' pre-visit; teachers' packs; audiovisual facilities; indoor/outdoor eating area; disabled access; workshops; car park; toilets
Open: Daily, 10.00 am–5.00 pm. Closed 24–26 December
Admission: Group rates apply during term time of 10+ children £3.00; adults/teachers £3.00. Essential carers free, other concessions available upon application
Group size: Up to 10 classes of 30–35
Length of visit: 3 hours

FLAMINGOLAND FAMILY FUN PARK

Address: Kirby Misperton, Malton, North Yorkshire YO17 0UX
Tel: (01653) 668287   Fax: (01653) 668280

Description:
Flamingoland is not only a theme park but Europe's largest privately owned zoo, providing a well-protected environment for hundreds of different animals – lions, tigers, polar bears, elephants, monkeys and reptiles. There is also a selection of some exciting rides, many of which are only for the brave and include the log flume, sky flyer, terrorizer and bullet. Lots of opportunity to use

many aspects of the park in the National Curriculum and lots of advice available from the staff.

Ages: All ages

Subjects: Mathematics; Science; Technology; Geography

Facilities: Free teachers' pre-visit; teachers' packs; educational workshop; exhibitions; talks; indoor/outdoor eating areas; shop; toilets; car park; disabled access

Open: Contact for opening times

Admission: Group rates upon application

Group size: Upon application

Length of visit: Full day

HAREWOOD HOUSE

Address: The Estate Office, Harewood, Leeds, West Yorkshire LS17 9LQ

Tel: (0113) 288 6331   Fax: (0113) 288 6467

Description:

Harewood House, designed by John Carr in 1759, has a plethora of furniture and decor including collections of Italian and English paintings, Chippendale furniture, ceramics and family memorabilia, making it an inspiration for any arts or cultural studies course. Outdoors among the 1,000-acre parkland there are formal gardens, woodland walks providing environmental resources and also a bird garden with exotic species plus an ongoing conservation and breeding programme.

Ages: 5+

Subjects: English; Science; Technology; History; Geography; Art; P.E.; R.E.

Facilities: Free teachers' pre-visit; teachers' packs; quiz sheet; audiovisual facilities; teacher on site; talk; study room; guided tours; worksheets; fieldwork; free inspection; trails; indoor/outdoor eating areas; disabled access; car park; toilets; shop

Open: Daily, 10.00 am–5.00 pm

Admission: Children £2.25. One teacher free for every 10 children. Additional adults £2 each

Group size: Upon application

Length of visit: Full day

JORVIK VIKING CENTRE

Address: Coppergate, York, North Yorkshire Y01 1NT

Tel: (01904) 543402

Description:

A fascinating educational encounter meets all those who visit the Viking Centre in York. Climb aboard a time car as it transports you back through the centuries to the medieval city of Jorvik, where the sounds, smells and atmosphere of a Viking-age York are authentically recreated from archaeological finds. And after your time travel there is an invitation to visit the gallery, where you will find over 500 artefacts discovered during the dig.

Ages: 5+

Subjects: English; Science; Technology; History; Geography; Music; Art; P.E.; R.E.

Facilities: Free teachers' pre-visit; audiovisual facilities; shop; disabled access; toilets; exhibitions

Open: Daily from 9.00 am. Closed Christmas Day

Admission: Children £2.75; adults/teachers £4.95. One teacher free for every 10 children. Discounts available

Group size: Max 50

Length of visit: 1 hour

LIGHTWATER VALLEY COUNTRY THEME PARK

Address: North Stainley, Ripon, North Yorkshire HG34 3HT
Tel: (01765) 635321   Fax: (01765) 635359

Description:
Covering 175 acres, Lightwater Valley provides an ideal educational environment with endless resources where learning is fun and where pupils can enjoy themselves and discover in relaxed surroundings. There are lots of rides, plus other attractions that can complement most subjects and there is plenty of opportunity for older students who may be involved in a Leisure & Tourism course to integrate their studies.

Ages: 5+

Subjects: Geography; Art; History; Design & Technology; Mathematics; Science; English

Facilities: Worksheets; educational pack; disabled access; first aid post; car park; outdoor eating area; rides and attractions; refreshments; shops; toilets

Open: Contact for opening times

Admission: Group concessions available by ringing (01765) 635334

Group size: Upon application

Length of visit: Whole day

MIDDLETON RAILWAY

Address: Moor Road, Hunslet, Leeds LS10 2JQ
Tel: (01904) 633906

Description:
Middleton Railway is a perfect place to learn about transport, conservation and many other subjects. Opened in 1758, the Middleton Railway was the first railway in the world and ran its very first steam engine in 1812. For 35 years it has been in the hands of the preservationists and has acquired a number of wagons, steam engines and other engines. There is also a collection of Leeds-built loco-motives that show the industrial past of Leeds.

Ages: Up to 15 years

Subjects: History; English; Mathematics; Science; Technology

Facilities: Free teachers' pre-visit; teachers' packs; quiz sheets; audiovisual facil-ities; education officer; resource material for loan; study room; guided tours/talk; worksheets; outdoor eating areas; guided fieldwork; trails; disabled access limited; shop; car park; refreshments

Open: April–December

Admission: Children £1.20; adults/teachers free

Group size: Max 150

Length of visit: 1½–2 hours

NATIONAL CENTRE FOR POPULAR MUSIC

Address: The Workstation, 15 Paternoster Row, Sheffield, South Yorkshire S1 2BX
Tel: (0114) 279 8941   Fax: (0114) 249 4328

Description:
Using sound, film and up-to-the-minute technology this new arts and education centre relates the story of popular music in an exciting way. With hands-on exhi-bitions visitors can learn the whole process involved in the music business – from recording and performing to distribution. And there is a three-dimensional sound auditorium, which transports students on a memorable journey through the world of sound.

Ages: 5+

Subjects: Music

Facilities: Free teachers' pre-visit; teachers' packs; quiz sheet; audiovisual facilities; teacher on site; talk; classroom; guided tours/talk; indoor/outdoor eating areas; disabled access; car park; shop; exhibitions are interactive and require hands-on participation

Open: Daily, 10.00 am–6.00 pm

Admission: Children £3 (minimum 10 children); adults/teachers free

Group size: Max 60
Length of visit: 2½ hours

NATIONAL FISHING HERITAGE CENTRE

Address: Alexandra Dock, Great Grimsby, North East Lincolnshire DN31 1UZ
Tel: (01472) 323345   Fax: (01472) 323355

Description:
A look at the life of Grimsby's fishermen and their families during the 1950s, when the town was known as the world's leading fishing port. There are a reconstructed trawler radio room and bridge, displays, documents and many other hands-on pieces of equipment clearly reflecting the important role fishing played.
Ages: All ages
Subjects: English; Mathematics; Science; Technology; History; Music; Geography; Art
Facilities: Free teachers' packs: audiovisual facilities; education officer; resource materials for loan; guided tours/talk; worksheets; free teachers' pre-visit; indoor eating area; trails; shop; disabled access; toilets
Open: All year. Monday–Sunday, 10.00 am–6.00 pm. Closed 25–26 December and 1 January
Admission: Group rates upon application
Group size: Max 60
Length of visit: 1–2½ hours

NATIONAL RAILWAY MUSEUM

Address: Leeman Road, York Y02 4XJ
Tel: (01904) 621261   Fax: (01904) 611112

Description:
Study the important role railway transport has played in all of our lives; explore and appreciate the theories behind the railway as the National Railway Museum introduces you to the world's finest collection of locomotive power under one roof.
Ages: All ages
Subjects: English; History; Mathematics; Science; Design & Technology; Information Technology; Art; Geography
Facilities: Free teachers' pre-visit; teachers' packs; guides; library; indoor eating area; exhibitions; workshop; car park; gallery tours; demonstrations; school coach as a study base; disabled access; shop; hands-on activity learning gallery; exhibitions and events
Open: Daily, 10.00 am–6.00 pm. Closed 24–26 December

Admission: School season ticket is available
Group size: Upon application
Length of visit: Upon application

NATIONAL TRUST PROPERTIES

The National Trust Yorkshire Region covers North, South and West Yorkshire, Cleveland and North Humberside. For further information contact: National Trust Regional Office, Goddards, 27 Tadcaster Road, Dringhouses, York Y02 2QG (tel: 01904 702021).

Beningbrough Hall
Bridestones Moor
Brimham Moor and Rocks
East Riddlesden Hall
Fountains Abbey and Studley Royal
Hardcastle Crags
Ormesby Hall
Ravenscar
Treasurer's House
Upper Wharfedale

PIECE HALL ART GALLERY

Address: Halifax, West Yorkshire HX1 1RE
Tel: (01422) 358087

Description:
A superb art gallery inviting pupils to meet and work alongside various artists covering a variety of activities: printing, paper making, textiles, clay and plaster exercises. There are also connections with creative writing and the world of music, all of which are linked in with the National Curriculum.
Ages: All ages
Subjects: Art; Science; Music; English
Facilities: Free teachers' pre-visit; workshops; worksheets; tours; toilets; shop; disabled access; project room
Open: Tuesday–Sunday, 10.00 am–5.00 pm. Closed Monday
Admission: Free. Small charge for workshops
Group size: Upon application
Length of visit: 1–2 hours

RIPLEY CASTLE ESTATE

Address: Ripley Castle Estate Office, Ripley, nr Harrogate, North Yorkshire HG3 3AY
Tel: (01423) 770152   Fax: (01423) 771745

Description:
For over 600 years Ripley Castle was home to the Ingilby family and it is now divided into two wings, Tudor and Georgian. See the ornate ceiling erected for James I's stay; find out how Thomas de Ingilby saved King Edward III's life; find the hidden priest hole; uncover Ingilby's involvement in the Gunpowder Plot; and touch the musket shot holes which remain, the result of Oliver Cromwell's visit.

Ages: 6+

Subjects: English; Science; Technology; History; R.E.

Facilities: Free teachers' pre-visit; teachers' packs; quiz sheet; audiovisual facilities; guided tours/talk; indoor/outdoor eating areas; car park; disabled access; shop; exhibitions; study room; trails; toilets

Open: Daily, 9.30 am–5.00 pm

Admission: For parties of 25+ children £1.75; adults/teachers: two are admitted free but additional adults £3.50 each

Group size: Max 250

Length of visit: 1½ hours

ROYAL ARMOURIES

Address: Armouries Drive, Leeds, West Yorkshire LS10 1LT
Tel: (0113) 220 1888   Fax: (0113) 220 1997

Description:
Over 1,000 years of history from around the world are displayed at the Royal Armouries Museum which relates to all subjects on the National Curriculum, contained within five themed galleries: Self-Defence; War; Tournament; Oriental; and Hunting. Excellent workshops and resource material available.

Ages: All ages

Subjects: English; Mathematics; Science; Technology; History; Geography; Music; Art; R.E.

Facilities: Free teachers' pre-visit; teachers' packs; audiovisual facilities; education officer; classroom; worksheets; outdoor eating area; trails; car park; shop; disabled access; exhibitions; toilets

Open: Monday–Friday in term time only, 10.00 am–4.00 pm. Closed Mondays 1 November–28 February

Admission: Group rates upon application

Group size: Min 10

Length of visit: 3–4 hours

SKIPTON CASTLE

Address: Skipton, North Yorkshire BD23 1AQ
Tel: (01756) 792442

Description:
A medieval castle which dates back to 1090, covering the history of the Norman Conquest, Tudor England, the Civil War and life in a medieval castle. There are woods behind the castle for exploring.
Ages: All ages
Subjects: English; History; Geography; Art; R.E.; P.E.
Facilities: Free teachers' pre-visit; worksheets; resource pack; outdoor eating area; classroom; shop; car park
Open: Daily from 10.00 am (Sunday 12 noon). Closed 25 December
Admission: Children £1.80; adults/teachers free
Group size: Upon application
Length of visit: 1 hour

SNEATONDALE HONEY FARM

Address: Racecourse Road, East Ayton, Scarborough, North Yorkshire YO13 9HT
Tel: (01723) 864001   Fax: (01723) 862455

Description:
A remarkable experience, the world's finest exhibition of the honey bee, with professional bee-keepers taking visitors on a tour they won't forget to see how the bees produce the honey.
Ages: All ages
Subjects: History
Facilities: Informative talk; quiz sheets; worksheets; adventure playground; animal farm; car park; shop; refreshments
Open: Daily, 9.00 am–5.00 pm
Admission: Children £1.50. One teacher free for every 10 children
Group size: Max 40
Length of visit: Bee tour lasts 30 minutes

ST LEONARD'S FARM PARK

Address: Chapel Lane, Esholt, Bradford, West Yorkshire BD17 7RB
Tel: (01274) 598795   Fax: (01274) 598795

Description:
Children who have never been on a working farm will enjoy a visit to St Leonard's Farm Park, a working dairy farm with a selection of animals, some of which are rare

breeds. There are outdoor paddocks and large covered areas, barns and buildings, a room set in a 16th-century farmhouse and viewing of the milking parlour.

Ages: All ages

Subjects: English; Mathematics; Science; Technology; History; Geography; Art; P.E.; R.E.

Facilities: Free teachers' pre-visit; classroom; guided tours/talk; indoor/outdoor eating areas; shop; car park; disabled access; toilets; trails

Open: April–end October: Tuesday–Sunday, 10.00 am–6.00 pm

Admission: Children £1.00. One teacher free for every five pupils

Group size: Max 75

Length of visit: 1½ hours

THACKRAY MEDICAL MUSEUM

Address: 131 Beckett Street, Leeds LS9 7LN

Tel: (0113) 244 4343   Fax: (0113) 247 0219

Description:

Medical healthcare has undergone so many changes over the years and a visit to Thackray Museum will demonstrate just how many. See how people lived in a typical Victorian street in Leeds, select a character and seek out a treatment for your character's illness, find out how the battle against infections was won, the horrors of surgery in the 1840s, and explore modern developments in the world of medicine through a doctor's professional eye. There are lots of activities, exhibitions and interactive displays.

Ages: 5+

Subjects: History; Science

Facilities: Classroom; free teachers' pre-visit; audiovisual facilities; disabled access; toilets; indoor/outdoor eating areas; education packs; car park; toilets; shop

Open: Daily. Tuesday–Sunday, 10.00 am–5.30 pm. Monday: school groups only

Admission: Junior school £2.50; senior school £2.75; students £3.00; non-school groups £2.75. Teachers free

Group size: N/A

Length of visit: 3 hours

YORK BOAT GUIDED RIVER TRIPS

Address: The Boatyard, Lendal Bridge, York Y01 2DP

Tel: (01904) 628324   Fax: (01904) 674204

Description:

Step on board the York Boat and enjoy a peaceful cruise through the centre of the walled City of York. You can enjoy learning over 2,000 years of history with tales to inform and entertain you of York both past and present.

Ages: 5+

Subjects: Geography; History; English; Mathematics; Art; Design & Technology; Information Technology; GNVQ

Facilities: Teachers' work packs; worksheets; commentary while on board; refreshments; shop; toilets

Open: Trips may be booked all year round with daytime departures between 9.30 am and 6.45 pm

Admission: Children and teachers £1.40

Group size: Upon application

Length of visit: Guided river trip lasts 1 hour

YORK CASTLE MUSEUM

Address: The Eye of York, York, North Yorkshire YO1 1RY
Tel: (01904) 633932   Fax: (01904) 671078

Description:
Discover over 400 years of the history of York from 1580 to 1980 with the help of a combination of everyday life and objects. Roam through reconstructed streets and shops of old York and perceive life from the Civil War to World War II. There is also an opportunity to glimpse prison life of 200 years ago. York Castle Museum is renowned for housing some of the finest art collections in the country.

Ages: 5+

Subjects: English; Mathematics; Technology; History

Facilities: Free teachers' pre-visit; teachers' packs; education officer; classroom; worksheets; indoor eating area; disabled access; shop

Open: November–March, 9.30 am–4.00 pm. April–October, 9.30 am– 5.30 pm

Admission: Children £3.15; adults/teachers £4.50. Discounts available for groups of 10+

Group size: Max 60

Length of visit: 2 hours

13 | The North East

ALNWICK CASTLE

Address: Estates Office, Alnwick, Northumberland NE66 1NQ
Tel: (01665) 510777   Fax: (01665) 510876

Description:
The second largest inhabited castle in England, home of the Percy family since 1309, Alnwick Castle provides the opportunity to study medieval fortification, the lifestyle of the nobility, old master paintings, fine furniture and fitments dating from the 1800s to the present.
Ages: 5+
Subjects: Geography; History; Art
Facilities: Car park; indoor/outdoor eating areas; toilets
Open: Easter to end September, 11.00 am–5.00 pm
Admission: Children £3.30; teachers free
Group size: Min 12
Length of visit: 2 hours

ARBEIA ROMAN FORT

Address: Baring Street, South Shields
Tel: (0191) 456 1369

Description:
Ancient history is revealed at the museum which provides an invaluable look at the life, death and burial of a Roman soldier, together with the West Gate reconstruction exhibiting a history of the site from Stone Age to modern day excavations. The Time Quest, a new hands-on archaeology centre, allows children a look into how archaeologists work. A visit to Arbeia Roman Fort will appeal to children of all ages.
Ages: All ages
Subjects: History; Science; Design & Technology

Facilities: Classroom; indoor eating area; toilets; workshops; audiovisual facilities; teachers' packs of activity sheets (£2.50); guidebook (1.95); activity book (£1.50); disabled access; resource materials for hire; refreshments; shop
Open: Daily. Easter–September: Monday–Saturday, 10.00 am–5.30 pm. Sundays, 1.00 pm–5.00 pm
Admission: Free
Group size: N/A
Length of visit: 2–3 hours

AUCKLAND CASTLE

Address: Market Place, Bishop Auckland, Co. Durham DL14 7NP
   Tel: (01388) 601627   Fax: (01388) 605264

Description:
   For over 800 years the castle has been home to the Bishops of Durham. There is a 17th-century chapel converted from a 14th-century banqueting hall.
Ages: 5+
Subjects: History; R.E.; Mathematics
Facilities: Free teachers' pre-visit; audiovisual facilities; guided tours/talk; toilets; car park; classroom; outdoor eating area
Open: All year. Pre-booking essential
Admission: Special school rates: pupils £1.00
Group size: N/A
Length of visit: 1 hour

BAMBURGH CASTLE

Address: The Administrator, Bamburgh Castle, Bamburgh, Northumberland NE69 7DF
   Tel: (01668) 214515   Fax: (01668) 214060

Description:
   One of the finest castles in England, dominating the Northumbrian landscape with many an exciting tale to tell from 547AD when the first of the Anglo-Saxon kings built his wooden fortress upon the great rock. In the 18th century it was turned into a school for children of the poor and a much-needed hospital with provision for shipwrecked sailors.
Ages: 7–10
Subjects: History; Geography; Science
Facilities: Guided tour; educational pack; worksheets; car park; indoor eating area; disabled access; toilets
Open: April–October, daily, 11.00 am–5.00 pm

Admission: Children £1.00; adults/teachers £2.50. One teacher free with every 15 children

Group size: Min 15

Length of visit: 1–1½ hours

BEAMISH, THE NORTH OF ENGLAND OPEN AIR MUSEUM

Address: Beamish, Co. Durham DH9 0RG

Tel: (01207) 231811   Fax: (01207) 290933

Description:

Climb aboard the ancient trams or vintage bus; step into the Drift Mine; taste some of the delicious treats for sale at the Jubilee Confectionery; and pop into the working farm and see the animals. These are just a sample of the many authentic attractions to be found at Britain's favourite open-air museum, which is packed with an assortment of exhibitions reflecting life in northern England during the early 1800s and 1900s.

Ages: 5+

Subjects: Geography; History; Art; English; Science; Mathematics; Design & Technology; Leisure & Tourism

Facilities: Free teachers' pre-visit; car park; teachers' guides; archive reproduction packs; free loan boxes; study aids; special events; video loan; refreshments; disabled access; toilets; exhibitions; indoor/outdoor eating areas

Open: Summer: 4 April–1 November, daily, 10.00 am–5.00 pm; 18 July–6 September, daily, 10.00 am–6.00 pm. Winter: 2 November–26 March, 10.00 am–4.00 pm, closed Mondays and Fridays. Also closed 14 December 1998–1 January 1999 inclusive

Admission: £4 per child. Under 11 years one adult free for every 5 children. Over 11 one adult free for every 10 children. Extra adults £7 each

Group size: N/A

Length of visit: Summer 4–5 hours. Winter 2 hours

BEDE'S WORLD MUSEUM

Address: Church Bank, Jarrow, Tyne & Wear NE32 3DY

Tel: (0191) 489 2106   Fax: (0191) 428 2361

Description:

Lots of opportunities to find out how the Venerable Bede (673–735 AD) lived. Together with genuine crops, animals and wooden buildings, the Anglo-Saxon farm reveals what conditions were really like.

Ages: 5+

Subjects: Archaeology; R.E.; History

Facilities: Classroom; free teachers' pre-visit; audiovisual facilities; working demonstrations; guided tour; work pack; indoor/outdoor eating areas; car park; resource material for hire; specialized programmes; disabled access limited; shop; toilets

Open: All year. Monday–Friday, 10.00 am–2.45 pm. Special opening times can be arranged

Admission: Group rates upon application

Group size: Min 30

Length of visit: Half–full day

DISCOVERY MUSEUM

Address: Blandford Square, Newcastle upon Tyne
Tel: (0191) 232 6789

Description:

Browse around the Turbinia gallery, which reveals the tale of Charles Parson's turbine design and how it altered maritime history. Other exhibitions include Fashion and Great City, and there is a look into the life of a north-eastern soldier from recruitment into the forces until his death.

Ages: All ages

Subjects: Science; Technology; History; Art; Geography

Facilities: Teachers' packs; disabled access; audiovisual facilities; workshops; toilets; activity room; indoor eating area; shop; activity sheets; free teachers' pre-visit; resource materials for hire

Open: All year. Tuesday–Friday, 10.00 am–5.30 pm. Saturday, 10.00 am–4.30 pm. Sundays, 2.00 pm-5.00 pm

Admission: Free

Group size: Upon application

Length of visit: 2 hours

ENGLISH HERITAGE

Before making a visit to any of the English Heritage listed buildings in the North East of England contact them for further information: English Heritage, Historic Properties North, Bessie Surtees House, 41–44 Sandhill, Newcastle upon Tyne NE1 3JF (tel: 0191 261 1585; fax: 0191 261 1130).

Aldborough Roman Town
Aydon Castle
Barnard Castle
Beeston Castle
Belsay Hall, Castle and Gardens

Berwick-upon-Tweed Barracks
Bessie Surtees House
Brinkburn Priory
Brougham Castle
Byland Abbey
Brodsworth Hall – near Doncaster. Tel: (01302) 722598. Fax: (01302) 337165
Carlisle Castle
Chesters Fort and Museum
Clifford's Tower, York
Conisborough Castle
Corbridge Roman Site
Derwentcote Steel Furnace
Dunstanburgh Castle
Easby Abbey
Etal Castle
Finchale Priory
Furness Abbey
Gisborough Priory
Goodshaw Chapel
Helmsley Castle
Housesteads Roman Fort
Kirkham Priory
Lanercost Priory
Lindisfarne Priory
Middleham Castle
Mount Grace Priory
Norham Castle
Pickering Castle
Prudhoe Castle
Richmond Castle
Rievaulx Abbey
Roche Abbey
Scarborough Castle
Stott Park Bobbin Mill
St Paul's Monastery and Bede's World Museum
Tynemouth Priory and Castle
Warkworth Castle
Whitby Abbey

HANCOCK MUSEUM

Address: Barras Bridge, Newcastle upon Tyne
Tel: (0191) 222 7418

Description:
The North's premier natural history museum is the ideal location to find out everything you ever wanted to know about the Living Planet, exploring ecology, the water cycle, food chains, animal habitats, etc. The Land of the Pharaohs permanent display explores how the Ancient Egyptians once lived and the Earth Galleries reveal all you ever wanted to know about the Earth. There is also a programme of temporary exhibitions throughout the year.

Ages: All ages
Subjects: History; Science; Geography
Facilities: Classroom; free teachers' pre-visit; audiovisual facilities; indoor/outdoor eating areas; toilets; education packs; workshops; resource materials for hire; audio guides; shop; disabled access
Open: All year. Monday–Saturday, 10.00 am–5.00 pm. Sunday, 2.00 pm–5.00 pm
Admission: Group rates upon application
Group size: Upon application
Length of visit: Half day

KIELDER FOREST

Address: Kielder Castle Visitor Centre, Kielder, Hexham, Northumberland NE48 2BQ
Tel: (01434) 250209

Description:
A range of cross-curriculum lessons can be combined with outdoor activities, the study of wildlife and conservation, as these and other educational resources are available at Kielder Castle. Built in 1775 as a former hunting lodge, the Kielder Forest Visitor Centre is now the focal point for a visit to Europe's largest man-made forest.

Ages: 5+
Subjects: Outdoor Education; Geography
Facilities: Classroom; audiovisual facilities; guided tour; outdoor eating area; work pack; car park; toilets
Open: April–October
Admission: Special school rate £15.00 per visit. Higher Education £52.00 half day
Group size: Max 60
Length of visit: Up to 3 hours

KIELDER WATER CRUISES

Address: Tower Knowe Visitors Centre, Kielder Water, Falstone, Hexham NE48 1BX
Tel: (01434) 240398   Fax: (01434) 240060

Description:
There is a lot to both see and do at Kielder Water: an educational cruise around one of the largest lakes in Northern Europe accompanied by a commentary and quiz; a dam and hydro-electric tour; a water exhibition; and guided conservation and wildlife walks; full educational packages can be arranged to suit.
Ages: 5+
Subjects: Geography; Art; Science; Outdoor Activities
Facilities: Classroom; car park; free teachers' pre-visit; audiovisual facilities; talk; toilets; demonstrations; indoor/outdoor eating areas
Open: Easter–October
Admission: Children £2.20; teachers free
Group size: Max 60
Length of visit: 2 hours

MONKWEARMOUTH STATION MUSEUM

Address: North Bridge Street, Sunderland, Tyne & Wear
Tel: (0191) 565 0723

Description:
Find out what being a station master of a Victorian railway station was like at the turn of the century; see an authentic ticket office; stand on the platform and imagine how terrified the young evacuees must have felt when embarking upon their journey in World War II.
Ages: All ages
Subjects: History; English; Design & Technology; Science
Facilities: Teachers' packs; quiz sheets; workshops; special exhibitions; free teachers' pre-visit; eating area; shop; car park; play area; toilets
Open: Monday–Friday, 10.00 am–5.00 pm. Saturday, 10.00 am–4.30 pm. Sunday, 2.00 pm–5.00 pm. Open Bank Holidays
Admission: Free
Group size: Upon application
Length of visit: 1½ hours

NATIONAL TRUST PROPERTIES

The National Trust Northumbria Region covers Durham, Northumberland and Tyne and Wear and has quite a number of sites to visit. For further information

212

contact: National Trust Regional Office, Scots' Gap, Morpeth, Northumberland NE61 4EG (tel: 01670 774691).

Cragside House, Gardens and Grounds
The Farne Islands
Hadrian's Wall and Housesteads Fort
Souter Lighthouse and The Leas

THE OTTER TRUST NORTH PENNINES RESERVE

Address: Vale House Farm, nr Bowes, Barnard Castle, Co. Durham DH12 9RH
Tel: (01833) 628339

Description:
A 230-acre wildlife reserve is the ideal venue to study the importance of wildlife, conservation and habitat management using environmentally friendly farming methods. There are British otters, domestic livestock, red and fallow deer, Exmoor ponies and bird-watching hides.

Ages: 5+
Subjects: Science
Facilities: Classroom; guided tour; indoor/outdoor eating areas; shop; visitor centre; car park; toilets
Open: April–October
Admission: Children £1.50; teachers free
Group size: Max 100
Length of visit: 3 hours +

PAXTON HOUSE

Address: Paxton, Berwick-upon-Tweed, Northumberland TD15 1SZ
Tel: (01289) 386291   Fax: (01289) 386660

Description:
Built in 1758 for a princess, Paxton House, situated in the delightful Northumbrian countryside, has 80 acres of grounds to explore and also the most extensive art gallery with the finest examples of Chippendale furniture to be seen in the area.

Ages: 5+
Subjects: History; Art; Technology
Facilities: Work pack; disabled access; car park; classroom; free teachers' pre-visit; guided tour/talk; indoor/outdoor eating areas; toilets
Open: April–October
Admission: House and grounds: children £1.75; adults/teachers £3.00

Group size: N/A
Length of visit: 4 hours

THE RISING SUN COUNTRYSIDE CENTRE

Address: Whitley Road, Benton, Newcastle upon Tyne NE12 9SS
Tel: (0191) 200 7841   Fax: (0191) 200 7851

Description:
A 400-acre natural oasis is the ideal location for students to study the environment, conservation and nature, available at the Rising Sun Countryside Park in Tyne and Wear. There is a nature reserve, a countryside centre which plays host to many animals and birds throughout the year, and an organic farm where visitors can get involved in organic agriculture and learn about farm life.
Ages: All ages
Subjects: Science
Facilities: Education service; activity room; education handbook; organized activities; disabled access; workshops; play sculpture; willow maze; waterfall; car park; café; shop; outdoor eating area
Open: Park open all year. Centre and grounds times may vary
Admission: Free
Group size: Any number
Length of visit: Half–full day

SHIPLEY ART GALLERY

Address: Prince Consort Road, Gateshead, Tyne & Wear
Tel: (0191) 477 1495   Fax: (0191) 478 7917

Description:
One of the most extensive collections of contemporary craft in the north of England can be seen on display at the Shipley Art Gallery, where there is a permanent 'Made in Gateshead' exhibition following 300 years of local industry with hands-on exhibits. There is always a range of temporary exhibitions.
Ages: All ages
Subjects: History; Geography; English; Art; Technology
Facilities: Workshops; toilets; classroom; library; quiz sheets; guided tours; indoor eating areas; demonstrations; disabled access; shop
Open: Daily. Monday–Saturday, 10.00 am–5.00 pm. Sunday, 2.00 pm–5.00 pm. Open Bank Holidays
Admission: Free
Group size: Upon application
Length of visit: 1½ hours

SOUTH SHIELDS MUSEUM AND ART GALLERY

Address: Ocean Road, South Shields, Tyne & Wear
Tel: (0191) 456 8740   Fax: (0191) 456 7850

Description:
South Tyneside is steeped in history, much of which can be seen at the South Shields Museum and Art Gallery. The Catherine Cookson gallery celebrates the life and work of the famous author. Visitors can see a reconstruction of her house and even the kitchen of her childhood home. There is also a hands-on exhibition exploring the history of South Tyneside together with temporary exhibitions.

Ages: All ages
Subjects: History; English; Geography; Science; Art; Design & Technology
Facilities: Audiovisual facilities; activity worksheets; teachers' packs; resource loans; workshops; education room; shop; toilets; disabled access; refreshments
Open: Contact for opening times
Admission: Free
Group size: Max 70
Length of visit: 2 hours

ST MARY'S LIGHTHOUSE VISITOR CENTRE

Address: St Mary's Voluntary Marine Nature Reserve, St Mary's Island, Whitley Bay, Tyne & Wear NE26 4RS
Tel: (0191) 200 8650   Fax: (0191) 200 8654

Description:
A unique way to learn about nature and wildlife and many other National Curriculum subjects is to spend a day at St Mary's Lighthouse, which can only be reached via a causeway at low tide. Visitors can see exhibitions on wildlife and maritime themes; explore the rock pools and pond areas or there are always the 137 steps to climb to the top of the lighthouse. When not being visited the Island becomes a sanctuary for many birds and marine life. Remember to pack the wellingtons and warm clothing.

Ages: 5+
Subjects: Science; History; Art; Geography
Facilities: Free teachers' pre-visit; audiovisual facilities; guided tour; teachers' packs; worksheets; toilets; small cinema; various activities: rock pooling, scavenger hunts, fossil hunts, weathering; brass rubbings; classroom; shop; indoor/ outdoor eating areas
Open: Daily throughout the year
Admission: Wardened – half day (up to 2 hours): children £1.25 + VAT. Full day (up to 4 hours) children £1.75 + VAT. One teacher for every six children free, extra

£2.00 each. Un-wardened – children £1.00; adults/teachers £2.00. Groups of 15+ qualify for a 10 per cent discount. VAT is already included in these prices. For students aged 16+, a wardened half day costs £2.50 + VAT, a wardened full day (up to 4 hours) costs £3.00 + VAT. One teacher free for every 10 students. Un-wardened – students £1.00; adults/teachers £2.00

Group size: Max 80

Length of visit: 45 mins–1 hour

THE WILDFOWL AND WETLANDS TRUST

Address: District 15, Washington, Tyne & Wear NE38 8LE
Tel: (0191) 416 5454   Fax: (0191) 416 5801

Description:
Covering 102 acres, home to over 1,000 birds of 100 different species with a 70-acre wild reserve, Washington's Wildfowl and Wetlands Trust is one of the eight centres throughout the United Kingdom which offer a comprehensive educational programme covering conservation, wildlife and many other related aspects of environmental studies.

Ages: All ages

Subjects: Science; Art; Technology; History; Geography; English; Mathematics

Facilities: Free teachers' pre-visit; worksheets; indoor/outdoor eating areas; shop; disabled access; education officer; exhibitions; car park; resource packs; toilets

Open: All year. Summer, 9.30 am–5.30 pm. Winter, 9.30 am–4.30 pm. Closed 25 December

Admission: Education group rate £1.90

Group size: Upon application

Length of visit: Up to full day

14 Scotland

BLAIR CASTLE

Address: Blair Atholl, Pitlochry, Perthshire PH18 5TL
Tel: (01796) 481207   Fax: (01796) 481487

Description:
Home of the Dukes of Atholl and Scotland's most visited privately owned home for over 725 years, Blair Castle has many fine treasures depicting Scottish life from the 16th century to the present time. Among its collections in the 32 fully furnished rooms are valuable paintings, china, furniture, arms and armour and other treasures.
Ages: All ages
Subjects: History; Art
Facilities: Guided tour; guides; worksheets; special events; outdoor eating area; car park; parkland; deer park; highland cattle; nature trails; shop; guide/quiz book; toilets
Open: 1 April–30 October, 10.00 am–6.00 pm
Admission: Separate charges for grounds and castle. Group rates upon application
Group size: Max 200
Length of visit: Up to 2 hours

CALDERGLEN COUNTRY PARK

Address: Strathaven Road, East Kilbride G75 0QX
Tel: (01355) 236644

Description:
Find out the history of Calderglen and the surrounding area; step inside the conservatory with its fine collection of plants and animals from around the world. There are over 8 miles of nature trails, a children's zoo, monthly animal magic sessions, play areas, and throughout the year in the visitor centre there is a history room staging a wildlife experience entitled 'Hidden Worlds'.
Ages: All ages

Subjects: Science; History

Facilities: Ranger service; animal handling sessions; disabled access; refreshments; ornamental garden; audiovisual facilities; shop; gallery

Open: Country park open all year. Conservatory: April–September, daily, 10.00 am–8.30 pm; October–March, daily, 10.00 am–4.30 pm. Visitor Centre: summer Monday–Friday from 10.30 am–5.00 pm; Saturday, Sunday and Public Holidays, 11.30 am–6.30 pm. Winter: Monday–Sunday, 11.30 am–4.00 pm

Admission: Free

Group size: N/A

Length of visit: 2–3 hours

CAMERA OBSCURA

Address: Castlehill Royal Mile, Edinburgh EH1 2LZ

Tel: (0131) 226 3709   Fax: (0131) 225 4239

Description:

Experience the wonders of science as you step into the rooftop chamber of the 17th-century tenement tower and see moving images of Edinburgh projected onto a viewing table through a huge periscope. See the UK's only permanent gallery dedicated to the art and science of holography; examples of the earliest type of cameras made from biscuit tins. There are also detailed paintings and photographs of day-to-day life in the city between 1780 and 1900.

Ages: All ages

Subjects: History; Art; Science

Facilities: Shop; free teachers' pre-visit; exhibitions

Open: 7 days a week. April–June: Monday–Friday, 9.30 am–6.00 pm; Saturday–Sunday, 10.00 am–6.00 pm. July–August: Monday–Sunday, 9.30 am–7.00 pm or later. September–October: Monday–Friday, 9.30 am–6.00 pm; Saturday–Sunday, 10.00 am–6.00 pm. November–March: Monday–Sunday, 10.00 am–5.00 pm

Admission: Group rates upon application. One adult free for every 10 children

Group size: Min 10; max 70

Length of visit: 45 minutes–1 hour

CHATELHERAULT

Address: Chatelherault Heritage and Countryside, Carlisle Road, Ferniegair, Hamilton ML3 7UE

Tel: (01698) 426213   Fax: (01698) 421532

Description:

Once a hunting lodge and summer house for the Dukes of Hamilton, Chatelherault, built 250 years ago, is now a museum and country park, with the kennels transformed into a modern museum containing exhibitions on the area's history and wildlife. Walks and various activities are organized by the ranger service with the aim of helping to increase awareness of the varied scope of wildlife found in the park.

Ages: All ages

Subjects: History

Facilities: Interactive exhibitions; visitor centre; nature trails; exhibition gallery; adventure playground; car park; woodland/guided walks; disabled access limited; activity sheets; shop; outdoor eating area; rare white cattle; gardens; café

Open: Visitor centre: All year. Monday–Saturday, 10.00 am–5.00 pm; Sunday, 12 noon–5.00 pm. House: Monday–Thursday, 10.00 am–4.30 pm; Saturday, 10.00 am–4.30 pm; Sunday, 12 noon–4.30 pm. Closed Fridays

Admission: Group rates upon application

Group size: Upon application

Length of visit: Up to 3 hours

DISCOVERY POINT

Address: c/o Dundee Heritage Trust, Discovery Quay, Dundee DD1 4XA
   Tel: (01382) 201245   Fax: (01382) 225891

Description:

Discovery Point, home of Scott of the Antarctic's famous research ship *Discovery*, transports visitors on the epic journey to the Antarctic in 1901, where they can find out about the amazing discoveries revealed by Ferrar, Bernacchi, Hodgson and Wilson. The highlight of the visit is stepping on board the *RRS Discovery*.

Ages: All ages

Subjects: History; Technology

Facilities: Film show; exhibitions; shop; café; play area; classroom; indoor eating area; education pack; drama workshops; activity sessions; education officer

Open: 7 days a week: 10.00 am–5.00 pm (11.00 am Sunday) April–October; 10.00 am–4.00 pm (11.00 am Sunday) November–March. Closed 25 December and 1–2 January

Admission: Children £2.75. One adult free for every 10 pupils. Additional adults will be charged the group discount rate of £4.00 each

Group size: Max 100

Length of visit: Without activities – 1 hour

EDINBURGH BUTTERFLY AND INSECT WORLD

Address: Dobbies Garden World, Melville Nursery, Lasswade, Midlothian EH18 1AZ
Tel: (0131) 663 4932   Fax: (0131) 654 2548

Description:
Enter a fascinating world at the Edinburgh Butterfly and Insect World, where hundreds of exotic butterflies are flying free in the indoor tropical rainforests. There are koi carp fish swimming in the ponds; the opportunity to see scorpions, tarantulas, leaf-cutting ants and other insects; even a honeybee display where you are free to observe close up the amazing life of this everyday insect through glass-fronted hives.

Ages: All ages

Subjects: Science

Facilities: Exhibitions; handling sessions; outdoor/indoor eating areas; car park; children's playground; education pack; talks/guided tours; disabled access; shop; toilets

Open: 7 days a week. Summer, 9.30 am–5.30 pm. Winter, 10.00 am–5.00 pm. Closed 25–26 December and 1–2 January

Admission: Group rates upon application

Group size: Min 10

Length of visit: 2 hours

FRIGATE UNICORN

Address: c/o Dundee Heritage Trust, Discovery Point, Discovery Quay, Dundee DD1 4XA
Tel: (01382) 201245   Fax: (01382) 225891

Description:
The oldest British-built warship still afloat provides the ideal opportunity for pupils to learn about the developments in ship building which were taking place during the early 19th century and to find out what life aboard a frigate was really like.

Ages: All ages

Subjects: History

Facilities: Artefact handling sessions, drama workshops and activity sessions can all be tailored to individual needs by the education officer; education pack currently being written

Open: Upon application

Admission: Group rates upon application

Group size: Upon application

Length of visit: Up to 1 hour

GLAMIS CASTLE

Address: The Castle Administrator, Estates Office, Glamis, Forfar, Angus DD8 1RJ
Tel: (01307) 840393   Fax: (01307) 840733

Description:
Home to the Earls of Strathmore and Kinghorne, a royal residence since 1372, Glamis Castle is steeped in history: the childhood home of Her Majesty The Queen Mother, birthplace of Her Royal Highness Princess Margaret and also the legendary setting of the famous Shakespearean play *Macbeth*.

Ages: All ages

Subjects: History; Art

Facilities: Exhibitions; guided tours; Italian garden and nature trail; restaurant; shops; car park; outdoor eating area; play park; disabled access; guide books; education packs; free teachers' pre-visit; toilets

Open: Check for opening times. Special visits can be pre-arranged

Admission: Group rates upon application. One teacher free for every 10 children

Group size: Max 40

Length of visit: 50–60 minutes

HISTORIC SITES IN SCOTLAND

There are over 300 sites in the care of Historic Scotland, which together cover over 5,000 years of Scottish history. Among its many attractions are castles, fortresses, tower houses, abbeys, tombs and other religious buildings, together with some beautiful gardens and notable buildings of historic interest. For further information contact Historic Scotland, Longmore House, Salisbury Place, Edinburgh EH9 1SH (tel: 0131 668 8800).

HUNTER HOUSE

Address: Maxwellton Road, East Kilbride G74 3LW
Tel: (01355) 261261

Description:
Visit the home of brothers John and William Hunter, born and bred in East Kilbride and whose contributions to the medical world were of great importance. Combining the past and present, interactive displays provide a fascinating insight into medicines with two CD ROM terminals enabling you to explore the human body.

Ages: All ages

Subjects: Science

Facilities: Seminar room; refreshment area; soft play area; car park; disabled access; shop; toilets

Open: Contact for opening times
Admission: Group rates upon application
Group size: Upon application
Length of visit: Up to 1 hour

MUSEUM OF CHILDHOOD

Address: 42 High Street, Royal Mile, Edinburgh EH1 1TG
   Tel: (0131) 529 4142   Fax: (0131) 558 3103

Description:
   A museum said to be the noisiest in the world devoted to the history of childhood is an enchanting and delightful place to visit. There are five galleries of displays located on four floors, exhibiting an assortment of dolls, trains, models, games and books.
Ages: All ages
Subjects: History
Facilities: Shop; disabled access (most floors accessible apart from Galleries 4–5)
Open: Monday–Saturday, 10.00 am–5.00 pm. During the Edinburgh International Festival Sundays, 2.00 pm–5.00 pm
Admission: Free
Group size: If bringing more than 10 pupils please advise before arrival
Length of visit: 2 hours

THE NATIONAL BIBLE SOCIETY OF SCOTLAND

Address: 7 Hampton Terrace, Edinburgh EH12 5XU
   Tel: (0131) 337 9701   Fax: (0131) 337 0641

Description:
   In 1991 Bibleworld was launched, bringing the story of the Bible to life for today's youth in an exciting innovative way. In 1996 the National Bible Society of Scotland launched Bibleworld II, a mobile version of its former learning method but on this occasion inside a converted lorry decked out to resemble a time capsule. With the help of Commander Hope, a million megahertz robot, and the crew, amazing revelations are uncovered about the Bible. The mobile van is available to all schools beyond 1½ drive from Edinburgh.
Ages: 5+
Subjects: R.E.; English; History
Facilities at Bibleworld: Preview video; souvenirs; artefacts; computer games; free teachers' follow-up pack
Open: Monday–Friday
Admission: Pupils £1.50
Group size: Min 24; max 36

Length of visit: 2 hours
Facilities at Bibleworld II: Video guide
Admission: Children £1.50
Group size: Min 16; max 32
Length of visit: 80 minutes

NATIONAL TRUST PROPERTIES

The National Trust has a number of places to visit in Scotland which are ideal for educational day visits and have over 185,000 acres of countryside in their care – farmland, forest, mountain and moor, waterfalls and islands as well as cliffs, rugged coastlines and delightful gardens. For further information about the following locations contact The National Trust For Scotland, 5 Charlotte Square Edinburgh EH2 4DU (tel: 0131 226 5922).

Islands – Canna, St Kilda, Staffa, Mull, Iona
Alloa Tower
Angus Folk Museum
Arduaine Garden
Bachelors' Club
Balmacara Estate and Lochalsh Woodland Garden
Bannockburn
Barrie's Birthplace
Barry Mill
Branklyn Garden
Brodick Castle, Garden and Country Park
Brodie Castle
Broughton House and Garden
Carlyle's Birthplace
Castle Fraser and Garden
Crathes Castle and Garden
Culloden
Culross
Culzean Castle and Country Park
Drum Castle and Garden
Dunkeld
Falkland Palace
Fyvie Castle
The Georgian House
Gladstone's Land
Glencoe
Glenfinnan Monument

Greenbank Garden
Haddo House
Hill of Tarvit Mansionhouse and Garden
House of the Binns
Hugh Miller's Cottage
Hutchesons' Hall
Inveresk Lodge Garden
Inverewe Garden
Kellie Castle and Garden
Killiecrankie
Kintail and West Affric
Leith Hall and Garden
Malleny Garden
Pitmedden Garden
Preston Mill and Phantassie Doocot
Priorwood Garden and Dried Flower Shop
Provost Ross's House
Robert Smail's Printing Works
Souter Johnnie's Cottage
St Abb's Head
The Tenement House
Threave Garden and Estate
Torridon
Weaver's Cottage

ROYAL OBSERVATORY VISITOR CENTRE

Address: Blackford Hill, Edinburgh EH9 3HT
Tel: (0131) 668 8045

Description:
Explore the universe, find out about space and astronomy in the computer gallery using the latest CD ROMs. Discover all about light and lenses in the Discovery Zone and see one of the largest telescopes in Scotland.

Ages: All ages
Subjects: Science
Facilities: Temporary exhibitions; shop; teachers' pack; worksheets
Open: Monday–Saturday, 10.00 am–5.00 pm. Sunday, 12 noon–5.00 pm
Admission: Children £2.00; adults/teachers £2.50. One adult admitted free for every 10 children
Group size: Min 10; max 50
Length of visit: 2 hours

TRAQUAIR HOUSE

Address: Innerleithen, Peebleshire EH44 6PW

Tel: (01896) 830323/831370   Fax: (01896) 830639

Description:

The oldest continually inhabited house in Scotland, having many associations with Mary, Queen of Scots and the Jacobites; once a refuge for Catholic priests in times of terror. A visit to the house enables visitors to relive a bit of history, explore the spooky cellars deep beneath the vaults, follow the secret staircase and browse the art gallery.

Ages: All ages

Subjects: History; Art; R.E.

Facilities: Guided tours (charge); exhibitions; refreshments; craft workshops; shop; woodland walks; maze

Open: Daily, 11 April–30 September. October: Fridays–Sundays only, 12.30 pm–5.30 pm. June, July and August, 10.30 am–5.30 pm

Admission: Group rates (minimum of 20 people). Children: house and grounds £1.80. Adults: house and grounds £3.50. One free adult for every 20 paying children.

Group size: Min 20; max 50

Length of visit: 1 hour

15 Northern Ireland

ARMAGH COUNTY MUSEUM

Address: The Mall East, Armagh, Co. Armagh BT61 9BE
Tel: (01861) 523070   Fax: (01861) 522631

Description:
The oldest museum in Ireland with collections based on specimens gathered by the Armagh Natural History and Philosophical Society during the 19th century reveals the rich and varied history of the county. Displays range from prehistoric artefacts to more recent materials.

Age: All ages

Subjects: Useful for Key Stages 1–2 pupils looking at History of Toys, Life In Early Times, Life In Recent Past, Victorian School Days

Facilities: Shop; disabled access (limited); exhibitions; workshops

Open: Monday–Friday, 10.00 am–5.00 pm. Saturday, 10.00 am–1.00 pm and 2.00 pm– 5.00 pm. Sundays closed

Admission: Free

Group size: Upon application

Length of visit: 1¼ hours each topic

ARMAGH PLANETARIUM

Address: College Hill, Armagh, Co. Armagh NT61 9DB
Tel: (01861) 523689   Fax: (01861) 524725

Description:
Fascinating exploration of the universe with hands-on computers in the Hall of Astronomy. There are astronomical instruments on display and outside the Astropark features a model solar system and the Eartharium displays a global view of the Earth and its place in the universe.

Age: All ages

Subjects: Science
Facilities: Shop; café; disabled access (limited); theatre shows
Open: Monday–Friday, 11.30 am–5.00 pm. Saturday–Sunday, 1.30 pm–5.00 pm.
Extra shows throughout the year – contact for further information
Admission: Contact for charges
Group size: N/A
Length of visit: 2½ hours

BELFAST ZOO

Address: Antrim Road, Belfast BT36 7PN
Tel: (01232) 776277   Fax: (01232) 370578

Description:
There are lots of animals to see at Belfast Zoo: chimpanzees, gorillas, marmosets, spectacled bears, manned wolves and red pandas, as well as a walk-through free flight aviary. Specific topics can be catered for and whenever possible there are guided tours available.
Ages: 5+
Subjects: Science; Geography
Facilities: Toilets; car park; shop; schoolroom; playground; alpine garden; rose garden; worksheets and teachers' packs; restaurant; teahouse
Open: 1 April–30 September, 10.00 am–5.00 pm. 1 October–31 March, 10.00 am–3.30 pm
Admission/Group size: Summer (from 1 April): adults £4.90; children £2.45. Family Day: two children and two adults £13.50. Schools £2.20 per child; every 10 children paying, 1 adult goes free. Groups of over 25 people, adults £3.80, children £2.20. Groups of over 250 people, 30 per cent discount. Winter (from 1 October): adults £3.70; children £1.85. Family Day: two children and two adults £10.00. Schools £1.50 per child; every 10 children paying, 1 adult goes free. Upper limit of 30
Length of visit: Half day

BELLEEK POTTERY VISITOR CENTRE

Address: Belleek, Co. Fermanagh BT93 3FY
Tel: (01365) 658501   Fax: (01365) 658625

Description:
One of the most popular tourist attractions in Northern Ireland, a tour around the Pottery Centre transports you back in time to see the methods originally adopted by the Belleek craftspeople to create the finest craftsmanship, and which are still followed today
Ages: All ages

Subjects: Art; History
Facilities: Car park; toilets; disabled access; restaurant; guided tours; museum; video presentation
Open: School tours: 1 October–31 March, Monday–Friday, 9.30 am–12.15 pm and 2.15 pm–4.15 pm. The last tour is at 3.15 pm
Admission: £1.00 per person
Group size: N/A
Length of visit: Tour lasts 25 minutes; video presentation lasts 20 minutes

CARRICKFERGUS CASTLE

Address: Marine Highway, Carrickfergus, Co. Antrim BT38 7BG
Tel: (01960) 365190   Fax: (01960) 365190

Description:
Built in 1180 by John de Courcy, this is the most complete ancient castle in Northern Ireland together with a keep, gate-house, portcullis and chapel. There are exhibitions throughout the castle, with life-size models and themed displays.
Ages: All ages
Subjects: History. Day in the Life of a Medieval Castle package suitable for projects on Defences through the Ages
Facilities: Toilets; car park; audiovisual theatre; visitors' centre; disabled access limited
Open: 1 April–30 October: Monday–Saturday, 10.00 am–6.00 pm; April, May, September and October, Sunday, 2.00 pm–6.00 pm; June, July and August, Sunday, 11.00 am–8.00 pm. 1 November–31 March: Monday–Saturday, 10.00 am–4.00 pm; Sunday, 2.00 pm–4.00 pm
Admission: Free
Group size: 60–80, depending on numbers of tour guides available
Length of visit: 1–1½ hours

DOWN COUNTY MUSUEM

Address: The Mall, Downpatrick, Co. Down BT30 6AH.
Tel: (01396) 615218   Fax: (01396) 615590

Description:
Located in the restored buildings of the previous Down County Gaol, the museum holds exhibitions on the social, human and natural history of County Down from earliest times to the present and is the most complete surviving Irish gaol of its time.
Ages: All ages
Subjects: History; Art and Design; Cultural Heritage; English; Geography; R.E.; Technology

Facilities: Free teachers' pre-visit; shop; guided tour; classroom; disabled access limited; indoor eating area; art exhibitions; worksheets; in service training

Open: Tuesday–Friday, 11.00 am–5.00 pm. Saturdays, 2.00 pm–5.00 pm throughout most of the year. Monday–Friday, 11.00 am–5.00 pm, Saturdays and Sundays, 2.00 pm–5.00 pm, June–August

Admission: General visits free. £1.00–£1.50 per pupil for special focus visits; £1.50 per pupil for guided tours; teachers' sessions free

Group size: N/A

Length of visit: Up to 2 hours

ENVIRONMENT AND HERITAGE SERVICE

There are a number of listed monuments in state care in and around Northern Ireland which would combine with making an educational day out for pupils of all ages. Many of these provide guided tours. For further information about these places contract: Environment and Heritage Service, 5–33 Hill Street, Belfast, BT1 2LA (tel: 01232 235000; fax: 01232 543111).

Co. Antrim
Dunluce Castle
Romantic ruins of the largest and most sophisticated castle in Northern Ireland situated on a prominent position.

Co. Fermanagh
White Island Monastic Site
Seven stone figures. Can be reached by ferry from Castle Archdale Marina.
Tully Castle
Built in 1613 by Scottish planter Sir John Hume, the castle was only lived in for 30 years before it was burnt down and everyone killed. For 350 years it lay in a state of decay until work began on clearing it in the 1970s. Is now a much-visited site.
Devenish Monastic Site
Said to be a little bit of heaven on earth, this is the site of Lough Erne's most important monastery. One of the island's most notable features is the 30-metre-tall rounded tower from which the bells for prayers were rung.

Co. Down
Ballycopeland Windmill
Late 18th-century tower mill, one of the only two working in the country. There is a visitor centre at the miller's house with an electrically operated model of the mill, hands-on experience of milling, computers and films.
Nendrum Monastery
Ruins of a pre-Norman monastery together with a small museum.

Grey Abbey
Founded in 1193 by Affrecxa, daughter of the King of Man and wife of John de Courcy, a knight from Somerset, this is the extensive remains of a Cistercian Abbey, which was colonized by monks from Holm Cultural in Cumbria.

Hillsborough Fort
An artillery fort built in 1650 by Colonel Arthur Huill and later remodelled in the 18th century for banquets and parties.

Kilclief Castle
Oldest surviving tower house in Co. Down.

Inch Abbey
The remains of a Cistercian monastery on the island of Quoile Marshes, which can be reached by a causeway.

Dundrum Castle
An outstanding Norman castle, one of the finest in Northern Ireland, which was built by John de Courcy in the 12th century.

Narrow Water Castle
Located on a river bend promontory downstream from Carlingford Lough, this fine tower house dates back to 1560.

Greencastle
A royal 13th-century castle, it once protected the entrance to Carlingford Lough and was besieged by Edward Bruce in 1316.

Jordan's Castle
A well-maintained four-storey tower house, the largest of a cluster of castles built in Ardglass in the Middle Ages to protect the port.

FORD FARM PARK AND MUSEUM

Address: 8 Low Road, Islandmagee, Co. Antrim BT40 3RD
Tel: (01960) 353264

Description:
Located in a former farm outhouse, this small country museum houses a selection of farming implements, fishing pots and lobster pots. There is also a collection of farm animals, and butter-making and spinning demonstrations are available on request, with wool from the sheep farm being used. There are also pleasant walks around the area.

Ages: All ages
Subjects: Science
Facilities: Disabled access on ground floor
Open: March–October, daily, 2.00 pm–6.00 pm
Admission: Children £1.75; adults £1.75
Group size: N/A
Length of visit: Half day

GIANT'S CAUSEWAY

Address: Causeway Centre, 42 Causeway Road, Bushmills, Co. Antrim BT57 8SU
Tel: (01265) 731855

Description:
An amazing place to visit, Ireland's first World Heritage Site. There are coast and cliff paths and unusual rock formations form a wealth of local and natural history. The wreck site of the Armada Treasure ship *Gorona* lies east of the Giant's Causeway, at Port-na-Spaniagh. There are waymarked walks and guided walks available. The visitors' centre provides an interpretive exhibition and a 25-minute audiovisual show of the flora and fauna around the area. Also, an exhibit of a replica of the hydro-electric tram which ran until 1949 between Portrush and the Causeway.

Ages: All ages

Subjects: Geography; History; Geology; Science; Biology

Facilities: Shop; tearoom (open March–October); disabled access limited; minibus available from visitor centre to the Giant's Causeway; guided walks; audiovisual theatre

Open: Apply to the visitors' centre regarding opening times. The Giant's Causeway is open at all times

Admission/Group size: Contact for details

Length of visit: Half day or more

IRISH LINEN CENTRE AND LISBURN MUSEUM

Address: Market Square, Lisburn, Co. Antrim BT28 1AG.
Tel: (01846) 663377   Fax: (01846) 672624

Description:
Irish linen is known and respected throughout the world for its sheer quality and elegance, and here at the museum, established for the study of the linen industry and to understand its heritage, there is the opportunity to learn how linen cotton was made from flax and to watch the experts spinning and weaving. Step inside the spinner's cottage, see the mill girls of Victorian times and hear them talk about their lives. And through displays and exhibitions learn all about the cultural heritage of the Lagan valley and its important role in the history of Irish linen.

Ages: All ages

Subjects: English; Mathematics; Science; Technology; Art; Music; History; Geography; Drama; Language Skills

Facilities: Free teachers' pre-visit; restaurant; café; shop; car park; toilets; disabled access; exhibitions; workshops; demonstrations; interactive displays; work-sheets; Braille synopsis of the Flax to Fabric exhibition available on request; there is a loop system in the audiovisual show in the basement

Open: April–September: Monday–Saturday, 9.30 am–5.30 pm; Sunday, 2.00 pm–
   5.30 pm. October–March: 9.30 am–5.00 pm; closed on Sunday
Admission: Adults £2.75; young people under 17 years £1.75. Group rates during
   normal opening hours: adults £2.25; young people under 17 years £1.25
Group size: N/A
Length of visit: 2 hours

KNIGHT RIDE AND HERITAGE PLAZA

Address: Antrim Street, Carrickfergus, Co. Antrim BT38 7DG
   Tel: (01960) 366455   Fax: (01960) 350350

Description:
   History is really brought to life as the Knight Ride, the only monorail themed ride
   in Ireland, transports passengers in a special car on a tour and whisks them away
   back through over 800 years of Carrickfergus history. First pass through sailing
   ships and shoals of fish, hearing about Carrickerfergus' maritime past, before you
   descend on to the Dark Ride, where history is truly recreated in a mind-spinning
   charade of life from the past: a market scene; the landing of William of Orange
   and a haunted house.
Ages: All ages
Subjects: History
Facilities: Shop; disabled access
Open: 1 April–September: Monday–Saturday, 10.00 am–6.00 pm; Sunday, 12
   noon–6.00 pm. June–September: Monday–Friday, 10.00 am–1.00 pm and 2.00
   pm–6.00 pm; Saturday–Sunday, 2.00 pm–6.00 pm. 1 October–31 March:
   Monday–Saturday, 10.00 am–5.00 pm; Sunday, 12 noon–5.00 pm
Admission: Child £1.15; child + worksheet £1.25; teachers free
Group size: N/A
Length of visit: 2 hours

MARBLE ARCH CAVES

Address: Marlbank Scenic Loop, Florencecourt, Co. Fermanagh, BT92 1EW
   Tel: (01365) 348855   Fax: (01365) 348928

Description:
   A fascinating world will be unveiled in an underground boat trip past stalactites
   and stalagmites, past winding passages and lofty caverns with a guided tour of
   limestone formations.
Ages: 5+
Subjects: Geography

Facilities: Car parking; shop; toilets; café; audiovisual facilities; exhibitions; disabled access; boat trip lasts 10 minutes; guided tour lasts 1¼ hours
Open: Daily mid-March–September (weather permitting) from 10.00 am
Admission/Group size: Contact for details
Length of visit: 2 hours

THE NAVAN CENTRE

Address: Naval at Armagh, Killylea Road, Armagh, Co. Armagh BT60 4LD
   Tel: (01861) 525550   Fax: (01861) 522323

Description:
   Located within a specially constructed building, which blends in with the surrounding countryside, the Navan Centre provides the visitor with a multi-faceted understanding of the ancient seat of Ulster's kings. The exhibition explores the history, mythology and archaeology of the ancient capital of Ulster. Visitors can empathize with people in the past, and develop an interest in Celtic rituals and beliefs.
Ages: All ages
Subjects: Geography; English; Drama; EMU; Cultural Heritage; History
Facilities: Toilets; car parking; disabled access; restaurant; packed lunch/picnic facilities; classroom; guided tour; audiovisual facilities; interactive exhibition; translation tapes of audiovisual available in French, German, Italian and Spanish.
Open: Monday–Saturday, 10.00 am–5.00 pm; Sunday, 11.30 am–4.30 pm (will open earlier for school visits provided pre-booked)
Admission: Primary and secondary schools and further education colleges £1.80 per pupil. Undergraduates, postgraduates £2.50 per student
Group size: N/A
Length of visit: Tour of exhibition 1 hour 15 minutes; tour of the site 45 minutes

SPRINGHILL

Address: Moneymore, Co. Londonderry BT45 7NQ
   Tel: (01648) 748210

Description:
   Built and occupied by the Conynghams until it was acquired by the National Trust in 1959, Springhill, an elegant 17th-century manor house, was the home of 10 generations of the family, who came from Ayrshire, and still has many portraits, furniture and family belongings. The house is set amidst delightful woodland and some of the trees are remains of the ancient Forest of Ulster.
Ages: 5+
Subjects: Contact for details

Facilities: Car parking; tearoom; disabled access limited; toilets; picnic area; costume museum

Open: Daily, 2.00 pm–6.00 pm April–June and September. Weekends and Bank Holidays, 2.00 pm–6.00 pm. July–August daily, 2.00 pm–6.00 pm (ex Thursday)

Admission: Contact for school rates

Group size: N/A

Length of visit: 1–2 hours

ST PATRICK'S TRAIN VISITOR CENTRE

Address: English Street, Armagh, Co. Armagh, BT61 7BA
Tel: (01861) 527808

Description:

The Armagh Story is revealed at the interpretative centre and also the fascinating Land of Lilliput (adaptation of Jonathan Swift's *Gulliver's Travels*). There are temporary exhibitions on St Patrick's confessions together with the historic Armagh battles.

Ages: All ages

Subjects: History; English

Facilities: Toilets; car parking; disabled access; shop; restaurant

Open: Monday–Saturday, 10.00 am–5.00 pm; Sunday, 2.00 pm–5.00 pm. July–August: Monday–Saturday until 5.30 pm; Sunday, 1.00 pm–6.00 pm

Admission/Group size: Contact for details

Length of visit: 1¼ hours

THE ULSTER AMERICAN FOLK PARK

Address: Mellon Road, Castletown, Omagh, Co. Tyrone BT78 5QY
Tel: (01662) 243292   Fax: (01662) 242241

Description:

Five miles north of Omagh lies the Ulster American Folk Park, an outdoor museum that reveals the story of the emigrant's life and experiences on both sides of the Atlantic in the 18th and 19th centuries. Inside the fully furnished buildings there are costumed demonstrators, a ship and dockside gallery plus a full-size reconstruction of an early 19th-century sailing ship which transported thousands of emigrants across the Atlantic Ocean, and an indoor exhibition entitled 'Emigrants' which complements the outdoor exhibition buildings.

Ages: 7+

Subjects: History; P.E. (Dance); EMU; Home Economics; Technology; Cultural Heritage

Facilities: Free teachers' pre-visit; car park; outdoor/indoor eating areas; shop; toilets; disabled access; special focused themed visits; in-service courses; residential-based programmes; general guided tours; craft workshops; exhibitions; audiovisual facilities; library; work/activity booklets; teachers' guide

Open: 1 September–31 March, 10.30 am–5.00 pm daily. Closed weekends and public holidays October–March
Admission/Group size: Contact for details
Length of visit: Up to full day

THE ULSTER HISTORY PARK

Address: Cullion, Omagh, Co. Tyrone BT79 7SU
Tel: (016626) 48188   Fax: (016626) 48011

Description:
Situated on a 35-acre site, the Ulster History Park transports visitors back in time to reveal how people lived and survived through 10,000 years of settlement, with full-scale models of homes recreated from authentic materials, based on extensive archaeological and historical research. There is an indoor exhibition gallery accommodating a display of models and artefacts, which demonstrate the theme of settlement and everyday life in the past.

Ages: All ages
Subjects: History; Art; Home Economics; Design and Technology; Environmental Studies; Leisure & Tourism
Facilities: Car parking; picnic area; café; shop; resource room; toilets; room available for lunch; disabled access; theme visits; workshops; general guided tours; exhibitions; audiovisual presentation; residential courses; special events throughout the year
Open: October–March: Monday–Friday, 10.30 am–5.00 pm. April–September: Monday–Saturday, 10.30 am–6.30 pm; Sunday, 11.30 am–7.00 pm; Public Holidays, 10.30 am–7.00 pm
Admission: General tour £1.70 per pupil. Workshop activities/environmental studies £1.95 per pupil including materials. Teachers and classroom assistants free
Group size: N/A
Length of visit: Up to full day

PART 3
SUBJECT-BY-SUBJECT LISTING, BY REGION

16 Subject-by-subject listing, by region

Beachy Head Countryside Centre
Beckonscot Model Village
Bentley Wildfowl and Motor Museum
The Bethnal Green Museum of Childhood
Bexhill Museum
Bexhill Museum of Costume and Social History
Blenheim Palace
Bodiam Castle
Booth Museum of Natural History
Brighton Museum and Art Gallery
The British Museum
Brooklands Museum
Buckleys Yesterday's World
Canterbury Roman Museum
Chelsea Physic Garden
The *Cutty Sark*
Dover Castle
Drusillas Park
Fishbourne Roman Palace
Foredown Tower Visitor's Centre and Camera Obscura
Geffrye Museum
Hampton Court Palace
Hastings Museum and Art Gallery
The Historic Dockyard
Imperial War Museum
Leeds Castle
Paultons Park
Penhurst Place and Gardens
The Royal Pavilion
RSPB Nature Reserve at Dungeness
Shipwreck Heritage Centre
The Shuttleworth Collection
Verulamium Museum
Victoria and Albert Museum
The Weald and Downland Museum
Woburn Abbey

Wales

Anglesey Sea Zoo
Bodelwyddan Castle
Cardiff Castle

Dan-yr-ogof Showcaves
King Arthur's Labyrinth
National Museum and Gallery
Rhyl Sea Life Centre
Turner House Gallery

The Midlands

The Aerospace Museum
Chatsworth
Drayton Manor Theme Park
Harvington Hall
The Ironbridge Gorge Museums Trusts
Museum of Advertising and Packaging
The National Waterways Museum
Rockingham Castle
The Shugborough Estate
Twycross Zoo
Walsall Leather Museum

East Anglia

Anglesey Abbey and Gardens
Bressingham Steam Museum Trust and Gardens
British Birds of Prey and Conservation Centre
Burghley House
Caithness Crystal
Christchurch Mansion and Wolsey Art Gallery
Easton Farm Park
Elton Hall
Ely Cathedral
Fitzwilliam Museum
Gainsborough's House
Lincoln Castle
Manor House Museum
Museum of East Anglian Life
National Horse-racing Museum
Natureland Seal Sanctuary
Norwich Castle Museum
Norwich Cathedral
Pensthorpe Waterfowl Park
Thetford Forest Park

The Thursford Collection
Wingfield Old College and Gardens

The North West

Bolton Museum, Art Gallery and Aquarium
Chester Zoo
The Conservation Centre
Hall I'th 'Wood
Jodrell Bank, Science Centre and Arboretum
Lancashire Mining Museum
Mirehouse
Muncaster Castle, Gardens and Owl Centre
The Museum of Science and Industry in Manchester
Ordsall Hall Museum
Salford Museum and Art Gallery

Yorkshire

Allerton Park
Archaeological Resource Centre
Bankfield Museum
Bolton Abbey Estate
Brontë Parsonage Museum
Calderdale Industrial Museum
Castle Howard
Cleethorpes Humber Estuary Discovery Centre
The Colour Museum
Deep Sea Experience Centre
Duncombe Park
Eden Camp Modern History Theme Museum
Eureka! The Museum for Children
Harewood House
Jorvik Viking Centre
Lightwater Valley Country Theme Park
National Fishing Heritage Centre
National Railway Museum
Piece Hall Art Gallery
Royal Armouries
Skipton Castle
St Leonard's Farm Park
York Boat Guided River Trips

The North East

Alnwick Castle
Beamish, the North of England Open Air Museum
Discovery Museum
Kielder Water Cruises
Paxton House
Shipley Art Gallery
South Shields Museum and Art Gallery
St Mary's Lighthouse Visitor Centre
The Wildfowl and Wetlands Trust

Scotland

Blair Castle
Camera Obscura
Glamis Castle
Traquair House

Northern Ireland

Belleek Pottery Visitor Centre
Irish Linen Centre and Lisburn Museum
The Ulster History Park

Architecture

The Midlands

Ludlow Castle

Archaeology

The North East

Bede's World Museum

Art and Design

Northern Ireland

Down County Museum

CDT and Art

London and the South East

The Royal Marines Museum

Design & Technology

The South West

The American Museum in Britain
Bristol Zoo Gardens
Dairyland Farm World
Dingle Steam Village
Fleet Air Arm Museum
Longleat
Poole Pottery
The Tutankhamun Exhibition
Wells Cathedral

London and the South East

Basingstoke Canal
Bentley Wildfowl and Motor Museum
The Bethnal Green Museum of Childhood
Booth Museum of Natural History
The British Museum
Canterbury Roman Museum
The Canterbury Tales Visitor Attraction
The *Cutty Sark*
Drusillas Park
Geffrye Museum
Herstmonceux Science Centre
Howletts and Port Lympne Wild Animal Park
Legoland Windsor
The Weald and Downland Museum

Wales

Bodelwyddan Castle
Centre for Alternative Technology
Dan-yr-ogof Showcaves
Museum of the Welsh Woollen Industry
Rhyl Sea Life Centre

The Midlands

Cadbury World
Drayton Manor Theme Park
The Ironbridge Gorge Museum Trusts
Walsall Leather Museum

East Anglia

The Long Shop Museum
Museum of East Anglian Life

The North West

The Beacon
Chester Zoo
Granada Studios Tour
Hall I'th 'Wood
Jodrell Bank, Science Centre and Arboretum
Lancashire Mining Museum
The Museum of Science and Industry in Manchester
North West Water Ltd
Ordsall Hall Museum
Salford Museum and Art Gallery

Yorkshire

Bolton Abbey Estate
Bradford Industrial and Horses At Work Museum
Duncombe Park
Lightwater Valley Country Theme Park
National Railway Museum
York Boat Guided River Trips

The North East

Arbeia Roman Fort
Beamish, the North of England Open Air Museum
Monkwearmouth Station Museum
South Shields Museum and Art Gallery

Northern Ireland

The Ulster History Park

Drama

London and the South East

Dan-yr-ogof Showcaves
The *Golden Hinde*

Northern Ireland

Irish Linen Centre and Lisburn Museum
The Navan Centre

English	*see also Humanities (page 250)*

The South West

Bristol Zoo Gardens
Dairyland Farm World
Fleet Air Arm Museum
Helicopter Museum
Longleat
Paignton Zoo
Pennywell Farm
Rode Bird Gardens
SS Great Britain Project
The Tutankhamun Exhibition
Wells Cathedral
Wookey Hole Caves

London and the South East

1066 Story in Hastings
Arcturus Day Cruises
Audley End House Park and Garden
Bateman's
Beckonscot Model Village
Bentley Wildfowl and Motor Museum
Blenheim Palace

Brooklands Museum
Canterbury Roman Museum
The Canterbury Tales Visitor Attraction
Cathedral and Abbey Church of St Alban
Chelsea Physic Garden
Chessington World of Adventures
The *Cutty Sark*
The Dickens House Museum
Dover Castle
Drusillas Park
Geffrye Museum
Gunnersbury Park Museum
Hampton Court Palace
Hastings Museum and Art Gallery
The Historic Dockyard
Howletts and Port Lympne Wild Animal Park
Imperial War Museum
Leeds Castle
Legoland Windsor
Museum of Kent Life
Paultons Park
The Royal Marines Museum
Shipwreck Heritage Centre
A Smuggler's Adventure in St Clement's Caves
The South of England Rare Breed Centre
Sussex Wildlife Trusts
Victoria and Albert Museum
The Weald and Downland Museum

Wales

Anglesey Sea Zoo
Dan-yr-ogof Showcaves
King Arthur's Labyrinth
Penrhyn Castle
Rhondda Heritage Park

The Midlands

The Aerospace Museum
Drayton Manor Theme Park
Museum of Advertising and Packaging

The National Waterways Museum
The Shrewsbury Quest
The Tales of Robin Hood

East Anglia

British Birds of Prey and Conservation Centre
Broads Tours Ltd
The Butterfly and Falconry Park
Easton Farm Park
Elton Hall
Fitzwilliam Museum
Gainsborough's House
Lincoln Castle
The Muckleburgh Collection
Museum of East Anglian Life
National Horse-racing Museum
The Norfolk Rare Breeds Centre
Norwich Castle Museum
Norwich Cathedral
Pensthorpe Waterfowl Park
Thetford Forest Park

The North West

Chester Zoo
Granada Studios Tour
Jodrell Bank, Science Centre and Arboretum
Lancashire Mining Museum
Mirehouse
The Museum of Science and Industry in Manchester
North West Water Ltd
Ordsall Hall Museum
Royal Mail
Salford Museum and Art Gallery
Windermere Steamboat Museum

Yorkshire

Archaeological Resource Centre
Bankfield Museum
Bolton Abbey Estate

Bolton Castle
Brontë Parsonage Museum
Calderdale Industrial Museum
Castle Howard
Cleethorpes Humber Estuary Discovery Centre
Duncombe Park
Eden Camp Modern History Theme Museum
Elsecar Barnsley
Eureka! The Museum for Children
Harewood House
Jorvik Viking Centre
Lightwater Valley Country Theme Park
Middleton Railway
National Fishing Heritage Centre
National Railway Museum
Piece Hall Art Gallery
Ripley Castle Estate
Royal Armouries
Skipton Castle
St Leonard's Farm Park
York Boat Guided River Trips
York Castle Museum

The North East

Beamish, the North of England Open Air Museum
Monkwearmouth Station Museum
Shipley Art Gallery
South Shields Museum and Art Gallery
The Wildfowl and Wetlands Trust

Scotland

The National Bible Society of Scotland

Northern Ireland

Down County Museum
Irish Linen Centre and Lisburn Museum
The Navan Centre
St Patrick's Train Visitor Centre

Humanities

The North West

Catalyst: The Museum of the Chemical Industry

| Geography | *see also Environmental Studies (page 253); Geology (page 254)* |

The South West

Brewers Quay
Bristol Zoo Gardens
Clovelly
Dairyland Farm World
Longleat
Paignton Zoo
Pennywell Farm
Rode Bird Gardens
SS Great Britain Project
The Tutankhamun Exhibition
Wookey Hole Caves

London and the South East

1066 Story in Hastings
Arcturus Day Cruises
Audley End House Park and Garden
Bentley Wildfowl and Motor Museum
Bexhill Museum
Blenheim Palace
Bodiam Castle
The Body Shop Tour
Bowman's Open Farm
The British Museum
Brooklands Museum
Canterbury Roman Museum
The Canterbury Tales Visitor Attraction
Cathedral and Abbey Church of St Alban
Chelmer Cruises
Chelsea Physic Garden
The *Cutty Sark*
Dover Castle

Drusillas Park
Farming World
Hastings Museum and Art Gallery
Hastings Sea Life Centre
Hatfield House
Heathrow Airport
The Historic Dockyard
Howletts and Port Lympne Wild Animal Park
Kelvedon Hatch Secret Ex-government Underground Bunker
Leeds Castle
Natural History Museum
Newhaven Fort
Paultons Park
Royal Engineers Museum
The Royal Marines Museum
Royal Navy Submarine Museum
RSPB Nature Reserve at Dungeness
Shipwreck Heritage Centre
A Smuggler's Adventure in St Clement's Caves
The South of England Rare Breed Centre
Sussex Wildlife Trusts
The Weald and Downland Museum
White Cliffs Experience

Wales

Anglesey Sea Zoo
Big Pit
Dan-yr-ogof Showcaves
Llechwedd Slate Caverns
Penrhyn Castle
Rhondda Heritage Park

The Midlands

The Aerospace Museum
The Ironbridge Gorge Museum Trusts
The National Waterways Museum

East Anglia

British Birds of Prey and Conservation Centre
Broads Tours Ltd

Bure Valley Railway
The Butterfly and Falconry Park
Oliver Cromwell's House
Easton Farm Park
Ely Cathedral
Flag Fen Bronze Age Excavations
Lincoln Castle
The Muckleburgh Collection
Museum of East Anglian Life
Nene Valley Railway
The Norfolk Rare Breeds Centre
Norwich Castle Museum
Pensthorpe Waterfowl Park
Pleasurewood Hills Family Theme Park
Railworld
Rutland Water
Sizewell Power Station Visitor Centre
Thetford Forest Park
Tropical Butterfly Gardens
Wingfield Old College and Gardens

The North West

Aquarium of the Lakes
The Beacon
Catalyst: The Museum of the Chemical Industry
Lancashire Mining Museum
Mirehouse
Muncaster Castle, Gardens and Owl Centre
North West Water Ltd
Salford Museum and Art Gallery

Yorkshire

Archaeological Resource Centre
Bankfield Museum
Bolton Abbey Estate
Calderdale Industrial Museum
Castle Howard
Cleethorpes Humber Estuary Discovery Centre
Duncombe Park
Eden Camp Modern History Theme Museum

Elsecar Barnsley
Eureka! The Museum for Children
Flamingoland Family Fun Park
Harewood House
Jorvik Viking Centre
Lightwater Valley Country Theme Park
National Fishing Heritage Centre
National Railway Museum
Royal Armouries
Skipton Castle
St Leonard's Farm Park
York Boat Guided River Trips

The North East

Alnwick Castle
Bamburgh Castle
Beamish, the North of England Open Air Museum
Discovery Museum
Hancock Museum
Kielder Forest
Kielder Water Cruises
Shipley Art Gallery
South Shields Museum and Art Gallery
St Mary's Lighthouse Visitor Centre
The Wildfowl and Wetlands Trust

Northern Ireland

Belfast Zoo
Giant's Causeway
Irish Linen Centre and Lisburn Museum
Marble Arch Caves
The Navan Centre

Environmental Studies

Northern Ireland

The Ulster History Park

Geology

Northern Ireland

Giant's Causeway

History

The South West

The American Museum in Britain
Bath Industrial Heritage Centre
The Bournemouth Bears
Bristol Zoo Gardens
The Bygones Museum
Clovelly
Dairyland Farm World
Fleet Air Arm Museum
Longleat
Paignton Zoo
Pennywell Farm
Rode Bird Gardens
Roman Baths and Pump Room
Royal Albert Memorial Museum
Shipwreck and Heritage Centre
Smeaton's Tower
SS Great Britain Project
The Tutankhamun Exhibition
Wells Cathedral

London and the South East

1066 Story in Hastings
Apsley House
Arcturus Day Cruises
Arundel Castle
Audley End House Park and Garden
Bank of England Museum
Basingstoke Canal
Bateman's
Battle Abbey
Beachy Head Countryside Centre
Beckonscot Model Village

The Bethnal Green Museum of Childhood
Bexhill Museum
Bexhill Museum of Costume and Social History
Blenheim Palace
Bodiam Castle
Booth Museum of Natural History
The British Museum
Brooklands Museum
Broughton Castle
Buckleys Yesterday's World
Canterbury Cathedral
Canterbury Roman Museum
The Canterbury Tales Visitor Attraction
Cathedral and Abbey Church of St Alban
Chelmer Cruises
Chelmsford Cathedral
Chelsea Physic Garden
The *Cutty Sark*
D-Day Museum and Overlord Embroidery
The Dickens House Museum
Dover Castle
Drusillas Park
Farming World
Fishbourne Roman Palace
Foredown Tower Visitor's Centre and Camera Obscura
Fort Amherst Heritage Park and Caverns
Geffrye Museum
The *Golden Hinde*
Groombridge Place Gardens and the Enchanted Forest
Gunnersbury Park Museum
Hampton Court Palace
Hastings Museum and Art Gallery
Hatfield House
The Historic Dockyard
Howletts and Port Lympne Wild Animal Park
Imperial War Museum
Kelvedon Hatch Secret Ex-government Underground Bunker
Kennet Horse Boat Company
Leeds Castle
The London Dungeon
Newhaven Fort
The Oxford Story Exhibition

Paultons Park
Penhurst Place and Gardens
Preston Manor
Romney, Hythe and Dymchurch Railway
Royal Engineers Museum
The Royal Marines Museum
Royal Navy Submarine Museum
The Royal Pavilion
Rye Heritage Centre
Shipwreck Heritage Centre
The Shuttleworth Collection
A Smuggler's Adventure in St Clement's Caves
Southsea Castle
Thorpe Park
Tonbridge Castle
The Twickenham Experience
Verulamium Museum
Victoria and Albert Museum
The Weald and Downland Museum
Wembley Stadium Limited
White Cliffs Experience
The Wimbledon Lawn Tennis Museum
Woburn Abbey

Wales

Anglesey Sea Zoo
Big Pit
Bodelwyddan Castle
Cardiff Castle
Celtica
Dan-yr-ogof Showcaves
Elan Valley Visitor Centre
King Arthur's Labyrinth
Llancciach Fawre Living History Museum
Llechwedd Slate Caverns
Museum of the Welsh Woollen Industry
Museum of Welsh Life
Penrhyn Castle
Rhondda Heritage Park
Roman Legionary Museum

Segontium Roman Museum
Turner House Gallery
Welsh Slate Museum

The Midlands

The Aerospace Museum
Avoncraft Museum of Historic Buildings
Black Country Living Museum
Bosworth Battlefield Visitor Centre and Country Park
Broadway Tower Country Park Limited
Cadbury World
Chatsworth
Clearwell Caves
Cotswold Farm Park
Dudley Zoo and Castle
Harvington Hall
The Ironbridge Gorge Museums Trusts
Museum of Advertising and Packaging
Museum of British Road Transport
The National Tramway Museum
The National Waterways Museum
Rockingham Castle
The Shrewsbury Quest
The Tales of Robin Hood
Tamworth Castle
Walsall Leather Museum
Warwick Castle

East Anglia

Anglesey Abbey and Gardens
Battle of Britain Memorial Visitors Centre
Bressingham Steam Museum Trust and Gardens
Broads Tours Ltd
Burghley House
Christchurch Mansion and Wolsey Art Gallery
Cockley Cley Iceni Village and Museums
Oliver Cromwell's House
Easton Farm Park
Elton Hall
Ely Cathedral

Fitzwilliam Museum
Flag Fen Bronze Age Excavations
Gainsborough's House
Hermitage Hall
Holkham Hall and Bygones Museum
Imperial War Museum
Lincoln Castle
The Long Shop Museum
Lowestoft Maritime Heritage Museum
Mannington and Wolterton Estate
Manor House Museum
Moyse's Hall Museum
The Muckleburgh Collection
Museum of East Anglian Life
National Horse-racing Museum
Nene Valley Railway
The Norfolk Rare Breeds Centre
Norwich Castle Museum
Norwich Cathedral
Pensthorpe Waterfowl Park
Pleasurewood Hills Family Theme Park
Railworld
Rutland Water
Thetford Forest Park
The Thursford Collection
Tolly Cobbold and the Brewery Tap
Wingfield Old College and Gardens

The North West

Appleby Castle Limited
Barton Aerodrome
The Beacon
Bolton Museum, Art Gallery and Aquarium
Catalyst: The Museum of the Chemical Industry
The Conservation Centre
Granada Studios Tour
Hall I'th 'Wood
Jodrell Bank, Science Centre and Arboretum
Lancashire Mining Museum
Manchester United Museum and Tour Centre
Maritime Museum

Merseyside Maritime Museum
Mirehouse
Muncaster Castle, Gardens and Owl Centre
The Museum of Science and Industry in Manchester
North West Water Ltd
Ordsall Hall Museum
Salford Museum and Art Gallery
Tullie House Museum and Art Gallery
Windermere Steamboat Museum

Yorkshire

Allerton Park
Archaeological Resource Centre
Bankfield Museum
Bolton Abbey Estate
Bolton Castle
Bradford Industrial and Horses At Work Museum
Brontë Parsonage Museum
Calderdale Industrial Museum
The Colour Museum
Duncombe Park
Eden Camp Modern History Theme Museum
Elsecar Barnsley
Embsay and Bolton Abbey Steam Railway
Harewood House
Jorvik Viking Centre
Lightwater Valley Country Theme Park
Middleton Railway
National Fishing Heritage Centre
National Railway Museum
Ripley Castle Estate
Royal Armouries
Skipton Castle
Sneatondale Honey Farm
St Leonard's Farm Park
Thackray Medical Museum
York Boat Guided River Trips
York Castle Museum

The North East

Alnwick Castle
Arbeia Roman Fort
Auckland Castle
Bamburgh Castle
Beamish, the North of England Open Air Museum
Bede's World Museum
Discovery Museum
Hancock Museum
Monkwearmouth Station Museum
Paxton House
Shipley Art Gallery
South Shields Museum and Art Gallery
St Mary's Lighthouse Visitor Centre
The Wildfowl and Wetlands Trust

Scotland

Blair Castle
Calderglen Country Park
Camera Obscura
Chatelherault
Discovery Point
Frigate *Unicorn*
Glamis Castle
Museum of Childhood
The National Bible Society of Scotland
Traquair House

Northern Ireland

Armagh County Museum
Belleek Pottery Visitor Centre
Carrickfergus Castle
Down County Museum
Giant's Causeway
Irish Linen Centre and Lisburn Museum
Knight Ride and Heritage Plaza
The Navan Centre
St Patrick's Train Visitor Centre
The Ulster American Folk Park
The Ulster History Park

| Mathematics | *see also Information Technology (page 263)* |

The South West

Dairyland Farm World
Fleet Air Arm Museum
Helicopter Museum
Paignton Zoo
Pennywell Farm
Rode Bird Gardens
SS Great Britain Project
The Tutankhamun Exhibition
Wookey Hole Caves

London and the South East

Arcturus Day Cruises
Audley End House Park and Garden
Bank of England Museum
Beachy Head Countryside Centre
Blenheim Palace
Brooklands Museum
Canterbury Roman Museum
Cathedral and Abbey Church of St Alban
Chelsea Physic Garden
The *Cutty Sark*
Drusillas Park
Geffrye Museum
Hatfield House
Howletts and Port Lympne Wild Animal Park
Imperial War Museum
Kelvedon Hatch Secret Ex-government Underground Bunker
Leeds Castle
Museum of Kent Life
Paultons Park
The Royal Marines Museum
RSPB Nature Reserve at Dungeness
Shipwreck Heritage Centre
The South of England Rare Breed Centre
Sussex Wildlife Trusts
Thorpe Park
Victoria and Albert Museum
The Weald and Downland Museum

Wales

Anglesey Sea Zoo
Centre for Alternative Technology
Rhondda Heritage Park

The Midlands

The Aerospace Museum
Drayton Manor Theme Park
The National Waterways Museum

East Anglia

Ely Cathedral
Lincoln Castle
Museum of East Anglian Life
The Norfolk Rare Breeds Centre
Norwich Cathedral
Pensthorpe Waterfowl Park
Pleasurewood Hills Family Theme Park
Thetford Forest Park
Tropical Butterfly Gardens

The North West

Catalyst: The Museum of the Chemical Industry
Chester Zoo
Jodrell Bank, Science Centre and Arboretum
Lancashire Mining Museum
North West Water Ltd
Royal Mail

Yorkshire

Archaeological Resource Centre
Bolton Abbey Estate
Cleethorpes Humber Estuary Discovery Centre
Duncombe Park
Eden Camp Modern History Theme Museum
Eureka! The Museum for Children
Flamingoland Family Fun Park
Lightwater Valley Country Theme Park

Middleton Railway
National Fishing Heritage Centre
National Railway Museum
Royal Armouries
St Leonard's Farm Park
York Boat Guided River Trips
York Castle Museum

The North East

Auckland Castle
Beamish, the North of England Open Air Museum
The Wildfowl and Wetlands Trust

Northern Ireland

Irish Linen Centre and Lisburn Museum

Information Technology

London and the South East

Chelsea Physic Garden
Legoland Windsor
Paultons Park

Yorkshire

Calderdale Industrial Museum
National Railway Museum
York Boat Guided River Trips

Music

The South West

Bristol Zoo Gardens

London and the South East

Cathedral and Abbey Church of St Alban
The *Cutty Sark*
Dover Castle

Drusillas Park
Geffrye Museum
Hampton Court Palace
Leeds Castle
Paultons Park
The Royal Pavilion
The Weald and Downland Museum
Wembley Stadium Limited

Wales

Anglesey Sea Zoo
Dan-yr-ogof Showcaves

The Midlands

The National Waterways Museum

East Anglia

Ely Cathedral
Norwich Cathedral
Thetford Forest Park
The Thursford Collection

Yorkshire

Bankfield Museum
Calderdale Industrial Museum
Eden Camp Modern History Theme Museum
Eureka! The Museum for Children
Jorvik Viking Centre
National Centre for Popular Music
National Fishing Heritage Centre
Piece Hall Art Gallery
Royal Armouries

Northern Ireland

Irish Linen Centre and Lisburn Museum

R.E.

The South West

Fleet Air Arm Museum
Paignton Zoo
Rode Bird Gardens
The Tutankhamun Exhibition
Wells Cathedral

London and the South East

1066 Story in Hastings
Audley End House Park and Garden
Battle Abbey
Bexhill Museum
Canterbury Cathedral
The Canterbury Tales Visitor Attraction
Cathedral and Abbey Church of St Alban
Chelmsford Cathedral
Hampton Court Palace
Hastings Museum and Art Gallery
Howletts and Port Lympne Wild Animal Park
Leeds Castle
Victoria and Albert Museum

Wales

Anglesey Sea Zoo
The Shrewsbury Quest
The Tales of Robin Hood

East Anglia

Ely Cathedral
Fitzwilliam Museum
Lincoln Castle
Norwich Cathedral
Wingfield Old College and Gardens

The North West

Mirehouse

Yorkshire

Archaeological Resource Centre
Bolton Abbey Estate
Castle Howard
Duncombe Park
Eden Camp Modern History Theme Museum
Harewood House
Jorvik Viking Centre
Ripley Castle Estate
Royal Armouries
Skipton Castle
St Leonard's Farm Park

The North East

Auckland Castle
Bede's World Museum

Scotland

The National Bible Society of Scotland
Traquair House

Northern Ireland

Down County Museum

| Science | *see also Biology (page 271); Technology (page 271)* |

The South West

Blazes – Fire Museum
Brewers Quay
Bristol Zoo Gardens
Dairyland Farm World
The Dinosaur Museum
Helicopter Museum
Longleat
Pennywell Farm
Rode Bird Gardens
Royal Albert Memorial Museum
SS Great Britain Project

Woodlands Leisure Park
Wookey Hole Caves

London and the South East

1066 Story in Hastings
Arcturus Day Cruises
Audley End House Park and Garden
Basingstoke Canal
Battle Abbey
Beachy Head Countryside Centre
Bentley Wildfowl and Motor Museum
Bewl Water
Bexhill Museum
Blenheim Palace
Bodiam Castle
The Body Shop Tour
Booth Museum of Natural History
Bowman's Open Farm
Brooklands Museum
Buckleys Yesterday's World
Canterbury Roman Museum
Cathedral and Abbey Church of St Alban
Chelmer Cruises
Chelsea Physic Garden
Chessington World of Adventures
Cotswold Wildlife Park
The *Cutty Sark*
Drusillas Park
Farming World
Foredown Tower Visitor's Centre and Camera Obscura
Geffrye Museum
Groombridge Place Gardens and the Enchanted Forest
Gunnersbury Park Museum
Hastings Museum and Art Gallery
Hastings Sea Life Centre
Hatfield House
Herstmonceux Science Centre
Howletts and Port Lympne Wild Animal Park
Kelvedon Hatch Secret Ex-government Underground Bunker
Kennet Horse Boat Company
Leeds Castle

Legoland Windsor
Mill Green Museum and Mill
Museum of Kent Life
Natural History Museum
Paradise Family Leisure Park
Park Lodge Farm Centre
Paultons Park
Royal Navy Submarine Museum
RSPB Nature Reserve at Dungeness
The Shuttleworth Collection
A Smuggler's Adventure in St Clement's Caves
The South of England Rare Breed Centre
Sussex Wildlife Trusts
Thorpe Park
Victoria and Albert Museum
The Weald and Downland Open Air Museum
Woburn Safari Park

Wales

Anglesey Sea Zoo
Big Pit
Centre for Alternative Technology
Dan-yr-ogof Showcaves
Elan Valley Visitor Centre
First Hydro
King Arthur's Labyrinth
Museum of Welsh Life
National Museum and Gallery
Rhondda Heritage Park
Rhyl Sea Life Centre
Techniquest

The Midlands

The Aerospace Museum
Broadway Tower Country Park Limited
Chatsworth
Drayton Manor Theme Park
The Ironbridge Gorge Museum Trusts
Museum of Advertising and Packaging
The National Waterways Museum

Stratford Shire Horse Centre
Stratford-upon-Avon Butterfly Farm
Twycross Zoo

East Anglia

Banham Zoo Limited
Bressingham Steam Museum Trust and Gardens
British Birds of Prey and Conservation Centre
Broads Tours Ltd
Bure Valley Railway
The Butterfly and Falconry Park
Caithness Crystal
Easton Farm Park
Ely Cathedral
Fitzwilliam Museum
Flag Fen Bronze Age Excavations
Hamerton Wildlife Park
Imperial War Museum
Inspire Hands-on Science Centre
Lincoln Castle
The Long Shop Museum
Mablethorpe Animal Gardens
Manor House Museum
Museum of East Anglian Life
National Horse-racing Museum
Natureland Seal Sanctuary
The Norfolk Rare Breeds Centre
Norwich Castle Museum
Norwich Cathedral
Pensthorpe Waterfowl Park
Pleasurewood Hills Family Theme Park
Railworld
Rutland Water
Sizewell Power Station Visitor Centre
Thetford Forest Park
The Thursford Collection
Tolly Cobbold and the Brewery Tap
Tropical Butterfly Gardens
Wingfield Old College and Gardens

The North West

Animal World, Butterfly House and Moss Bank Park
Aquarium of the Lakes
The Beacon
Bolton Museum, Art Gallery and Aquarium
Catalyst: The Museum of the Chemical Industry
Chester Zoo
The Conservation Centre
Jodrell Bank, Science Centre and Arboretum
Lancashire Mining Museum
Manchester Airport
Maritime Museum
Mirehouse
The Museum of Science and Industry in Manchester
North West Water Ltd
Windermere Steamboat Museum

Yorkshire

Archaeological Resource Centre
Bankfield Museum
Bolton Abbey Estate
Calderdale Industrial Museum
Castle Howard
Cleethorpes Humber Estuary Discovery Centre
Deep Sea Experience Centre
Duncombe Park
Eden Camp Modern History Theme Museum
Elsecar Barnsley
Eureka! The Museum for Children
Flamingoland Family Fun Park
Harewood House
Jorvik Viking Centre
Lightwater Valley Country Theme Park
Middleton Railway
National Fishing Heritage Centre
National Railway Museum
Piece Hall Art Gallery
Ripley Castle Estate
Royal Armouries
St Leonard's Farm Park
Thackray Medical Museum

The North East

Arbeia Roman Fort
Bamburgh Castle
Beamish, the North of England Open Air Museum
Discovery Museum
Hancock Museum
Kielder Water Cruises
Monkwearmouth Station Museum
The Otter Trust North Penines Reserve
The Rising Sun Countryside Centre
South Shields Museum and Art Gallery
St Mary's Lighthouse Visitor Centre
The Wildfowl and Wetlands Trust

Scotland

Calderglen Country Park
Camera Obscura
Edinburgh Butterfly and Insect World
Hunter House
Royal Observatory Visitor Centre

Northern Ireland

Armagh Planetarium
Belfast Zoo
Ford Farm Park and Museum
Giant's Causeway
Irish Linen Centre and Lisburn Museum

Biology

Northern Ireland

Giant's Causeway

Technology

The South West

Helicopter Museum
Rode Bird Gardens
Roman Baths and Pump Room
Wookey Hole Caves

London and the South East

1066 Story in Hastings
Arcturus Day Cruises
Audley End House Park and Garden
Battle Abbey
Bewl Water
Bexhill Museum
Bexhill Museum of Costume and Social History
Blenheim Palace
Bowman's Open Farm
Brooklands Museum
Buckleys Yesterday's World
Cathedral and Abbey Church of St Alban
Chelmer Cruises
Dover Castle
Hastings Museum and Art Gallery
The Historic Dockyard
Imperial War Museum
Kennet Horse Boat Company
Leeds Castle
Mill Green Museum and Mill
Museum of Kent Life
Royal Engineers Museum
RSPB Nature Reserve at Dungeness
Shipwreck Heritage Centre
The Shuttleworth Collection
Thorpe Park
Verulamium Museum
Victoria and Albert Museum

Wales

Anglesey Sea Zoo
Museum of Welsh Life
Segontium Roman Museum
Turner House Gallery

The Midlands

Black Country Living Museum
Chatsworth
Museum of Advertising and Packaging

The National Waterways Museum
The Tales of Robin Hood

East Anglia

Anglesey Abbey and Gardens
Battle of Britain Memorial Visitors Centre
Bressingham Steam Museum Trust and Gardens
British Birds of Prey and Conservation Centre
Broads Tours Ltd
Bure Valley Railway
Caithness Crystal
Easton Farm Park
Fitzwilliam Museum
Flag Fen Bronze Age Excavations
Imperial War Museum
Inspire Hands-on Science Centre
Lincoln Castle
Manor House Museum
The Muckleburgh Collection
National Horse-racing Museum
Nene Valley Railway
The Norfolk Rare Breeds Centre
Norwich Castle Museum
Norwich Cathedral
Pleasurewood Hills Family Theme Park
Railworld
Rutland Water
Sizewell Power Station Visitor Centre
Thetford Forest Park
Tolly Cobbold and the Brewery Tap

The North West

Catalyst: The Museum of the Chemical Industry

Yorkshire

Allerton Park
Archaeological Resource Centre
Brontë Parsonage Museum
Cleethorpes Humber Estuary Discovery Centre

Deep Sea Experience Centre
Eden Camp Modern History Theme Museum
Elsecar Barnsley
Embsay and Bolton Abbey Steam Railway
Eureka! The Museum for Children
Flamingoland Family Fun Park
Harewood House
Jorvik Viking Centre
Middleton Railway
National Fishing Heritage Centre
Ripley Castle Estate
Royal Armouries
St Leonard's Farm Park
York Castle Museum

The North East

Discovery Museum
Paxton House
Shipley Art Gallery
The Wildfowl and Wetlands Trust

Scotland

Discovery Point

Northern Ireland

Down County Museum
Irish Linen Centre and Lisburn Museum
The Ulster American Folk Park

Appendix: Useful names and addresses

Guide to Health and Safety at School No. 5: Out and About – School Trips Part 1, available from Royal Society for the Prevention of Accidents (RoSPA), The Priory, Cannon House, Queensway, Birmingham B4 6BS.

Health Advice to Travellers Anywhere in the World, published by the Department of Health and available free from most post offices, libraries and travel agents.

Health and Safety Fact Sheet on Off Site Activities, available free from Further Educational Development Agency, Publications Department, Coombe Lodge, Blagdon, Bristol BS18 6RG (tel: 01761 462503).

Minibus Safety: A code of practice, available from RoSPA.

Safety on School Journeys, available free from National Union of Teachers, Hamilton House, Mabledon Place, London WC1H 9BD (tel: 0171 388 6191).

School Minibuses: A Safety Guide, available free from National Union of Teachers (address as above).

Taking Students Off-Site, available free from Association of Teachers and Lecturers, 7 Northumberland Street, London WC2N 5DA (tel: 0171 930 6441).

There are also many informative leaflets produced by the Health and Safety Executive, HSE Information Centre, Broad Lane, Sheffield S3 7HQ. If you require the local numbers for HSE offices telephone HSE Infoline: 0541 545500.

Other useful addresses

Association of British Travel Agents (ABTA)

55–57 Newman Street
London W1P 4AH
Tel: (0171) 637 2444

The Central Bureau for Educational Visits and Exchanges

10 Spring Gardens
London SW1A 2BN
Tel: (0171) 389 4004
Fax: (0171) 389 4426
They provide information and advice on educational visits and exchanges.

The Foreign & Commonwealth Office's Travel Advice Unit

Consular Division
1 Palace Street
London SW1E 5HE
Tel: (0171) 238 4503/4504 (Monday–Friday, 9.30 am–4.00 pm)
Fax: (0171) 238 4545

The Heritage Education Trust

Pickwick
Vicarage Hill
Badley
Daventry
NN11 3AP
Tel: (01327) 77943

Historic Houses Association

Chester Street
London SW1X 7BB
Tel: (0171) 259 5688

HSE Books

PO Box 1999
Sudbury
Suffolk CO10 6FS
Tel: (01787) 881165
Fax: (01787) 313995
They produce a number of relevant publications.

National Association for Outdoor Education

12 St Andrew's Churchyard
Penrith
Cumbria CA11 7YE
Tel: (01768) 65113

National Association of Farms for Schools

164 Shaftesbury Avenue
London WC2H 8HL

School Journey Association

48 Cavendish Road
London SW12 0DG
Tel: (0181) 675 6636

The Historic Royal Palaces

Hampton Court Palace
Surrey KT8 9AU
Tel: (0171) 259 5590

Tourist Boards

Cumbria Tourist Board

Ashleigh
Holly Road
Windermere
Cumbria LA23 2AQ
Tel: (01539) 444444
Fax: (01539) 444041

East of England Tourist Board

Toppesfield Hall
Hadleigh
Suffolk IP27 5DN
Tel: (01473) 822922
Fax: (01473) 823063

English Tourist Board

Thames Tower
Black's Road
London W6 9EL
Tel: (0181) 846 9000

Heart of England Tourist Board

Larkhill Road
Worcester WR5 2EZ
Tel: (01905) 763436
Fax: (01905) 763450

North West Tourist Board

Swan House
Swan Meadow Road
Wigan Pier
Wigan
Greater Manchester WN3 5BB
Tel: (01942) 821222
Fax: (01942) 820002

Northern Ireland Tourist Board

St Anne's Court
59 North Street
Belfast BT1 1NB
Tel: (01232) 231221
Fax: (01232) 240960

Northumbria Tourist Board

Aykley Heads
Durham DH1 5UX
Tel: (0191) 375 3000
Fax: (0191) 386 0899

Scottish Tourist Board

23 Ravelston Terrace
Edinburgh EH4 3EU
Tel: (0131) 332 2433
Fax: (0131) 343 1513

South East Tourist Board

The Old Brew House
Warwick Park
Tunbridge Wells
Kent TN2 5TU
Tel: (01892) 540766
Fax: (01892) 511008

Southern Tourist Board

40 Chamberlayne Road
Eastleigh
Hampshire S050 5JH
Tel: (01703) 620006
Fax: (01703) 620010

Wales Tourist Board

Production Services Department
Davis Street
Cardiff CF1 2FU
Tel: (01222) 475226
Fax: (01222) 482436

West Country Tourist Board

60 St David's Hill
Exeter
Devon EX4 4SY
Tel: (01392) 276351

Yorkshire Tourist Board

312 Tadcaster Road
York Y02 2HF
Tel: (01904) 707961
Fax: (01904) 701414

Miscellaneous

English Heritage Education Service

Keysign House
429 Oxford Street
London W1R 2HD
Tel: (0171) 973 3442/3

The National Trust

36 Queen Anne's Gate
London SW1H 9AS
Tel: (0171) 222 9251

Index

Note: *add* = address

Index of advertisers

Visit Kogan Page on-line

Comprehensive information on
Kogan Page titles

Features include

- complete catalogue listings,
  including book reviews and
  descriptions

- special monthly promotions

- information on NEW titles and
  BESTSELLING titles

- a secure shopping basket facility
  for on-line ordering

PLUS everything you need to know about
KOGAN PAGE

http://www.kogan-page.co.uk